The United States and the Americas

Lester D. Langley, General Editor

*This series is dedicated to a broader
understanding of the political, economic, and
especially cultural forces and issues that have
shaped the Western Hemispheric experience—
its governments and its peoples. Individual
volumes assess relations between the United
States and its neighbors to the south and north:
Mexico, Central America, Cuba, the Dominican
Republic, Haiti, Panama, Colombia, Venezuela,
the Andean Republics (Peru, Ecuador, and
Bolivia), Brazil, Uruguay and Paraguay,
Argentina, Chile, and Canada.*

The United States and the Americas

Venezuela and the United States

Judith Ewell

Venezuela and the United States: From Monroe's Hemisphere to Petroleum's Empire

The University of Georgia Press
Athens and London

© 1996 by the University of Georgia Press
Athens, Georgia 30602
All rights reserved

Set in 10 on 14 Palatino by Books International
Printed and bound by Thomson-Shore, Inc.

The paper in this book meets the guidelines
for permanence and durability of the Committee on
Production Guidelines for Book Longevity of the
Council on Library Resources.

Printed in the United States of America

00 99 98 97 96 C 5 4 3 2 1

00 99 98 97 96 P 5 4 3 2 1

Library of Congress Cataloging in Publication Data

Ewell, Judith, 1943–
    Venezuela and the United States : From Monroe's
hemisphere to petroleum's empire / Judith Ewell.
        p.   cm. — (The United States and the Americas)
    Includes bibliographical references and index.
        ISBN 0-8203-1782-9 (alk. paper). — ISBN 0-8203-1783-7
(pbk. : alk. paper)
        1. United States—Relations—Venezuela. 2. Venezuela—
Relations—United States.   I. Title.   II. Series.
E183.8.V3E9   1996   95-2808
327.73087—dc20

British Library Cataloging in Publication Data available

Contents

Acknowledgments   ix

Introduction   1

1. The Origins, 1790–1830   11

2. Gunboats and Caudillos, 1830–1866   37

3. Rogues and Heroes, 1866–1896   63

4. Venezuela Dodges the Big Stick, 1897–1912   91

5. Oil and the Democratic Caesar, 1912–1935   117

6. Good Neighbors and the Dismantling
   of Democracy, 1936–1958   144

7. The Hydrocarbon Economy and the
   American Way of Life, 1936–1958   168

8. From Hemispheric to Global Perspectives,
   1958–1990s   199

Notes   225

Bibliographical Essay   243

Index   259

Acknowledgments

Over the years, a number of funding agencies have supported my work. I am deeply grateful to the American Association of University Women, the Organization of American States, the National Endowment for the Humanities, the Council for International Exchange of Scholars (Fulbright Program), and the College of William and Mary for various opportunities to conduct research in Venezuela and in Washington. I also gratefully acknowledge the support of the Newton family, which has so generously funded the endowed chair that I hold at the College of William and Mary.

Colleagues and friends have given intellectual and emotional support over the years. I will always be grateful for the "camaraderie around the campfire" with the Lobos, Bill and Blue Beezley, Rick Hopper and the SR bunch, the Monday Night Football gang, the Friday Afternoon Seminar members, and all of my colleagues in the Department of History at William and Mary. Cam Walker pointed out a source that I would have missed, and Ed Crapol deserves a special vote of thanks for reading the entire manuscript, spotting some egregious errors, and suggesting additional sources.

Friends in Venezuela have enriched my time there and my efforts to understand their nation's history. I have very much enjoyed my association with Ramón Escovar Salom, Carlos Romero, Nikita Harwich, Oscar and Rosario Abdala, and all the students in the History of the Americas master's program at the Universidad Católica Andrés Bello in 1979–80. Nor can I forget to mention some of my favorite "adopted Venezuelans": Steve Ellner, Susan Berglund, Ralph and Carmen Van Roy, Ilmar Luks, and Elsa Dirickx.

I also appreciate Lester Langley's role in putting together and editing this series, and especially his assigning a complete volume to Venezuela. Lester's forbearance through my many delays was exemplary; it is indeed a tribute to his patience that he did not inflict the "kneecapping" that he once threatened. Editors and staff at the University of Georgia Press—especially Kelly Caudle, Melinda Conner, and Molly Thompson—have been professional and pleasant to work with. I also am grateful to David Carr for the suggestions he made when he was translating the manuscript into Spanish.

Needless to say, like all historians, I would be utterly lost without the good cheer and helpfulness of librarians and archivists, editors, and secretaries. For this project, the staff has been especially helpful at the United States National Archives, the Library of Congress, the Archive of the Ministry of Foreign Relations in Caracas, the Biblioteca Nacional and Hemeroteca in Caracas, the Biblioteca del Estado de Zulia in Maracaibo, and Swem Library and the Law Library of the College of William and Mary. In this day and age, I could not forget to acknowledge the computer technicians who can miraculously recover the deleted file and the secretaries who have contributed directly and indirectly to the completion of the manuscript. Doris Emerson and Sara Gross deserve special thanks for their help with manuscript and index preparation.

Venezuela and the United States

Introduction

> With the majestic qualities of Bolívar, Washington would have awakened fears among the fervent puritans of the North; with the modest virtues of Washington, Bolívar would not have advanced by one day the cause of Independence in the South.
>
> —Juan Vicente González

Historians have recently used concepts from cultural anthropology to analyze "a relatively coherent, emotionally charged, and conceptually interlocking set of ideas" that form the core of foreign policy ideas.[1] In the case of the United States, Michael Hunt has argued for the constancy of three core ideas: racism, distrust of revolution, and the notion of American exceptionalism or mission, imbued with Protestant virtues and the English parliamentary and common law traditions. Especially with regard to Latin America, the core U.S. foreign policy ideas have resulted in assertions of superiority interspersed with quixotic efforts to "export democracy."

If cultural ideas do indeed drive much of a nation's international projection, one might expect a degree of discordance between the United States and Venezuela. Venezuela's core concepts have included a relatively tolerant experience with racial mixture, a fatalistic acceptance or endorsement of revolution, and a distaste for intervention. Traditions of Roman law and Catholic faith and philosophy have schooled Venezuelans to value universal values of community over individual competition.

It would be foolish, however, to suggest that cultural patterns alone influence relations between the strong and the weak, the rich and the poor. National power—as measured by population, wealth and resources, military force, and political stability—sets the unavoidable context for international, or binational, relations.

Nearly from the outset, Venezuelans have been supplicants or irritants who have requested aid, refuted claims, or sought protection.

1

When supplication failed, they used the tools of the weak—an alternating barrage of subterfuge, delay, passivity, outrage, lobbying, and union with others. Traditional Venezuelan folktales glory in the modest victories of the clever rabbit, Tío Conejo, over the stronger and more ferocious tiger, Tío Tigre. Of course, *el conejo* could never definitively defeat *el tigre*, or alter the skewed power relationship between them. But his *astucia*, or cleverness, could ensure survival and a degree of independence beyond the reach of the tiger's powerful claws. The traditional folktale provides a metaphor for the history of Venezuela's relationship with the United States and an insight into Venezuelan cultural icons.[2]

Venezuelan National Identity

Three major elements have shaped Venezuela's national identity: geography, history, and petroleum. First, its eastern Caribbean location affords proximity to the United States and Europe and places Venezuela at the political, economic, and demographic crossroads of the Americas. Unlike the other mainland and isthmus nations (Mexico, Colombia, and the countries of Central America), Venezuela's capital and many of its resources and population lie near the long northern coast. Like the United States, Venezuela has viewed hostile governments in the Caribbean as a threat to national security. The twentieth-century petroleum age has accentuated the importance of Venezuela's geography. Most of the important oil fields are in the Caribbean coastal region, and petroleum tankers need neutral, open sea lanes to transport the oil to refineries and markets.

U.S. leaders recognized Venezuela's potential as the linchpin of the Caribbean's southern rim long before sea power, the Panama Canal, and petroleum drew the world's attention there. For years, U.S. dreamers had touted Venezuela's Orinoco River as a means of access to the markets of the entire South American continent. After 1898, the determined economic expansionism of the United States and its view of national security required unilateral domination over the enclosed sea, its islands, and its major coastal nations. The region became the proverbial "backyard" of political rhetoric.

Similarly, Venezuela's location influenced its outlook before the development of a conscious Caribbean identity. Yet, Venezuela, a weak nation with no possibility of dominating the zone, benefited most when several great powers vied there for trade, allies, and privileges. One of the few South American nations never to have gone to war with its neighbors, Venezuela found both challenge and opportunity in dealings with the insular enclaves of the great powers that remained in the Caribbean. For much of the nineteenth century, Venezuela traded primarily with British merchants while keeping a wary eye on expansionist activities in neighboring British Guiana to the east. When Britain threatened, Venezuela called on Washington for protection, a protection the United States was unable or unwilling to give until 1896. Neither isolationist nor concerned about "entangling alliances," Venezuela had a more complex vision of the Caribbean than did the United States.

Second, three hundred years of colonial history also contributed to Venezuela's national identity. As inhabitants of a neglected outpost of the Spanish empire until the late eighteenth century, Venezuelans acquired a taste for smuggling, independence, and sporadic obeisance to a distant crown and church. Still, the educated elite saw Catholic, Mediterranean Spain as their link to Western culture reaching back to Roman traditions of empire and law. The Spanish past also embraced the contradictory traditions of ethnic mingling among Catholic, Moslem, and Jew, and of brutal pogroms, expulsion, and intolerance. Venezuela's small population, dominated by the mercantile and landed elite in Caracas, consisted principally of racially mixed people, a significant number of Afro-Venezuelans, and a few isolated indigenous peoples. Without being racial egalitarians, Venezuelans accepted all ethnic groups as compatriots. With no distinguished colonial society or institutions to draw on, national pride grew to center on a mythologized version of Simón Bolívar's leadership of the nation—and the entire continent—into an independence inspired by Enlightenment liberalism. Educated Venezuelans assumed that they shared their Enlightenment values with U.S. citizens, although they came to realize that northern and southern priorities and interpretations differed. George Washington and Simón Bolívar epitomized different streams of liberalism.

True liberal democracy with universal suffrage, of course, did not arise in either nation in the nineteenth century. The white populations in both countries feared the results of voting by people of color. In Venezuela, persons of European extraction comprised only a small portion of the population, while they formed the overwhelming majority in the United States. Suffrage laws in the United States excluded African Americans and Native Americans from the definition of citizenship. Venezuelans did not count slaves or enclaved indigenous populations as citizens either, but they faced the additional dilemma of how to check the political potential of the people of color who formed the majority. Ultimately, the Venezuelan elite adopted the Latin American liberal formula of espousing democratic institutions while insisting that their citizens were not "ready" for full, direct political participation. Until the mid-twentieth century, most educated Venezuelans accepted the view that a strong man, a transitional "democratic caesar," should govern on behalf of the majority. U.S. observers fully concurred with that political formula, a formula that reinforced U.S. prejudices about nonwhite populations in general and those outside the Anglo-American tradition in particular. Until 1958, the United States usually cooperated with Venezuelan elites to discourage mass political participation.

Finally, petroleum—the devil's excrement, as some call it—reformed Venezuelan society, economy, and consciousness in the twentieth century. Venezuela depends more than any other Latin American nation on the revenues produced by exporting petroleum. Since the 1920s, petroleum issues have overshadowed all others in U.S. relations with Venezuela. To the United States, Venezuela has represented a frontier for the "American century," a reserve for a strategic mineral whose access must remain cheap and secure. The United States requires a steady supply of petroleum for consumers, for industry, and for military might. Venezuela, one of the wealthiest Latin American countries in the late twentieth century, relies on petroleum for an equally critical goal: to maintain political tranquility and, ideally, democracy by "sowing" the oil revenues in consumer benefits and economic diversification. Petroleum wealth has also helped to finance a global foreign policy whose goal is the redistribution of international wealth. In other words, Washington's petroleum perspectives are usually antithetical to those of Caracas. Venezuela wants high prices and a competitive world market, while the interests of the United States are best served by a controlled market and low prices.

Geography, history, and petroleum have thus facilitated a greater degree of "Americanization" in Venezuela than in any other Latin American nation. Venezuelans watch *Dallas* on television as avidly as *Cristal*; vacation in Miami as well as Margarita; drink *guiski* with Coca Cola; study at Harvard, MIT, and the Universidad Central de Venezuela; dance equally to the beat of Oscar d'León and Michael Jackson; display more enthusiasm for baseball than for soccer. A popular travel guide introduces a section on "the Venezuelans" with the comment that "Venezuelans seem to import culture wholesale from the United States."[3] The section concludes, however, with the observation that Venezuelans may travel and study abroad, but few emigrate. "While their gaze may be distracted by the latest North American cultural totems, their feet remain firmly fixed at home."[4] The strong U.S. presence in the economy, business, and popular culture has created in Venezuelans an ambivalent love/hate for the "American way of life." Surprisingly, however, there has been relatively little anti-Americanism. Venezuela also welcomed a large number of European immigrants after World War II, contributing to a more tolerant attitude toward all foreigners. On the surface, the Americanisms and lack of hostility make Venezuelans seem more familiar to U.S. citizens. Beneath the veneer, however, lurk five hundred years of national cultural patterns and an *astucia* that often confound English-speaking northerners. Maracaibo is, after all, Maracaibo and not Miami.

Venezuela's core cultural ideas have sometimes corresponded to and sometimes diverged from those of the United States, but the core ideas are hardly monolithic in either society. Nor can they encompass all national economic and political interests. Obviously, many U.S. citizens deplore the evidence of racism, ethnocentrism, and interventionism in their nation's foreign policy. Just as obviously, some Venezuelans are racists or isolationists, and, since 1959, some have even wanted to intervene in the affairs of their sister republics in order to "export democracy." At almost any moment in the binational history, transnational alliances have been evident. Many people in both North and South America believed Simón Bolívar to represent enlightened republicanism in Gran Colombia; yet, U.S. minister William Henry Harrison and some Gran Colombian conspirators charged that Bolívar was a tyrant with monarchical tendencies. In recent times, multinational companies such as Standard Oil have allied with Venezuelan importers to advocate the unrestricted entry of Venezuelan oil into the United States and of U.S. manufactures into Venezuela. In opposition, Venezuelan industrialists joined independent petroleum producers in the United States to call for trade restrictions to protect Venezuelan manufacturing and U.S. domestic oil producers from competition. Thus, particular power elites have found more effective allies abroad than at home and have used their foreign friends to secure their interests at home.

The United States, Venezuela, and the Inter-American Relationship

What is unique about the history of the Venezuela–United States relationship? Venezuela has hardly been the most important Latin American country to Washington, but at different times it has reflected, sometimes critically, all of the key transforming moments and issues of inter-American relations. Viewing hemispheric relations through a Venezuelan lens reveals a microcosm of U.S. goals and priorities regarding Latin America. At the same time, no other Latin American nation—especially in the Caribbean basin—has managed so adroitly, or luckily, to escape U.S. military and diplomatic intervention. Rather, Venezuela has felt the more gradual impact of a petroleum-driven cultural invasion bearing many superficial aspects of the "American way of life."

Through all the turns and twists of Venezuela's relations with the United States, the nation has avoided suffering any major military, diplomatic, or economic sanctions. In the nineteenth century, U.S. citizens generally saw less to covet in Venezuela than they did in their own vast western territory. Venezuela also benefited—mostly—from the counterweight of British trade and presence. After 1898 until World War II, when U.S. hegemony was at its height, Venezuelan dictators enforced an orderly peace and a relatively compliant petroleum and economic policy to avoid giving any cause for intervention. Since 1945, Caracas has used multilateral alliances and the forum of U.S. and international public opinion to bolster its own modest power quotient.

Venezuelan leaders have frequently employed tactics similar to the *Obedezco pero no cumplo* (I obey, but I will not execute) of Spanish colonial fame. They have delayed, diverted, ignored, or partially executed some demands instead of flaunting their recalcitrance. Like Tío Conejo, they have often seen and exploited weaknesses or divisions within U.S. political institutions. After 1959, Venezuelan presidents had the additional advantage of being able to call on the populace for support in disagreements with the United States. Obviously, no one wanted disorder or sabotage that would interrupt the flow of petroleum. Washington, the multinational oil companies, and Caracas all had incentives to conciliate their differences.

Venezuela's history illustrates much of the checkered pattern of inter-American relations. The 1820s aura of shared liberal values gave way to neglect, filibustering, and wrangling over claims, legal precedents, the actions of hucksters, and trade concessions. Simón Bolívar's assertion of an American republican identity paralleled Monroe's proclamation of a U.S. sphere of influence. The United States provided little assistance in the independence wars, but it recognized Gran Colombia (which included Venezuela) before any other independent Latin American nation and praised Bolívar as the George Washington of the Southern Hemisphere. As in much of the Caribbean by the 1830s, U.S. merchants competed, usually unsuccessfully, with the British for influence and markets. Washington's support of the Aves Island filibusterers, and of other sometimes dubious claims by U.S. citizens, and the pressure for a reciprocal trade treaty all roiled the Venezuelan political waters. Venezuela's request for assistance in the face of British expansionism met with stony silence until 1896, when Secretary of State Richard Olney warned the British that they must submit their territorial dispute with Venezuela to arbitration, marking Washington's new assertion of a Monroe Doctrine responsibility for the hemisphere.

Similarly in the twentieth century, Venezuela has represented all the classic issues in U.S. Latin American policy. President Theodore Roosevelt ached to invade Venezuela and root out "chronic wrongdoing" as he had done elsewhere in the Caribbean. Venezuelan dictator Juan Vicente Gómez (1908–35) became the national "policeman" who assured order, progress, and dollar diplomacy in lieu of the U.S. Marines just as Porfirio Díaz had done in Mexico and men like Anastasio Somoza would do in Nicaragua and other Caribbean countries. In the 1930s, Gómez's tenure became an issue in the U.S. debate over supporting dictators. Franklin Roosevelt's Good Neighbor policy tolerated Venezuela's first steps toward taxing and controlling the multinational oil companies. As the Good Neighbor policy was "dismantled" and the cold war began, Venezuela's anticommunist dictator hosted the inter-American meeting that issued the Caracas Declaration, which condemned communism in the hemisphere. That dictator, Marcos Pérez Jiménez (1950–58), exemplified the results of Washington's support of dictators, especially when Vice President Richard Nixon was nearly killed by angry Caracas mobs in 1958.

Since 1958, Venezuela's relations with the United States have reflected the growing weight and assertiveness of the developing world and its multilateral challenges to U.S. global hegemony. Venezuela also became a cold war battleground against communist guerrillas and a model for new democracies. President John F. Kennedy gave counterinsurgency aid to President Rómulo Betancourt and held him up as a democratic leader to be emulated. Venezuela joined with the Middle Eastern petroleum-producing countries to found the Organization of Petroleum Exporting Countries (OPEC) and led the call for a new international economic order that would shift resources from the rich to the poor nations. In that spirit of confidence Venezuela nationalized its petroleum industry in 1976, but then reeled under the weight of a massive foreign debt, 85 percent of which was owed to U.S. bankers. Venezuelan leaders have remained fully involved in hemispheric affairs, as witnessed by their participation in the Contadora effort to bring peace to Central America, but ever more frequently they have come to see hemispheric issues as part of more general global concerns.

Since at least the days of U.S. secretary of state James G. Blaine and the 1889 Pan-American Conference, multilateral initiatives have taken place in a hemisphere clearly dominated by U.S. military and economic power. Neither Blaine's Pan-American Union nor the Organization of American States (OAS) formed in 1948 constituted more than a facade of a multilateral union. From 1945, the United Nations, with all its flaws and weaknesses, has provided a competing forum, albeit one that Latin American nations can use only to the limits of Washington's tolerance. In the United Nations, Venezuela discovered that there might be more common ground with Saudi Arabia than with Paraguay. As some binational issues became global ones, the United Nations almost imperceptibly (and certainly erratically) diluted Washington's hegemony in the hemisphere.

The 1989 collapse of the Soviet empire marked the end of a bipolar cold war between East and West. In July 1994, when Washington asked the United Nations to endorse an invasion of Haiti, some perceived a parallel crumbling of the "American empire."[5] In a *Washington Post* column entitled "Goodbye, Monroe Doctrine," pundit Charles Krauthammer protested, "One does not ask permission to put out a fire in one's own backyard."[6] Other scholars counter that with or without permission, Washington will not stand by if the tinder of drug trafficking, trade friction, and illegal immigration stoke new flames; the ghosts of Olney and Roosevelt will be with those who take up the fire hoses.[7] Venezuelans in blue jeans and baseball hats may celebrate the demise of Monroe's legacy while they wonder whether their own ideal of Bolívar's Pan-Americanism has also become obsolete in a multipolar world.

Historians and policymakers in the United States have often assumed the existence of a concept called "Latin America." The idea of

"Latin America" derives from a geopolitical, strategic vision of a "hemisphere" as a kind of distant frontier over which the United States must project its power, and possibly its cultural traditions. Arguably that hemispheric frontier has existed only as a spurious mental construct. Looking at it from the perspective of one nation—in this case, Venezuela—makes it clear that the United States has not simply poured its power and values into an empty vessel. Venezuelans have influenced the tone and the content of the relationship as well. Nor have Venezuelan-U.S. relations taken place in a vacuum. Other players—from Great Britain to OPEC—have affected the course of the binational relationship. A new synthesis of inter-American relations will consider not only the multifaceted interaction of all American nations over time, but also the global context.

1   The Origins, 1790–1830

The United States showed Venezuela the path of liberty and social virtues.

— Telésforo de Orea

What hope can be entertained of the independence of such people!
— Alexander Macaulay

From the first booming trade of the 1790s to the breakup of Gran Colombia (comprised of Venezuela, Colombia, and Ecuador) in 1830, Venezuelans and U.S. citizens learned about each other. The learning came through trade, diplomacy, individual encounters, and war experiences. Unfortunately, the experiences of these four decades dashed Venezuelans' initial expectations that shared ideologies of free trade and bourgeois liberalism would inevitably draw the United States closer to its South American neighbors in a common American destiny. Instead, their formal and informal contacts between 1789 and 1830 drove Venezuela and the United States further from mutual understanding and natural alliance. Citizens of both countries alternated between a naive belief that they shared political and economic goals and a pessimistic recognition that divergent cultural values and national interests discouraged any alliance. Waves of pessimism frequently accompanied disgusted assessments of the other nation's honor and values.

The Dawn of Commercial Potential, 1790–1809

Contacts between the United States and the Spanish colony of Venezuela increased from the 1770s onward and intensified with the Spanish free trade decree of 1789.[1] At the outset, the creole elite of Venezuela and the U.S. political elite shared the assumption that the burgeoning trade between the two need not threaten Venezuela's colonial relationship with Spain, or Spain's relationship and trade with the United States. The disturbing example of the French Revolution—and its Haitian offshoot with the specter of racial warfare—dampened any potential enthusiasm for separatist movements.

Between 1790 and 1814 (especially from about 1803 to 1808) Caribbean commerce accounted for one-third of U.S. exports, and an even larger share in some U.S. cities. U.S. merchants supplied Venezuela with wheat flour, machinery, tools, numerous European products, and slaves, which were usually brought from the islands. A U.S. ship, the *Maria Elizabeth*, in May 1811 advertised a wide range of luxury goods to residents of La Guaira, Venezuela: wine, olive oil, 580 pounds of opium(!), figs, soap, saffron, sulphur, paper, dresses, hazelnuts, alpiste (canary seed), and almonds. U.S. shipping companies profited from the carrying trade as well as from the commerce itself since Venezuela had only a few small coastal vessels to carry livestock. From Venezuela, the ships carried home cacao, cotton, indigo, coffee, tobacco, sugar, mules, and cattle. Islands such as Saint Thomas and Saint Croix became transshipment points as well as recipients of the livestock, which provided draft animals and meat for island sugar plantations.[2]

The Spanish Crown authorized a Venezuelan *consulado* in 1785 to supervise the growing trade, but it did not begin to function until 1793. The merchants and hacendados who became *consulado* members, mostly *caraqueños*, generally agreed that there should be a balance of benefits between commerce and agriculture. Most peninsular merchants and political officials in Venezuela also welcomed the freer trade, which provided both private profits and provincial revenues from tariffs. Venezuelan historian Mercedes Alvarez stressed the importance of commerce to the development of a spirit of autonomy among the elite: "Without commerce, the independence movement would have been delayed."[3]

The weakness and inconsistent policies of Spain periodically interrupted the free trade. At times when Spain was at war and acknowledged that it could neither supply nor defend its American colonies, Madrid allowed either complete freedom of trade or limited trade with other colonies or neutrals. Arguably, Venezuela more than any other

Hispanic colony benefited from these periods of free trade, but the inconsistent and rapidly changing regulations frustrated the Venezuelans and their trading partners. In 1789 Spain allowed Venezuela to trade with the Antilles—as had been the case between 1777 and 1783—but cacao could not be traded with foreigners. In 1791 the crown allowed Venezuelans to use cacao to pay foreign shippers for slaves. Restrictions were fewest from 1793 to 1795 and from 1797 to 1799 while Spain and France were at war. In 1799 the Spanish Crown reestablished the traditional protectionist policy prohibiting foreign trade. The Venezuelan economy and revenues plunged, and the *consulado* and *intendente*, or governor, petitioned the crown to exempt Venezuela from the orders. In May 1801 the governor restored foreign commerce. Seven months later, in December, the crown again prohibited foreign ships from entering Venezuelan ports, excepting only foreign merchants who had purchased monopoly concessions. John Craig of Philadelphia secured one of the critical monopolies when he purchased the right to be the exclusive supplier of flour to the province. The Venezuelan *consulado* criticized the monopolies for keeping prices high and supplies uneven.

The complex and frequently changing rules invited corruption and disobedience. Customs authorities interpreted decrees as they wished and demanded extra payments and fees, catching shippers unaware. U.S. merchants, like other foreigners, hated the fluctuating rules and were disappointed in general at the nature of Venezuelan trade. French observer Francisco Depons reported that U.S. businessmen arrived in Venezuela between 1797 and 1801 with the mistaken idea that silver was abundant, that merchandise could be sold at exorbitant prices, and that warehouses were full of Venezuelan products awaiting shipment.

A Failed Effort to Export Republicanism, 1805–1810

Whatever their disappointment with their bilateral trading experience, the Venezuelan elite envied U.S. prosperity and associated it with U.S. independence and republican institutions, which many admired. Merchants and seamen from the United States eagerly propagandized for their new system and sometimes offered to finance separatist efforts. Travelers and seamen encouraged the founding of Venezuelan masonic lodges, formal and informal, which had ties with U.S. lodges. Venezuelans who had traveled to Philadelphia (as well as to London or Cádiz) frequently became Masons or members of Lautaro lodges. Francisco Miranda, Simón Bolívar and Simón Rodriguez all had associations with masonic lodges in Philadelphia. In 1777 in Caracas, Dr. José Ignacio Moreno, rector of the University of Caracas between 1787 and 1789 and a sympathizer with the separatist movement, translated and probably circulated a copy of the 1774 and 1775 proclamations of the Philadelphia Continental Congress.[4]

Venezuelan Francisco Miranda had the lack of foresight to urge Venezuelan independence in 1805–6, when U.S.-Venezuelan trade was at its height and before the Venezuelan elite saw the commercial and political advantages of independence. Miranda received support from influential U.S. citizens such as Alexander Hamilton, Rufus King, General Henry Knox, and William Smith and financial backing from merchants such as Samuel Ogden. In November 1805 Miranda met with Secretary of State James Madison, who informed him that the United States could not provide official support. Whether Madison privately encouraged Miranda to believe that he had the sympathy of the United States is a matter of debate. In any case, Miranda's agents John Fink and William Smith, who sought recruits to join the expedition, apparently gave the impression that Washington had blessed the mission. James Biggs, who provided a journal of the expedition in his letters home, wrote, "We are encouraged in the belief that our government has given its implied sanction to this expedition."[5] Biggs himself seemed skeptical of the claim.

Biggs wrote to a friend that he and the other volunteers were going to South America "to assist the inhabitants in throwing off the oppressive yoke of the parent country; and establishing a government for themselves, upon which we are told by our general they have resolved; and for which they are entirely disposed and prepared."[6] Biggs judged, however, that most of his companions, a rather motley crew in his opinion, had signed on because "they can hardly lose and may gain."[7]

Before the end of the adventure, Biggs also held nothing but scorn for Miranda, whom he considered "more fit for bedlam than for the command of an army." He lamented Miranda's fascination with himself, his "vanity and egotism."[8] The expedition was a fiasco. Two schooners, the *Bacchus* and the *Bee*, were captured with their crews and imprisoned at Cartagena. Even when Miranda's ship took La Vela de Coro in Venezuela, no Venezuelans came to join the invaders.

Venezuelan conservatives agreed with Biggs that Miranda and his U.S. allies were "thirteen hundred amateurs, failures, scoundrels, castoffs from other nations, corrupt men" who had among them "one hundred and thirty-three Jews and Protestants." The bishop of Mérida de Maracaibo further characterized Miranda as "an irreligious man, an atheist, a monster accompanied by a gang of madmen."[9] In spite of the initial apathy or criticism, however, the idea of independence began to gain currency in Venezuela as a result of the news of the Miranda invasion. Perhaps the involvement of the United States, controversial though it was, encouraged the Venezuelan elite to think more seriously about independence. Miranda, moreover, may have resented his compatriots for scorning his modest birth, but he was no Jacobin. He greatly admired the British system, and he criticized the United States because property rather than virtue "was given a high place" there, and because the legislative power was "placed in the hands of entirely ignorant persons."[10]

Whatever Secretary of State Madison's private instructions to Miranda might have been, neither President Thomas Jefferson nor the U.S. Congress did anything to save the captured U.S. citizens. The prisoners petitioned Congress to seek their release on the grounds that Miranda had deceived them. Republicans argued against intercession because the men had broken United States law, they had joined Miranda voluntarily, and, perhaps most important, because aiding them might imperil relations with Spain. At least one U.S. newspaper editor termed the *"banditti"* men "whose death can be no serious loss to any country."[11] Twelve of the thirty-nine men captured were executed.

Politicians and the press and public would be more cautious about support of independence efforts in Latin America in the future.

Newspapers in the United States followed the Miranda expedition closely, and its failure changed their prose from ecstatic praise for Miranda to bitter disappointment. At least three of the U.S. adventurers who accompanied Miranda (Biggs, Moses Smith, and John Sherman) published critical accounts of the expedition. Enthusiasm for a hemisphere of independent republics was tempered by the growing pessimism that Venezuelans might not be ready for or capable of independent government. Thomas Ritchie, the editor of the *Richmond Enquirer*, pointed out that differences existed between Anglo-American and Spanish-American colonies. The North Americans had been governed by a more enlightened king and had had a greater degree of self-government. The Spanish government and its subjects in America were, in Ritchie's opinion, "slaves to the clergy."[12]

Many U.S. spokesmen expressed a general anti-Spanish bias when referring to South Americans as well as to Spaniards. John Adams scoffed at Miranda's plans of 1797–98 when he noted that democracies were as likely to succeed among the birds, beasts, and fishes as among the South Americans. Thomas Pickering, a Federalist leader and Adams's secretary of state, thought Latin Americans "corrupt and effeminate beyond example."[13] Thomas Jefferson commented to Alexander Humboldt in 1813 that history "furnishes no example of a priest-ridden people maintaining a free civil government."[14] Jefferson also wrote to John Adams that "the enemy is within their [Latin Americans'] own breasts, ignorance and superstition will claim their minds and bodies under religious and military despotism."[15] John Quincy Adams believed that South Americans could not institute republican structures because "arbitrary power, military and ecclesiastical, was stamped upon their education, upon their habits, and upon all their institutions."[16]

Napoleon's invasion of Spain in 1808 provided a new opportunity for Venezuelans to consider independence. A small group of influential Caracas *mantuanos* (wearers of mantillas, or the elite) pressed the governor to form an autonomous Venezuelan junta to rule in the absence of a legitimate monarch. The intendant and his allies acted quickly and decisively, jailing or exiling many of the dissidents. The conspirators—the conde de Tovar, the conde de San Javier, and the marqués del Toro among others—represented mercantile interests and advocates of free trade and were not then or later identified with political radicalism.

Contact between the south and the north fell off after 1808 when the United States turned its attention to the Napoleonic Wars and the attacks on neutral shipping rights. The U.S. embargo of 1807 and the Non-Intercourse Act of 1809 effectively halted U.S. trade with Venezuela. Still, to Venezuelans, the example of U.S. republicanism must have become stronger every year that Joseph Bonaparte remained on the throne of Spain. Moderate Venezuelans who wanted freer trade and political control with no radical social program could base their arguments on the same principles that the U.S. patriots had used. U.S. and Venezuelan economic and ideological interests may not have been complementary, but they were parallel.

The Rise and Fall of Venezuela's First Republic, 1810–1812

When the Caracas elite finally proclaimed an independent junta on 19 April 1810, the rules governing the relations between Venezuela and the United States changed. Trade remained important, but the Venezuelan patriots more desperately needed diplomatic recognition, arms, and assistance. Venezuelans knew that they could not survive as an autonomous province without neutral trade, aid, and diplomatic support, and they looked toward Great Britain and the United States as the most logical sources of assistance.

Unfortunately, the United States would or could do less to assist the Venezuelan patriots in 1810 than it had in 1806. Many recalled the fiasco of the Miranda expedition. Moreover, between April 1810 and July 1811 Venezuela still remained a part of the Spanish empire, albeit with local autonomy and a local junta. Many U.S. leaders preferred to press the Venezuelan case diplomatically before the European powers without risking U.S. interests or provoking reprisals from Europe. Even the lure of Venezuelan trade was less appealing than it had once been. From 1808, Great Britain had had an ever increasing edge in Venezuelan trade and had been granted a 25 percent reduction in duties. At the same time, President Madison favored the lucrative Spanish peninsular grain trade over the less secure market to the south. In the face of a possible war with either England or France, South American trade and relations seemed less pressing. U.S. statesmen also increasingly set their sights on possessing Florida, which meant that they could neither alienate the Spanish nor condone any Latin American plans to "free" Spanish Florida. National interests thus dictated that the United States delay giving any overt assistance to the Venezuelans.

Venezuela's early efforts at diplomacy with the United States were clumsy, but the experience served the nation well in subsequent dealings with the republic to the north. Venezuelan diplomats also suffered by comparison with the skillful Spanish minister, Luís de Onís. Onís had replaced the thoughtless and arrogant Carlos Martínez de Irujo, the marqués de Casa Irujo, who had so botched Spanish interests in the years 1805–6. Onís kept a close eye on Venezuelan activities, and he pressed his interests privately and effectively with leaders in the United States, cleverly tempting them with the promise of a prize much sweeter than anything the Venezuelan patriots could offer: Florida.

Onís also outwitted the first Venezuelan agents to Washington, Juan Vicente Bolívar and Telésforo de Orea, who arrived seeking recognition and arms on 11 June 1810. Rebuffed at every turn, Orea returned to Caracas in August 1810 to inform the Venezuelan junta that there was no hope of aid as long as Venezuela remained part of the Spanish empire. Nudged by Orea and other young radicals, the Caracas political elite fairly rapidly accepted the idea of independence.

Juan Vicente Bolívar, apparently less of a firebrand than his younger brother Simón who had been dispatched to England to seek assistance, remained in the United States after Orea left. He did secure some arms through the intercession of merchants such as Stephen Girard, some of whom were less than scrupulous in their dealings with the Venezuelan.[17] Bolívar also began to negotiate the recognition of Venezuelan autonomy within the Spanish empire with Spanish minister Luís de

Onís. He remained unaware that the Caracas junta increasingly favored complete independence. When it became known that Juan Vicente Bolívar was endorsing Venezuela's continued imperial status, a patriotic outcry nearly forced the junta to condemn him as a traitor. In early 1811, his brother Simón warned him not to return to Venezuela. Tempers had cooled, however, by the time the Venezuelan Congress declared independence on 5 July 1811. Juan Vicente's perceived betrayal became moot when he and his cargo of fifteen hundred guns were lost at sea in August 1811 on the voyage home.

The United States hesitated to recognize Venezuela officially, but Washington did dispatch U.S. agents to South America to facilitate commerce and to gain information about the patriots' activities. Robert K. Lowry of Maryland, for example, carried the title of maritime agent, a less official position than consul. After the declaration of independence, apparently at Lowry's instruction, Venezuela regarded him as a consul, although no official confirmation of his official status was received. In November 1810 Lowry informed Washington that Venezuela was modeling its laws and institutions on those of the United States, but he expressed pessimism a year later about the new country's ability to survive without outside help. The patriots had no arms, and Lowry estimated that a troop of six thousand Europeans could easily defeat them.[18]

The second U.S. special agent, Alexander Scott, arrived in 1812, ostensibly to accompany goods that had been contributed toward earthquake relief. The Venezuelans hoped that Scott might bear certification and instructions to initiate formal diplomatic relations. If he had such instructions, however, he did not reveal them. Like Lowry, he kept Washington informed on the patriots' activities. To that end, he visited General Miranda's barracks in La Victoria, a critical military zone, without telling the Venezuelans his purpose.[19] Even in such chaotic times, the Venezuelans noted such deviations from diplomatic courtesy and practice. In 1819 Venezuelan foreign minister Juan Germán Roscio recalled the examples of Scott's unauthorized entry into a military zone and the discrepancy over Lowrey's credentials as examples of Venezuelan gullibility and U.S. duplicity.

Venezuelan agents so convinced themselves that Washington *must* recognize a fellow American republic that they frequently misread U.S. intentions. Telésforo de Orea returned to the United States in 1811, stressing the common history and interests shared by Venezuela and the United States when he presented his credentials on 17 May: "The United States showed Venezuela the path of liberty and social virtues, and the peoples of South America will also follow insofar as possible the Constitution of North America." He asserted that nature, "the political state" of Europe, and reciprocal American interests dictated an "intimate union." Venezuela's government, based on the will of its people, wanted to form mutually beneficial commercial ties and "a lasting union with the United States."[20] Orea informed the *Gazeta de Caracas* that people in Washington and Philadelphia expressed admiration for Venezuelans' actions, especially for their prudence and moderation. He optimistically hoped that the United States would recognize Venezuelan independence.

Yet Orea had moments of cynicism and pessimism as well. Although he admired the U.S. system, the Venezuelan agent reported that the relative autonomy of Congress and the state governments limited the president's actions. "The Government, like the people, want the liberty and independence of South America, but without a public commitment."[21] By September, Orea reluctantly concluded that Venezuela could not expect the United States to act on the basis of ideals: "Every day I am more persuaded that it is necessary for each country to rely on its own resources; foreign aid always depends upon the rewards that are expected. . . . I repeat to you that without money nothing can be done."[22]

When Caracas suffered a devastating earthquake in March 1812, Telésforo de Orea learned another lesson. He asked Secretary of State Monroe to lift the embargo so that private citizens could participate in a humane effort to ship goods and relief to Venezuelan ports,[23] but his request was refused. Instead the U.S. Congress voted to send a mere fifty thousand pesos worth of earthquake relief. The disappointed Venezuelan agent concluded, "If these United States were not in such difficult circumstances, I am certain that their generosity would not have been limited to dedicating such a small sum of money to such a worthy cause."[24] Still optimistic, however, Orea characterized the modest aid as a gesture of official friendship, an implicit action of recognition. He predicted that recognition, a commercial treaty, and the naming of resident ministers would soon follow.

The fall of the First Republic in July 1812 just after the United States entered the War of 1812 effectively concluded this period of intense diplomatic maneuvering. U.S. statesmen had perhaps confirmed their suspicion that Venezuela could not defend its independence and that intervention would have been a useless risk. The *Providence Gazette* heartlessly gloated that the "notorious malcontent Miranda . . . is imprisoned at Caracas, and, it is expected that an ignominious death will close the career of this restless unprincipled chief."[25] Venezuelans learned that ideological affinity and the argument of a peculiarly "American" interest were not strong enough to influence U.S. official policy. They felt disappointed and somewhat betrayed by the official U.S. policy of neutrality. The Venezuelan First Republic had simultaneously tested the possibility of an American alliance with the United States and the effectiveness of a federal constitution largely based on the U.S. model. Neither the alliance nor the model provided measurable benefits for Venezuela.

War, Realism, and Recognition, 1812–1822

In the decade that separated the fall of the First Republic from official U.S. recognition of Venezuelan independence, Venezuelan leaders abandoned idealism. They continued to solicit aid and recognition from the United States, but they assessed the chances of receiving aid from that quarter as minimal. U.S. leaders gave precedence to the War of 1812 and to urging the Spanish to cede Florida. Disappointment at being rebuffed by the United States, military necessity, and a closer look at their own society also led Simón Bolívar and his companions to look more critically at the U.S. political model. All the Venezuelan governments between 1812 and 1822 were much more centralist and authoritarian than the First Republic had been, and U.S. leaders and emissaries frequently voiced disapproval of this conservative tendency.

Consistent with Venezuela's new realism, Simón Bolívar and other patriots tried to attract privateers, filibusters, and mercenaries to aid their cause. Without funds or legitimacy to attract such adventurers, the Venezuelans instead offered generous shares in any booty taken from the royalists. Following his famous "war to the death" proclamation in 1813, Simón Bolívar promised that foreigners who fought for Venezuela would become Venezuelan citizens and be suitably compensated. In that same year, General A. Nicolás Briceño invited foreigners to join the campaign against the royalists. Any royalist property seized would be divided into four portions: one quarter to be divided equally among officers who commanded the operation, the second quarter for the soldiers, and the other half reserved for the state. An officer or soldier who displayed extraordinary heroism could expect an additional share of the spoils. Officers earned military promotions on the basis of the number of Spanish heads they accumulated. Twenty heads gained one the rank of second lieutenant, fifty heads earned a promotion to captain, and so forth.[26]

Relatively few U.S. soldiers responded to these attractive offers, and little was recorded about those who did enlist, perhaps because they came as individuals and not as a group like the famous British expedition of 1817. Few left records like that of U.S. citizen Felix Jastran, who received a colonel's commission around 1813 and fought in the Battles of Carabobo (Venezuela, 1821) and Ayacucho (Peru, 1824).[27]

Alexander Macaulay, born in Yorktown, Virginia, was infatuated with military life and had a short but meteoric career in the Gran Colombian army. A U.S. Army surgeon angry at his failure to earn promotion, Macaulay traveled to Venezuela in 1811. In La Guaira, Macaulay announced to U.S. agent Robert K. Lowry "that he had come to South America, for the purpose of espousing the cause of the patriots, in their struggles to emancipate themselves from the yoke of Spanish slavery."[28] After a spell of practicing medicine in the interior of Venezuela, Macaulay's scorn for the republican troops could not be contained: "What hope can be entertained of the independence of such people!"[29] He must have expressed his views publicly, for Colombian Antonio Nariño expelled Macaulay from Cudinamarca for criticizing the government. After leaving Cudinamarca, Macaulay joined some republican troops on the way to Quito. His hapless military career ended when Spanish troops captured and executed him. An account of Macaulay's disillusionment with the patriots and his death appeared in the *Portico* of Baltimore and was excerpted in the *National Intelligencer* of Washington in 1817 and may have discouraged other would-be recruits.

Most of the North Americans who fought for Venezuelan independence did so as privateers—the risks were fewer and the profits greater. Privateering did not boom until the conclusion of the War of 1812, but some adventurers had rushed to Venezuela as early as 1810. New Orleans–born Renato Beluche gained experience as a ship captain on the route between Vera Cruz, Campeche, and Belize and served France as a privateer from 1810 until that country lost its Caribbean bases. In 1812, Beluche secured a letter of marque from Cartagena, the only Caribbean base issuing letters of marque at that time. While continuing to use New Orleans as a base, Beluche piled up rewards and praise. General Andrew Jackson lauded Beluche's service in the Battle of New Orleans (18 January 1815), and Simón Bolívar, who promoted Beluche to commodore in the Gran Colombian navy in 1816, wrote of him: "He is superior to all the others because of his rank, knowledge and ability, enthusiasms, etc."[30]

Not all Venezuelans shared Bolívar's esteem of Beluche. Some Venezuelan military officers resented the foreigners, especially the privateers, because of the wealth they amassed and the preferential treatment they received. General José Padilla charged, for example, that Beluche had received unwarranted credit for his role in the Battle of Lake Maracaibo. Padilla said that Beluche was fighting "as a corsair; that is to say, so he could serve his own interests." Beluche responded that he served himself and Colombia at the same time, "and what is the matter with that?"[31]

Beluche was not the only North American to recognize the profits to be gained from assisting the Venezuelans on the seas. Baltimore and

Philadelphia had early benefited from Caribbean and Venezuelan trade, and both cities became havens for Venezuelan and Latin American exiles. Baltimore's mercantile activity and its role in the War of 1812 had fueled rapid urban expansion between 1790 and 1817. At the conclusion of the war, investors and shipowners looked for new ways to put their ships and crews to work. The letters of marque issued so freely by Latin American ports provided an opportunity to link political sympathies and profits. The ships that received such licenses were authorized to loot and destroy enemy shipping. U.S. law forbade either sailors or captains to participate in outfitting hostile ships in U.S. ports, but networks of merchants, shipowners, and customs officials found ways to circumvent the laws and press reluctant seamen into service.[32]

Anxious to keep the Spanish minister happy while the delicate negotiations for Florida were being conducted, the U.S. government took several measures to limit privateering. An 1817 law banned the sale of warships to privateers. In April 1818 Congress enacted legislation to fine and imprison any citizen—or foreigner in the United States—who aided the outfitting of hostile expeditions. On 7 December 1819 President Monroe recommended that only designated ports be open to foreign ships. Baltimore was not on his list.

The Venezuelan patriots bitterly resented the enforcement of U.S. neutrality legislation after 1817. It patently was *not* neutral, they argued, to take actions against those who would help Venezuela while allowing Spain to send all the military forces it wished to keep control of Latin America.

These U.S. actions were influential, but other factors also contributed to the decline of privateers after 1819. The twenty to thirty privateering ships outfitted in Baltimore between 1815 and 1819 found that Spanish trade to America had decreased so much that profits could not be had by merely harassing Spanish shipping. A few privateers, such as John Daniel Danels, became committed to the Venezuelan independence cause and continued to fight on. Danels became a captain in the Colombian navy under the Dutch admiral Luís Brion. In addition to his naval leadership, Danels procured military supplies for Simón Bolívar and gave the Venezuelans a corvette of war, two brigantines, and three schooners in addition to some of his prize ships. Danels later thought better of his generosity, however. In 1844 he asked the Venezuelan government to pay him 290,939 pesos 50 centavos, the value of the property he had donated in 1818 and 1820.[33]

One of the major disagreements between the United States and Venezuela in this period intersected the major issues of Florida, privateering, and the Venezuelan independence strategy. The Venezuelan exiles in Philadelphia—most prominently Pedro Gual and Lino de Clemente—suspected that the March 1817 neutrality legislation had been a down payment to Spain for the acquisition of Florida. Gual and his colleagues wanted to use Amelia Island (off the east coast of Florida) as a strategic northern Caribbean base to harry Spanish shipping and to provide a safe haven for South American exiles. They knew of the abortive 1812 independence movement on Amelia Island, which the United States had covertly supported, and they too aspired to establish a Florida republic. About 40 percent of East Florida's scant population of 3,729 resided on Amelia Island in 1815. Gual and Clemente may have naively assumed that the United States would not object to their temporary establishment of a base on the Spanish territory that the United States so avidly coveted.[34] The pair joined representatives of Argentina and Mexico in commissioning Gregor MacGregor (a Scot married to a cousin of Simón Bolívar) as a general in the Venezuelan and New Granadan Army. MacGregor was ordered to occupy Amelia Island, which he did on 30 June 1817 with recruits from Georgia and South Carolina.

MacGregor held the island for two and a half months amid conflict among the adventurers and slave traders who formed his force. General Louis Aury of France arrived in mid-September to restore order and raise the Mexican flag. Many of the Anglo-Americans resented the French faction, especially the 130 black Haitians who accompanied Aury. In early October, Pedro Gual and Vicente Pazos arrived, scheduled elections in November, and wrote a constitution that provided for, among other things, freedom of religion and freedom of the press.[35]

U.S. troops ended the short-lived republic in December, condemning both the occupation by a foreign power (Mexico) and the privateering and slave trading that the Amelia leaders had sponsored.

Gual and the Venezuelans were outraged. It was one thing for the United States to refuse to help the patriots, or even to enforce one-sided neutrality legislation. In this case, however, as Gual and others saw it, the United States had actually used force to defeat the patriots' effort. In January, Lino de Clemente instructed one of his allies, the Peruvian Vicente Pazos, to make a formal protest to the secretary of state.

Pazos's February statement summarized the grievances the Venezuelans had held against the United States since 1810. Pazos pointed out that Venezuela had emulated U.S. institutions and had asked for U.S. recognition of its independence in 1811. Since the United States had not "thought it convenient to take action" in the name of liberty, the unnecessary bloodshed had continued. Moreover, the northerners had abandoned all possibility of understanding Latin America when they remained aloof from the independence struggle. "The understanding of the habits and mental and physical capacity of peoples; of the hopes of their leaders; of the state of opinion, and finally, of the genius and ability of its inhabitants to undertake and execute deeds cannot be acquired except through a familiar communication acquired through long residence."[36]

More specifically on the Amelia Island incident, Pazos pointed out that the United States, as a neutral power, had no stake in Florida, which was Spanish territory. Amelia was under republican government, just like the United States, and if the United States had had a complaint, it should have appealed to the Latin American republics. Further, there was less slave trading and privateering under the leadership of MacGregor and Aury than had been the case under the Spanish. In any case, U.S. citizens in Georgia had both encouraged and benefited from most of the illicit activities. Finally, the Venezuelans were offended by Washington's characterization of the patriots as a "handful of adventurers." Irregular actions frequently accompany the struggle for liberty, Pazos asserted, and the South American patriots were no more "adventurers" than George Washington had been.[37]

Venezuelan privateering caused further conflict with the United States between 1817 and 1819. Venezuela's trade with the Antilles had declined greatly because of the Spanish blockade. On 6 January 1817 Bolívar decreed a blockade of various Venezuelan ports, including Guayana, or Angostura, and announced that all ships, regardless of flag, that came within three miles of these ports were liable to capture. In 1817 Venezuelans captured and condemned two U.S. ships (*Tigre* and *Libertad*, which belonged to the shipping company Peabody, Tucker, and Coulter) carrying arms and supplies when they violated the Orinoco blockade on their way to the royalists in Angostura. The United States had just fought a war to uphold the shipping rights of neutrals, and Secretary of State Adams sent a Baltimore journalist with political ambitions, John Baptiste Irvine, to Venezuela. Irvine was instructed to seek out Bolívar and courteously but firmly insist that the vessels be returned to their owners along with an indemnity for the lost cargo. The United States still had no immediate plans to establish relations with Venezuela, but Irvine was also to inform Washington about the population and resources of the zone controlled by Bolívar, the probable consequences of the freeing of the slaves, and Venezuela's commercial potential.

When Irvine arrived in Angostura on 12 July 1818, Bolívar received him graciously, perhaps because he thought that Irvine brought the coveted recognition. In his instructions to Lino Clemente, Bolívar had optimistically written "that we can expect to be recognized and even assisted with the military elements that we need, and with money to cover the credits that we have contracted with some commercial houses in England."[38] Irvine soon corrected Bolívar's misconceptions in a barrage of letters sent between late July and October. Bolívar stubbornly insisted that ships that provided arms and supplies to ports blockaded and under siege were not neutral; accepting the U.S. interpretation of neutrality was equivalent to surrender. Nor could Bolívar contain his bitterness at the lack of help from the United States: "I am speaking of the behavior of the United States with respect to the independence movements of the South, and of the rigorous laws promulgated with the purpose of preventing our securing any kind of aid there."[39] Bolívar concluded that he was satisfied that he had acted according to law, and, unless the United States wanted to submit the matter to arbitration, the affair was over.

Irvine did not take the frustration generated by his mission lightly. He stayed for several months, firing letters back to Adams that characterized Bolívar as a tyrant. "The wheels of his government," Irvine charged, "are clogged already with imbecility."[40] Moreover, he said, "since Bolívar heads up the Army, he has also put himself at the head of the nation. It is said that he hopes now to increase his power by using a Congress of ignorant men with pretensions to wisdom."[41] Others might save the nation, Irvine predicted, but it had been put in more peril by this "Don Quixote with ambition, but without military talents, than by a tireless and savage enemy."[42] Irvine finally gave up and left Venezuela in February 1819.

Secretary of State John Quincy Adams persisted in his interpretation of neutrality. He and President James Monroe decided that a more forceful emissary might jar loose the requested indemnities, and they sent Commodore Oliver Hazard Perry to Venezuela with two warships. If the Venezuelans should express chagrin at battleships coming to discuss a diplomatic matter, Adams told Perry, he was to assure the patriots that no pressure was intended: "Captain Perry will explain that the President of the U.S. prefers to give explanations through a naval officer rather than a special agent named for the purpose, precisely because he thinks that an unofficial communication, can be more friendly and confidential."[43] Perry was received by Vice President Francisco Antonio Zea when he arrived in Angostura in late July 1819, because Bolívar was away on a military campaign.

Whether it was through the U.S. show of force or Zea's relative mildness, Perry gained more satisfaction than Irvine had. Zea agreed to pay an indemnity for the two vessels only, citing the corsair regulations, which allowed seizure of illegal goods but not the ships that carried them. The United States continued to press for indemnities for the cargos as well, and in September 1819 Venezuela accepted the claim for the noncontraband cargo of one ship. To Perry's warnings about illegal privateers and slave trading the Venezuelans responded that they recognized the same laws on piracy and had prohibited the slave trade since 14 August 1810.

Perry never returned home with his news, however, for on 23 August he succumbed to a fever and died off the coast of Trinidad. Venezuelan historian Vicente Lecuna characterized Perry's mission as the "first of many acts of force which have victimized our defenseless countries, and the first act of weakness of our lamentable diplomacy."[44]

Perry's chaplain, John N. Hambledon, returned with views that could not have improved Venezuela's reputation in Washington. In his journal Hambledon termed the "natives" "the most indolent and inactive people in the world" and found the soldiers in the fortress so ignorant and lacking in discipline "that I am sure that two hundred good soldiers would be enough to take both forts." Hambledon saw no law in the land aside from the will of Bolívar, "who is an absolute dictator" whose "education leaves much to be desired." He noted that many of the people with whom he spoke had "prejudices" against the United States, but he believed that the prejudice had been fomented by the British, who "enthusiastically dedicated themselves to libeling the United States in Venezuela."[45]

Even though Venezuelans grew more wary of the United States, they could not afford to ease their pressure for diplomatic recognition. Before 1822, however, they still faced an impasse in Washington. Luís de Onís played a clever game, requiring that in exchange for Florida, the United States must promise not to recognize Latin American independence. U.S. presidents resisted making such a promise, but they remained noncommittal about Latin America until the Adams-Onís Treaty was secure. Spain signed the treaty in 1819 but did not ratify it until 1822.

The ratification of the Adams-Onís Treaty, Bolívar's military victories in Gran Colombia (Boyacá in 1819 and Carabobo in 1821), Britain's South American ambitions, and the European threat to retake the former Spanish colonies finally moved the United States to recognize Venezuela's independence as part of Gran Colombia. Venezuela's more skillful diplomatic efforts in the 1817–22 period no doubt also aided the cause. In 1819 Bolívar revoked Lino de Clemente's credentials (U.S. officials had refused to speak with him because of his involvement with the Amelia Island affair) and named Philadelphia resident (since the 1790s) Manuel Torres as the official agent of Gran Colombia. Venezuelans had learned that respected lobbyists had a higher value than principled arguments. Torres's Philadelphia circle and his friends in Washington knew well the machinations of the federal government, and of Onís, and made credible the argument that the United States finally accepted—and then claimed as its own: that European powers should not consider new colonization attempts in the Americas. On 19 June 1822, President Monroe received Torres as chargé d'affaires of Colombia, the first effective recognition of a Latin American diplomat. His dream fulfilled, Torres died less than a month later.

Pan-Americanism and Reactions, 1822–1826

Monroe's recognition of the Latin American republics is only part of the story of the origins of inter-American relations. Venezuelans had steadily proposed an inter-American alliance from 1810 onward, inspired both by the need for military aid and by their belief in an American republican destiny.

President Bolívar and his colleagues in Gran Colombia—most notably Francisco Paula de Santander, who became vice president of Colombia, and Pedro Gual, the minister of the treasury and foreign relations—agreed that an American confederation was more necessary than ever. Although the Spanish had been expelled from Venezuela and Colombia by 1821, Spain still retained strongholds in the Andean provinces of Ecuador, Peru, and Alta Peru (Bolivia), and in Cuba and Puerto Rico. Europe's Holy Alliance announced its intention to help Spain recapture its empire, heightening Venezuelans' fears that their fragile victories would evaporate. Bolívar's army marched to the south to engage the royalist troops and establish independent republics in the Andean region, a task that would occupy him until 1826. Santander and Gual pursued the fight on the diplomatic front, working to call an American congress that would defy European ambitions. An energetic correspondence kept the diplomatic and military fronts in contact.

Pedro Gual, who had previous experience in the United States as an agent of the patriots in 1812–13 and 1815–17, tried to persuade Washington to participate in the congress and alliance. He was heartened by President James Monroe's announcement of the Monroe Doctrine in December 1823. The doctrine announced that the Americas with their republican institutions differed from the tyrannies of Europe and warned that Europeans should cease to seek further colonization or recolonization in the New World. Pragmatically, Gual asked Minister Juan María Salazar of Colombia to test U.S. intentions regarding Latin America. Specifically, Gual wanted to know if the United States was prepared to use force to resist European efforts at reconquest in Latin America. Would Washington sign an offensive and defensive treaty of alliance with Colombia? Secretary of State Adams responded in August 1824 that any U.S. decision to act against foreign intervention was up to Congress; that the president would ask Congress to take action if armed attacks should threaten the liberty of the new republics; but the United States would need the active cooperation of some European powers to be able to resist the Holy Alliance. Adams's response could hardly have encouraged Gual, but he nevertheless instructed Salazar in October to invite the United States to attend the hemispheric conference in Panama.[46]

After the definitive victory at Ayacucho in Peru in December 1824, Simón Bolívar turned his attention to the proposed inter-American conference. In the same month, he issued an invitation to the Spanish-American republics to attend an assembly of plenipotentiaries in Panama. His correspondence took little note of the Monroe Doctrine, and he objected to inviting the United States to participate at Panama. He had concluded that only England could guarantee the independence of the Latin American republics, and he feared that an invitation to the United States would alienate the English. In a June 1825 letter to Santander the Liberator insisted that neither the Haitians nor the North Americans should be invited, because "the North Americans and the Haitians are foreigners to us."[47] He further predicted that the United States would be the congress's "greatest opponents, on the alleged grounds of independence and freedom, but their real reasons will be selfish ones, for they have nothing to fear at home."[48] Santander and Gual remained unconvinced and persisted in extending the invitation to the United States.

John Quincy Adams, now president of the United States and his secretary of state, Henry Clay, in 1825 proposed that Washington accept the invitation to Panama. Members of Congress objected, citing the dangers of abandoning strict neutrality. Some Venezuelans and Mexicans wanted the congress to consider joint military operations against Spanish forces in Cuba and Puerto Rico. The United States opposed that quixotic initiative because it feared that a weak Cuba could not maintain its independence and would tempt a major power to occupy the island.

Moreover, an ineffectual Cuban government might be unable to contain uprisings by slaves and people of color, uprisings that could affect racial peace in the U.S. South. Some U.S. politicians deplored the racial equality that most Spanish-American republics affirmed and objected to the possibility that antislavery issues might be debated at the congress. Senator Thomas Benton of Missouri argued that the U.S. Congress did not want to debate antislavery measures or encourage racial equality. Why, then, go to Panama "to advise and consult in council about it? Who are to advise and sit in judgment upon it? Five nations who have already put the black man upon an equality with the white, not only in their constitutions but in real life: five nations who have at this moment (at least some of them) black generals in their armies and mulatto senators in their congresses!"[49]

Indeed, the senator need not have worried. The Venezuelan elite were no more eager than Benton was to encourage racial democracy, or "pardocracy," as they sometimes referred to a feared rule by *pardos*, people of color. The 1824 Treaty of Peace, Friendship, Navigation, and Commerce between Colombia and the United States agreed to suppress the slave trade but omitted any mention of the institution of slavery itself. Simón Bolívar had freed Venezuelan slaves who fought in his army in 1816, both as a pragmatic military gesture and as fulfillment of his pledge to President Alexandre Pétion of Haiti. Venezuelans' reaction, beginning with the Congress of Angostura in 1819 and ratified in the constitution and laws of Cúcuta, then forced what historian John Lombardi called the "reconstruction of slavery in Venezuela."[50] Slaves were to be considered free at birth, but they owed their masters eighteen to twenty-one years of work. Of course, the Latin American elite, like many contemporary U.S. abolitionists, could oppose slavery while despising or fearing African Americans. In June 1825 Bolívar wrote that "my sister, who is quite capable, writes me that Caracas is uninhabitable because of the excesses and threats of domination by the people of color. She, who is poor, tells me that she wants to go to the United States."[51]

The Panama Congress, finally held in June 1826, proved anticlimactic. Only Peru, Colombia, Mexico, and Central America sent representatives. Great Britain and Holland sent observers. The two designated U.S. observers did not participate; one died en route, and the other arrived after the congress had adjourned. The Spanish-American delegates proved no more enthusiastic about a binding alliance than the United States was. Still, the congress lives in Venezuelan historical memory as the union that might have been and the precursor of all subsequent efforts to forge an autonomous Latin America alliance apart from U.S. domination.

Tyranny, Diplomacy, and the Collapse of Gran Colombia, 1826–1830

The Gran Colombian confederation fell into chaos with Bolívar's return from Peru in 1826. Regional and personal rivalries, and Bolívar's increasingly autocratic rule, fueled a constant atmosphere of crisis and conspiracy. Venezuelan José Antonio Páez led a rebellion against Bogotá's control in 1826 and again in 1829. Bolívar's enemies charged that the Liberator intended to establish a monarchy in Colombia. A conspiracy to assassinate Bolívar in 1828 failed, earning the death penalty for several men. Bolívar commuted the death sentence of Vice President Santander, who allegedly was involved in the plot.

U.S. politicians struggled to understand the issues and to sort out rumor from reality. At the dawn of the Jacksonian age of rough-hewn democracy in the United States, U.S. citizens and newspapers increasingly voiced suspicion of Bolívar's motives. One of Bolívar's aides-de-camp, Colonel Belford Wilson of Britain, reported in 1829 from the United States: "The majority hate your excellency for the same reason that the Greeks hated Aristides, because they are tired of hearing your virtues mentioned; others, because your excellency is not a federalist; others, because they don't want to see anyone compared with their Washington, and others because your excellency does not protect the contraband and other abuses that favored them."[52]

General William Henry Harrison, appointed U.S. minister to Colombia in 1828, reflected the distrust of Bolívar. With an enthusiasm that led Colombians to compare him with the meddling Joel Poinsett in Mexico, Harrison set to work to undermine perceived tyranny in Colombia. If Harrison's rank was exceptional among the lot of second-raters who customarily served in the U.S. diplomatic service in nineteenth-century Latin America, his judgment was no better. He foreshadowed a host of U.S. emissaries who self-righteously mixed in local politics that they only dimly understood. Bolívar's rumored plans to establish a monarchy especially concerned Harrison because he believed that the British were encouraging them. Harrison's general lack of discretion and his public disapproval of Bolívar led the Colombian government to ask that he be withdrawn because of his alleged involvement in a plot against the Liberator. President Andrew Jackson had already appointed Harrison's successor, who arrived in September 1829, but Harrison remained in Colombia for several months to refute the charges that he had aided the conspirators.

Before he left, he wrote a long letter to Bolívar, advising him to give up his monarchical ideas and turn his back on his political allies. To his credit, Harrison was one of the few nineteenth-century U.S. agents who judged that the people of Gran Colombia were capable of self-rule. He advised Bolívar that "the people of Colombia have many features of character suitable to a good republican government. A people more moderate, tolerant and well disposed, cannot be found anywhere."[53] Harrison judged the problems to be as follows. With "a multitude of comfortable and lazy friars and an army excessively disproportionate to the resources of the country, with a body of officers ten times more disproportionate to the army, all branches of industry are oppressed with burdens that deprive the industrious man of the profits of his labor and the farmer of his reward."[54] Bolívar ignored Harrison's advice and sent the letter, with an accompanying note, to his foreign minister: "This gentleman, a foreign agent, attempts to meddle very directly and through a semi-official note in our affairs. It seems to me that the Council should say something about this irregular conduct."[55]

Harrison shortly saw his goals realized in spite of himself. Bolívar resigned the presidency in April 1830 and made plans to go into exile. He died in December in the Colombian port of Santa Marta. Ecuador withdrew from the union in August 1830. José Antonio Páez headed Venezuela's definitive separatist movement, endorsing a republican constitution in May 1830. Ironically, Páez, an unschooled mulatto general who seized and held power by force, would epitomize Venezuelan democracy to the United States for the next two decades.

The possibility that an ideological affinity between the United States and South America might bring about a harmonious confederation of republics had been only a dim hope at best and had been shattered by the experiences of the first quarter of the nineteenth century. The official U.S. position of neutrality looked distinctly unneutral to the south. U.S. citizens, nurtured on anti-Spanish and anti-Catholic biases, believed that the South American independence struggles confirmed their views that Latin America was incapable of true democracy. Private U.S. citizens had found out that the streets were not paved with gold in the south, although opportunities existed for the hardworking and the unscrupulous.

Venezuelans, on the other hand, learned to suspect the republican idealism they heard in the United States Their northern neighbor was more likely to act from self-interest than from idealism and would opt for a show of force over formal diplomacy and international law. Moreover, the famous U.S. governing checks and balances often made decisive action abroad impossible. If Venezuelans had had relatively few anti-*yanqui* biases prior to independence, their experience with private citizens and official agents of the United States during the first two decades of intensive contact augured poorly for the future.

Venezuelan and U.S. leaders generally displayed a lack of imagination and empathy when they considered the issue of security from the other's point of view. Venezuela underestimated the fear in the United States that England would seize Cuba, Florida, or other bases in the Caribbean and thus threaten U.S. independence or expansion. The United States gave relatively little weight to Venezuelan concerns that their independence would not be secure as long as Spain retained control of Florida or Cuba. Security meant entirely different things on the northern and southern rims of the Caribbean Sea.

2   Gunboats and Caudillos, 1830–1866

> Not only the United States, but Venezuela and all the other American States, are struggling with reactionary agencies that threaten the very existence of the republican situation itself.
>
> —William Seward

Venezuela's independent relations with the United States unfolded at a time when most American nations embraced a romantic nationalism that celebrated the unique rather than the universal, the nation rather than the hemisphere. In turn, regional loyalties and interests threatened national unity. The Enlightenment universalism that had accompanied the Venezuelan independence period had faded on both sides of the Caribbean by the 1830s. Eighteenth-century principles, each state now saw, overlay centuries of divergent Hispanic and English colonial traditions and cultures. Both nations struggled to build on the positive elements of their traditions and to minimize or eliminate the negative.

The first thirty years of association set the tone for binational relations for nearly a century. Venezuela's trade and strategic location were more important to the United States than those of any other country in South America (except for Brazil), but the U.S. government maintained a firm official policy of noninvolvement. Until the 1860s, the State Department pragmatically extended diplomatic recognition to all Venezuelan presidents. United States citizens in Venezuela were less scrupulous. Naval officers, diplomatic representatives, and businessmen frequently sided with the factions that favored their interests, and they pleaded with Washington to threaten or chastise the recalcitrant. By one count, fewer than fifty U.S. citizens resided in Venezuela during this period.[1] Their informal relations no doubt influenced Venezuelans' perceptions of *yanquis*, but they probably contributed little to their own compatriots' views of Venezuelans. The few Venezuelans who resided or traded in New York, Philadelphia, or Baltimore made little impression on their English-speaking neighbors. Newspapers in both countries occasionally played a role in creating impressions of the other country and its citizens. Still, even by 1860 Venezuelan consul Simón Camacho could write to a New York newspaper: "But, to our detriment, the United States knows Venezuela only because of our wars, and your best geographers distinguish Caracas *only* for the terrible earthquake of 1812."[2]

Reciprocal impressions often depended on the exaggerated reputations of a few individuals. José Antonio Páez replaced Simón Bolívar as an admired symbol of Venezuela in the United States, and Andrew Jackson or Abraham Lincoln epitomized the positive side of Uncle Sam. More ambiguous, or negative, images became associated with U.S. diplomatic agents like John G. A. Williamson or adventurer Seth Driggs, and Venezuelan Liberals José Tadeo Monagas or Antonio Leocadio Guzmán.

Relations between Venezuela and the United States were among the smoothest in the hemisphere so long as José Antonio Páez remained in control. Strongman and president between 1830 and 1848, Páez held in check both the aristocratic, even royalist, partisans of Simón Bolívar and the allegedly ungovernable and volatile colored masses. Rather similar in image to President Andrew Jackson in his populism and military reputation, Páez pleased foreigners by maintaining order and encouraging relatively free trade with other nations. He allowed the Caracas oligarchy to direct most of the national business, contributing to a natural alliance between them and the foreign merchants. After Páez fell in 1848, the Liberal party ascended to power and changed some of the rules. Unable, or unwilling, to control the masses, the Liberals invited criticism because of the constant civil conflict and because they threatened the interests of foreign creditors. Slavery debates and sectionalism in the United States at the same time further encouraged U.S. citizens to view Venezuelan tensions through the lens of their own concerns.

Impressions and Prejudices

The few lonely chargés d'affaires, consuls, and naval officers who resided in Venezuela reflected the exceptionalism that took for granted
that they and their traditions were vastly superior to those of Venezuela. Chargé d'affaires John G. A.Williamson compared the Venezuelan and United States independence movements in his diary:

> But there was an immense difference between the principles that moti-
> vated the two peoples, so much so that they scarcely admit any compari-
> son. In North America, we fought for law and justice and our stimulus
> was patriotism and resistance against oppression. In Venezuela, the
> greater part of the people were not interested in a change, and many of
> their precursors . . . were motivated . . . by personal interests and am-
> bitions. They were ignorant of the sacred rights that make man a morally
> and politically free being.[3]

Throughout his rather churlish journal of the 1830s, Williamson criticized the many excesses of Venezuelans: they were sexually profligate
(and consequently "not as white as they could be"), religiously super-
stitious, wastefully spendthrift, ambitious, ignorant and prejudiced,
and greedy and dishonest. Although the chargé acknowledged that the
great gap between the few rich and the many poor contributed to Venezuelan decadence, he found the undesirable traits to be present across
all social boundaries. Evenhandedly, Williamson thought that the resident foreigners in Venezuela, including his own countrymen, were
little better, and he further criticized the Venezuelans for tolerating the
foreigners' peccadillos.

In truth, the U.S. citizens who resided in or passed through Venezuela did little to polish the image of their country. Many of them, including even the consuls and diplomatic representatives, were among
the adventurers and immoral scofflaws that Williamson described. Like
Williamson, however, most of his compatriots probably considered
themselves superior to the racially mixed and politically backward
Venezuelans. They feared civil conflicts except when they profited

from them, preferred predictable strong-arm rule, and demanded favorable treatment for their business endeavors. Rampant individualism, a frontier spirit, and their intention to get ahead drove others as much as they did Renato Beluche, the Louisiana-born privateer who became an admiral in the Venezuelan navy.

For their part, most Venezuelans had ceased to consider the United States as a political model for their own government. The idealistic liberalism of Venezuela's United States–inspired constitution of 1811 had given way to a more pessimistic view of the Venezuelan masses and sometimes to a more jaundiced view of U.S. republicanism. In his Angostura address of 1819, Simón Bolívar had asserted that it was impossible to apply Anglo-American constitutional principles to Venezuela. Citing Montesquieu, Bolívar concluded that "laws should be suited to the people for whom they are made." The Venezuelan statesmen who followed Bolívar similarly stressed the unique, and essentially conservative, origins of the U.S. Revolution. Fermín Toro wrote in 1839:

> There is no parallel between North and South America. . . . The Anglo-American colonies modeled their institutions and laws after those of the mother country, the only liberal ones then in the world; . . . In the English colonies there was no real revolution, nor change in ideas, nor moral conquests, nor access to new political and philosophical doctrines; there was no more than emancipation . . . and the leaders of this American movement did not have to create, but only to defend and conserve."[4]

In contrast, Toro pointed out, Hispanic-American independence leaders had to reject the absolutism, despotism, and illiberal traditions of Spain. Conservative Juan Vicente González agreed, speculating that "with the majestic qualities of Bolívar, Washington would have awakened fears among the fervent puritans of the North; with the modest virtues of Washington, Bolívar would not have advanced by one day the cause of Independence in the South."[5]

Sometimes drawing on Alexis de Tocqueville's work that analyzed and criticized U.S. democracy, Venezuelan writers pointed out the flaws in U.S. republicanism. How could a republic based on equality and liberalism permit slavery to continue, Toro queried? He also criticized the principle of majority rule, which left slaves, Indians, and people of color with no recourse to protect their basic humanity and rights. Referring to the famous "gag rule" to prohibit debate on slavery that passed by a vote of 198 to 6 in the U.S. Congress in 1836, Toro asserted that the vote revealed the "omnipotence that the majority exercises over opinions, even over thought."[6] In an 1860 critique of U.S. expansionism, Antonio Leocadio Guzmán disparaged the view that land occupied by non-Christian Indians could legally be seized by more "civilized" people.[7]

Venezuelans who resided in the United States, such as Simón Camacho in the 1850s, often expressed shock at what Mrs. Trollope termed "the domestic manners of the Americans." Camacho's soul "was saddened" by the image of democracy he found in the House of Representatives: The congressmen put their feet up on the desks, noisily interrupted each other, and ate during the debates; when one lot finished eating, they talked so that the others could eat. The Venezuelan doubted that this scene was what Plato had had in mind when he spoke of "legislative perfection." Remarking on the relationship between the capital and the nation, Camacho wrote: "The capital of the United States is Washington: the capital of Washington is Pennsylvania Avenue. . . . When the Avenue moves, Washington moves, but the United States does not move." In Washington, he observed, everyone had a civil or military title. Uniting all the men with military titles in Washington would result in an army larger than that of the Crimean allies, Camacho joked. Beyond the bounds of Washington, Camacho complained of the famous U.S. commercialism. When he went to Niagara Falls in 1858, he had to pay for everything: guide, carriage, food, and souvenirs. Americans traveled to the marvelous site, Camacho thought, more to say that they had been there than because they enjoyed the scenery. Like many of his compatriots, then and later, Camacho also found U.S. women lacking in femininity and attractivenes, citing as examples Lucy Stone and Elizabeth Cady Stanton.[8]

Many Venezuelan writers characterized their own Hispanic heritage as despotic and backward, but they took pride in the universal principles of justice and humanity, including the condemnation of slavery, espoused by Spanish writers and the Catholic church. Conservative writers like Fermín Toro and Juan Vicente González especially defended Iberian universalism over the more mechanistic process of majority rule that epitomized democracy in the United States. And Simón Camacho reflected the generations of Venezuelans who would take comfort in the belief that their own manners and genteel bearing were superior to those of the *yanquis*.

Despite their sometimes unfavorable views of the other, Venezuelan elites and U.S. citizens usually found common ground when they considered what form Venezuela's republican government should take. Both groups agreed that the president and his allies should control the lower orders who had not yet learned how to be responsible citizens and should facilitate the free commerce that would enrich those foreigners and Venezuelans who understood and appreciated freedom.

Diplomacy, Commerce, and British Rivalry

The European powers continued to compete for advantage, trade, resources, and territory in the Americas. Like the United States, European nations paid less attention to Venezuela than to Mexico, although the potential for harassment remained. Spain did not recognize Venezuela's independence until 1845. France shocked Venezuelans with its invasion of Mexico in 1837 and again in the 1860s under Louis Napoleon's expansionist program. British and European loans in the 1820s, and again after 1850, constructed international financial empires. Great Britain also used its Caribbean territories and its powerful navy to expand its influence in the entire region, and the colonies of Trinidad and British Guiana straddling the mouth of the Orinoco River were potential openings to Venezuela's Guayana region and the South American continent.

Venezuela's survival, then, was hardly a foregone conclusion when it withdrew from the Gran Colombian confederation in 1830. The United States delayed establishing relations with the new government, waiting to see whether Venezuela could maintain an independent existence and how the three Gran Colombian nations would apportion their common national debt. Washington hoped that Venezuela would abide by the terms of the 1824 Gran Colombian treaty in the meanwhile, but a rush of new tariffs aroused fear that U.S. merchants would lose even more ground to the British. In 1832 John G. A. Williamson left his post as consul in La Guaira and returned to the United States to join with Philadelphia and New York merchants in lobbying for early recognition and a favorable commercial treaty. Of the Gran Colombian nations, Venezuela's trade was the most valuable to the United States in the early 1830s, meriting consular posts in Maracaibo, Puerto Cabello, La Guaira, and Angostura (later Ciudad Bolívar).

In December 1834, Colombia and Venezuela signed a treaty that confirmed their separation, and Venezuela agreed to assume 28.5 percent of Gran Colombia's debt. Great Britain had extended recognition to Venezuela and secured a commercial treaty in October 1834. The United States dispatched Williamson as the first U.S. chargé d'affaires to the independent republic in June 1835. Much to his chagrin, Williamson found that his British counterpart, Robert Ker Porter, had stolen the advantage both commercially and socially in Caracas. Until Williamson's death in Caracas in 1840, his diplomatic and personal rivalry with Porter resembled that between Joel Poinsett and the Briton Henry Ward in Mexico in the 1820s. Williamson, a North Carolinian, came to his diplomatic post with some knowledge of Venezuela and a predisposition to favor José Antonio Páez. He had served as U.S. consul in La Guaira since 1826, arriving just as Páez was challenging Bolívar's leadership. Bolívar smoothed over the disagreement with Páez in 1827 but inadvertently awakened Williamson's ire with a speech that publicly praised Great Britain but neglected to mention the United States. Piqued, Williamson refused to attend a banquet in Bolívar's honor the following night. Bolívar's reputation in the United States had already declined, but Williamson's dislike of Bolívar and preference for Páez may have dated from those events in La Guaira.[9] In any case, Williamson's diary and dispatches as chargé d'affaires between 1835 and his death in 1840 praised Páez and criticized Páez's foes, many of them Bolívar's partisans, as self-interested and unpatriotic.

U.S. secretary of state John Forsyth instructed Williamson in 1835 to consider the negotiation of a commercial treaty his first priority. U.S. citizens had claims to lodge with the Venezuelan government, but they could wait until the commercial treaty was concluded. A revolt against the Venezuelan government between July and November 1835 delayed Williamson's conclusion of the Treaty of Peace, Friendship, Navigation, and Commerce until January 1836.

The United States recognized Venezuela's strategic importance but particularly valued its commercial potential in the Caribbean trade. A later U.S. chargé, Benjamin Shields, pointed out that "the natural advantages of Venezuela were inviting—her fine capacious harbors, healthy sites for commercial cities, . . . navigable rivers, extended varieties of surface and altitude from the tropical plain to the regions of perpetual snow, and with all, her fine commercial position on the most prominent part of the Atlantic coast of South America."[10]

Venezuela's location especially appealed to Philadelphia, Baltimore, and New York merchants and shippers as they expanded their carrying trade. U.S. manufactures did not compete effectively with British goods in the nineteenth-century Venezuelan market, but U.S. shipping, in contrast, more than held its own. Many of the prized British and European goods arrived at Venezuelan ports in U.S. ships.

Showing special concern for U.S. maritime interests, Secretary Forsyth suggested that Williamson extol the clear advantages that the United States held in shipping—an existing coastal trade, abundant raw materials, and skilled seamen. Venezuela needed to recover from its civil war, and "it would be highly injudicious to check its expansion and prosperity by paying an enhanced price for vehicles to transport its products to market and to carry back whatever she may want of the production of other countries."[11] Venezuelans did not necessarily accept this argument and sporadically tried to foster Venezuelan nautical industries and skills, even sending one Domingo Marcucci on a government fellowship to Philadelphia in the 1840s to study naval architecture. Its weakness, civil conflict, and lack of a maritime tradition, however, doomed Venezuela to costly dependence on foreign shippers.

The United States purchased from Venezuela coffee, cacao, indigo, and raw hides and sold principally flour, wheat, lard, rice, and corn. Unlike the British, who enjoyed a positive trade balance with Venezuela, the United States exported less valuable products than its Venezuelan imports for most of the nineteenth century. U.S. merchants complained bitterly that their sales suffered because they had to pay higher tariffs than the British did in Venezuela. The State Department termed Venezuelan trade "important and valuable" in 1844, but Venezuelans continued to prefer British goods over American.[12]

The British had also secured an advantage in Venezuela through merchant banking firms such as Herring, Powles and Graham and Hyslop and Company that became established in Gran Colombia in the 1820s. These mercantile firms and others sold arms, negotiated loans, and conducted an active commerce. Some of the British commercial houses, such as La Guaira's Casa Boulton (1826), handled United States trade and credit as well as British. The connection between credit and commerce gave British banking and mercantile agents a natural advantage, but they also proved to be skillful in cultivating ties with prominent Venezuelan families.

The nature of British-American-Venezuelan relations was complex. Each of the three players jockeyed for advantage, with the edge going to the British for most of the century. Mutual suspicion sometimes sparked rumors of fantastic plots. During the civil conflicts of the 1840s in Venezuela, U.S. chargé Benjamin Shields reported that he had read that Great Britain planned to bring African contract (not slave) labor to its Caribbean colonies. If this happened, Shields predicted, Caribbean free blacks would flee to Venezuela where their labor would have more value. Their presence would then enable a black majority to dominate Venezuela. Venezuelan white notables, Shields thought, would ask the British to assume a protectorate before they would tolerate black rule. Shields's warnings earned little serious consideration in Washington, but they creatively linked the two worst fears of many U.S. citizens living in Venezuela: British expansionism and Haitian-style black rule.

Often benefiting from the British-American competition, Venezuelans nonetheless also remained wary of England's intentions and reprisals. They turned to the United States as their natural protector in troubled times. For example, Williamson reported in February 1837 that Venezuelans were worried about a rumored deal between Spain and England by which the latter might take Venezuela's Guayana territory and the Isthmus of Panama in exchange for surrendering claims against Spain. In 1848, Chargé Benjamin Shields judged that Venezuelans would favor a United States protectorate over British seizure of their customs houses. Two years later, Chargé Isaac Steele reiterated that some Venezuelans had proposed a treaty under which the United States would guarantee their territorial integrity. Steele thought that the Venezuelans had interpreted a U.S. promise to mediate on behalf of the South American republics as a "willingness to become their bound protector." Apparently inspired by the Bidlack Treaty between the United States and Colombia (1846), which guaranteed the neutrality and sovereighty of Panama under Colombian control, in 1855 the Venezuelan foreign minister offered to trade free rights of navigation on the Orinoco River in exchange for a formal U.S. commitment to protect Venezuelan sovereignty. In 1865, President Antonio Guzmán Blanco reiterated the thesis: "Venezuela had come to regard the United States as a Protector of her principles and institutions, and to look up to her as the senior and most powerful Republic on the Continent."[13] Some U.S. diplomats were more sympathetic than others to the proposals and fretted that Venezuela's location and national debt, owed almost exclusively to British bondholders, placed the nation in jeopardy. The State Department steadily resisted all suggestions to play a stronger role in South America.

José Antonio Páez as "the Washington of His Country"

From 1835 until 1848, relations between Venezuela and the United States were perhaps more harmonious than they would be again until the long dictatorship of Juan Vicente Gómez (1908–35). Venezuela's political chief, independence hero José Antonio Páez, enjoyed great prestige in both the United States and Venezuela. A self-taught *llanero*, Páez relied on the Caracas oligarchy for his advisers, welcomed foreigners and their business, and cultivated a warm personal relationship with U.S. representatives like Williamson. He sent his son Ramón to school in the United States, and when the time came, he chose to spend his own political exile in New York. Páez proved his military prowess when he put down the rebellions of 1831, 1835, 1837, 1844, and 1846, but he generously conceded amnesty to his defeated foes.

Chargé John Williamson disapproved of both the rebels and Páez's generosity toward them. He characterized the 1835 rebel leaders, including José Tadeo Monagas, as militarily and morally bankrupt and believed that a civilized country would mete out justice in the form of "six yards of good mecate [rope]." He was also disgusted with the general citizenry, who passively stood by without taking up arms to protect their government. "Truly they don't deserve any better than to be governed by tyrants," Williamson fumed.[14]

Williamson believed that only Páez kept the nation from dissolving into chaos. He did not share William Henry Harrison's faith in the political capacity of Venezuelans, writing that "the influence of a few particular individuals in or out of employment, be it for good or evil, will more or less control the destinies of the country."[15] Twelve years later, in 1848, as Páez's hold was being challenged and civil war seemed imminent, Benjamin Shields judged that Páez "has more completely filled out the character, and is better entitled to the appellation, of the Washington of his country, than perhaps any other man who has gained public confidence in any one of the Spanish American Republics."[16] In the era of Andrew Jackson, William Henry Harrison, and Zachary Taylor, both Venezuelans and North Americans accepted and admired generals who combined political authority with military power. Racial and sectional tensions called for strong hands to contain them.

The confidence in Páez relieved the United States government of any temptation, or need, to intervene in Venezuela. Washington could afford to guard the cherished neutrality that some of its agents occasionally compromised. As Secretary of State Forsyth cautioned Williamson in April 1835, "You cannot be too careful in refraining from identifying yourself with or from appearing by your words and actions to favor or lean towards any of the political parties into which the country may be divided. One of the settled principles of this Government is that of non-interference in the domestic concerns of nations."[17] The exhortation was easier to adhere to before 1840, for there *were* no other parties in Venezuela. In 1840, however, Tomás Lander and Antonio Leocadio Guzmán, a journalist and former cabinet member, founded the Liberal party. They began an unrelenting attack on the party of the "oligarchs," as Páez's followers were termed. Like Páez and his cronies, observers in the United States perceived Guzmán's program both as an attack on private property and foreign merchants and as a demagogic call for blacks and *pardos* to rise up.

The specter of a race war frightened both Páez's allies and U.S. citizens residing in Venezuela after the uprising that accompanied the contentious presidential campaign in 1844. Carlos Soublette, the Páez designate, had won, but he confessed to Chargé A. A. Hall his concern about the Liberals' alliance with people of color. According to Hall, Soublette said that he did not want the United States to "interfere in the internal affairs of Venezuela," but that he would appreciate "any outward demonstrations of sympathy and good understanding between the two Governments." Hall continued that Soublette had "particularly requested that, when our men-of-war touch at La Guayra (and I am quite sure he would be glad at their doing so as often as practicable), the officers, or as many of them as can conveniently leave the vessel, should visit Caracas." Such a projection of force, Hall commented, would have a good effect, "especially on a certain class of the population of this city."[18]

This confidence in the salutary effects of U.S. warships looming on the horizon was hardly new. Clearly, the chargé and the Páez oligarchy understood that warships could intimidate domestic opponents as well as European predators. Venezuela's demography, with most of the population within easy reach of the Caribbean coast or the banks of the Orinoco River, made Venezuelans especially vulnerable to naval shows of force. Commodore Oliver H. Perry in 1819 set the precedent in the

Orinoco, but Washington remained less enthusiastic about dispatching ships than did the bombastic chargés and consuls about requesting them. Members of the U.S. West Indian Squadron, based at Saint Thomas, occasionally approached the Venezuelan coast, although less frequently than U.S. diplomatic agents would have wished. John Williamson thought that the warship *St. Louis* had helped to discourage piracy in 1835 during the rebellion, but he scoffed that some naval officers preferred to use their warships for pleasure cruises, choosing friendly ports over troubled waters.[19]

The 1840s, then, saw the stable Páez regime on the verge of crumbling. The U.S. chargés shared the *paecista* view that unprincipled Liberals and debtors, uncivilized blacks, and British machinations fueled the disorder. In the face of this crisis, Páez took some of the harsher, and surely undemocratic, measures that U.S. agents had sometimes urged. The government passed sedition and conspiracy laws, and then arrested Liberal politician Antonio Leocadio Guzmán in 1844 for having violated them by publishing a disrespectful poem. During his trial, a mob took over the courtroom, intimidated the jury, and then surged through the capital yelling "Death to the oligarchy." The U.S. chargé found nothing to criticize in the conspiracy laws or Guzmán's trumped-up arrest, but he predicted that Páez's amnesty toward the colored mob meant the end of institutional rule.

Following even more widespread social upheavals in 1846, the *paecistas* again charged the Liberal party leaders with conspiracy. This time Guzmán received a death sentence, although he had not instigated the spontaneous rural uprising. Benjamin Shields applauded the sentence and later criticized José Tadeo Monagas, Páez's successor, for commuting it to exile. Like Williamson, Shields shared with the *paecista* elite a distrust of both the colored population and the Liberal political opposition. The Liberal elite fought mostly with words, but their frustration with Páez's repression prepared them, like Thomas Jefferson, to tolerate watering the tree of liberty with blood. Party founder Tomás Lander counseled Venezuelans to be slow to judge that "revolutions are crimes simply for being revolutions."[20]

The Bugbears of Race, Revolution, and Sectionalism

Venezuela's "revolution of 1848" at the outset resembled Jefferson's "revolution of 1800" more than it did the French Revolution, but it did prompt a change in the tone of U.S. relations with Venezuela. Páez had designated José Tadeo Monagas, veteran of the 1831 and 1835 rebellions, as the presidential candidate in 1847. Monagas accepted the conciliatory nomination, but, on taking office, he brought Liberals into the cabinet and began to form a militia of the colored masses. Congress, still controlled by *paecistas*, began impeachment proceedings in January 1848. Monagas backers preempted the trial by forcibly taking over Congress, wounding several congressmen and killing three in the scuffle.

To U.S. citizens who had close personal and business ties with the *paecistas*, the Monagas accession represented rule by the uncivilized in cooperation with the xenophobic. Shields described the events of January 1848 as "some of the most horrible atrocities, ever perpetrated by the authorities or individuals of any civilized country on the face of the earth." He continued, "Never before in the history of nations, was such an act consummated—never such means employed." Not forgetting his suspicion of the British, Shields speculated that the British chargé had fomented the conflicts as a preliminary to seizing Venezuela. The United States should send warships with one or two companies of flying artillery, Shields entreated, to restore order and return the whites to power. Such a display of force would be "an act of humanity that would be worthy of the United States."[21]

Shields further emphasized his parallel fears of race and revolution when he advised State Department officials that they could understand the character of the Liberals if they took their impression of "the Mexican character" and imagined it modified by "the idleness, want of energy, ignorance and credulity natural to the African race." He added that "the small portion of the colored population, elevated by education and superior traits of character above the level of the mass, is generally identified with the opposite party."[22]

Washington again rebuffed Shields's demand for a fleet to aid his friends and keep the blacks in submission. The president was distressed to hear of the violence in a nation that professed to follow the U.S. model, but the United States would not intervene in the domestic affairs of a foreign country. The United States would send a warship, but Shields was cautioned, "You will remember that she is sent to Venezuela for the purpose of affording security to American interests, and will be careful to advise her employment on no service which may be justly regarded as inconsistent with the neutral character of the United States."[23] Shields went beyond his instructions in his efforts to help Páez. When Captain John Kelly and the warship *Albany* stopped at La Guaira on 12 May en route from Saint Thomas to Yucatán, Shields persuaded Kelly to disregard his orders and stay by the Venezuelan coast. He expected orders any day, the chargé told Kelly, to support Páez in a major invasion or to protect American lives and property. Kelly stayed for nearly three months before leaving for Yucatán in August, uneasy about his disregard of orders and his depleted provisions.

Both the British government and Monagas lodged complaints against Shields. The State Department reprimanded him in August 1848 and recalled him a year later, although he was allowed to save face by resigning. Shields protested that the British chargé had orchestrated the criticism of him and that he had achieved a good working relationship with the Monagas government in spite of his own preference for Páez. He reported that his house had been attacked in July 1849, but he denied that the attacks represented anti-Americanism. The State Department stood firm in the belief that Shields had become too compromised to be able to defend U.S. interests in Venezuela.[24]

The conflicts of the 1840s in Venezuela derived from internal causes, not foreign meddling. Still, the U.S. chargés, and presumably U.S. merchants as well, not only made their preferences for Páez obvious, they shared the *paecista* view that the Liberals, backed by the racially mixed mobs, were dangerous men. Naturally, the Liberals resented such attitudes and treated the foreigners less warmly than had the *paecistas*. Venezuela escaped the invasions and filibustering that Mexico, Cuba, and Nicaragua suffered at the hands of U.S. soldiers and adventurers. Still, the unofficial meddling of Shields and his compatriots contributed to

Venezuelan suspicion regarding the intentions of the North American republic.

Venezuela's mounting concerns about British encroachment and the fierce Federal War (1859–63) muffled open attacks on the United States. U.S. observers' pessimism about Venezuelan institutions and the Liberals received further confirmation as the civil conflict escalated. To oversimplify, José Tadeo Monagas, in his new guise as a Liberal, alternated in power with his brother, José Gregorio, until 1858, when Conservatives joined disgruntled Liberals to overthrow the Monagas duo. The ensuing Federal War ostensibly pitted advocates of local powers against centralists. A parade of presidents, acting presidents, and dictators held the executive office. General José Antonio Páez even returned from exile in New York to declare a dictatorship between 1861 and 1863. Páez abdicated in 1863, and the exhausted parties agreed to write a new constitution. The 1864 Constitution represented the high tide of federalism and states' rights in Venezuela and arguably was the most egalitarian and popular of all of Venezuela's constitutions. Venezuelans asserted that the bloody Federal War had purged the nation of its oligarchy, making way for a more authentic democracy.

Observers from the United States may have interpreted Venezuelan events during this period through the lens of their own racial fears and concerns for the disintegration of their own union. Surely Venezuela exemplified the lapse into anarchy that would follow a weakening of central authority and the unfettered actions of colored mobs. In 1859 U.S. minister Edward Turpin referred to "the lawless black rabble regiment, notoriously opposed to the existing Government," but he added: "It has been from the beginning a war of classes not of the black against the white, but of the idle, base, and profligate against the friends of Justice and Order."[25]

U.S. minister Henry T. Blow, a Virginian by birth and a fervent Missouri unionist by conversion, commented on the implications of an extreme states' rights position and black power in Venezuela. In February 1862 he observed that the white population in Venezuela had declined in proportion to the colored population since the early days of the republic.

Since then, the races have intermarried, there is still an exclusive class (mostly white) who are intent on ruling the country. They number one hundred and fifty thousand, while the opposing Sambos, Mestizos, Mulattos and Negroes estimated at a million, feel that they have been maltreated and are Proscribed. These latter are nearly all the Federales, and are not without the sympathies of a large number of the Whites. They cling closely to two ideas, viz. that as a majority, they have a right to control the affairs of the Republic, and once in Power, to provide a Constitution which will allow each state or province to choose its own Government and elect the other officers and magistrates.[26]

Blow conceded that the masses had some grievances, but their redemption lay not in self-government but "in the protection and ennobling influence of a superior people," a role that foreigners might fill.

After the Liberals' ascent in 1848, U.S. diplomats perceived not only an increase in racial tensions in Venezuela but also an unparalleled corruption. In 1853, Isaac N. Steele wrote, "Plunder of the national funds and corruption in all branches of the Government, Executive, Legislative and Judicial have during the past four years become so universal and notorious, that for some time past, it seems scarcely to have been thought necessary to make any effort to conceal them."[27] The frequent rotation of cabinet members paralyzed business, and the courts scarcely functioned at all—for foreigners, at least. Of the courts, Erastus Culver exclaimed, "Truth demands that I should say of them they are a stench in the nostrils of all honest men."[28]

No doubt considerable corruption did exist. Still, U.S. citizens resident in Venezuela had seldom complained of corruption under Páez, who had parlayed his political and military skills into extensive landholdings and wealth. After 1848, the Liberals' goals of putting their own partisans in office and reversing some of Páez's favoritism toward foreigners confused and angered foreigners. The Liberals, without opposing the principles of free trade, set out to modify the rules of the game slightly, especially to shield debtors, mostly landowners, during a time of economic crisis. Foreign creditors demanded that their governments protect their assets, setting off a flurry of new foreign claims against the Venezuelan government. A review of the claims records suggests that both Venezuelan officials and U.S. citizens engaged in corrupt behavior, but some of the Venezuelans' recalcitrance derived from alternative legal interpretations and administrative inefficiency as much as from corruption. Of course, the red tape and frequent changes in administrative personnel also allowed Venezuelan officials to resist foreign demands without denying them, a strategy that avoided at least temporarily the prospect of seeing foreign gunboats along their Caribbean coast. Corruption lay in the eyes of the beholder, and delays and inefficiency became the tools of the weak.

Political Legitimacy and Civil Wars

In spite of Washington's negative view of the Venezuelan governments after 1848, the Civil War in the United States and European threats influenced formal relations more than the character or legitimacy of the Venezuelan government. The United States pragmatically and nonjudgmentally extended diplomatic recognition to each Venezuelan government in turn until the 1860s. U.S. diplomats registered some ambivalence about the meaning and value of suffrage in Venezuela, but they appreciated the outcome of elections more than they did the democratic process. In 1848 Shields thought that too many of the "uneducated and destitute" were swayed by demagoguery to produce the Liberal victory and recommended that suffrage be further restricted.[29] On the other hand, in 1852 Isaac Steele criticized the "utter want of patriotism" that sent fewer than one quarter of the eligible voters to the polls. To him, Venezuelan elections were "a mortifying spectacle to the sincere advocates of Republican Government."[30]

Despite the criticism by Shields and Steele, the two Monagas brothers (1848–58) maintained some aspect of legitimacy through indirect, and highly restricted, elections. Venezuelan historian José Gil Fortoul estimated that only 342 voters (of a total eligible list of 128,785 in a national population of 1,273,155) cast ballots at the national level in the 1846 election that brought José Tadeo Monagas to power.[31] Once in power, the

Monagas brothers displayed no enthusiasm for wider suffrage, endorsing the Constitution of 1857, which specified that Congress would elect the president.

In the 1860s, government officials in Washington viewed Venezuelan legitimacy from the perspective of their own concern about foreign support of the rebellious southern Confederacy. They even shunned their old hero, José Antonio Páez, when he seized power in Venezuela again in 1861 during Venezuela's Federal War (1859–63). Henry Blow, on his arrival in Venezuela in November 1861, decided (apparently on his own initiative) not to present his diplomatic credentials to the Páez government because the old hero's rule had not been sanctioned by elections. He noted that he was aware that his action was "at variance with former usage and policy."[32] The State Department approved his action but issued such a weak trail of instructions that the subsequent minister, Erastus D. Culver, unwittingly recognized Páez by presenting his diplomatic credentials in September 1862. Much to Culver's embarrassment, Secretary of State William H. Seward notified him in November that his action had been ill-advised and instructed him to withdraw the recognition. In March 1863, Seward wrote that the United States wanted evidence of popular support before granting recognition and alluded to the U.S. domestic conflict: "For a considerable period, considerations, quite foreign from the domestic conditions of Venezuela, have hitherto forbidden the United States from recognizing new authorities arising in the Spanish American states through domestic revolution, and that the delay in regard to Venezuela is to be understood as implying no hostility, disfavor or distrust, in regard to the Government of General Páez."[33] Notwithstanding Culver's ambiguous position, Secretary of State Seward insisted that he continue to press aggressively the claims of U.S. citizens against the Venezuelan government.

Páez expressed hurt and surprise at this policy and reminded Culver of his affection for the United States. The minister reported, "On one occasion he [Páez] said with tears in his eyes that his earnest desire was when he retired to private life to go to die and be buried in the United States, adding there was no people or country like America."[34] Minister of Foreign Affairs Pedro José Rojas protested that the United States had always recognized de facto governments, even the spurious one of William Walker in Nicaragua.[35]

In spite of their disappointment, the members of Páez's government continued to treat Culver as if he had official standing, even entertaining his arguments on claims against the government. When a U.S. newspaper ran an article about the nonrecognition of Venezuela, however, Rojas believed that Venezuelan honor required him to break off all unofficial relations with Culver and hand him his passport. Since Culver was a close friend of Páez, he was allowed to remain in Venezuela.[36]

As they had from the time of Miranda's 1806 fiasco, press reports played a role in the binational relationship between Venezuela and the United States. The Monagas government had been outraged at the laudatory press articles written about Páez when he arrived in New York in 1851. The Liberals believed the U.S. government encouraged the newspaper stories, and Monagas interpreted the public praise of Páez as an attack on him and an intervention in Venezuela's domestic politics. The Venezuelan president forbade U.S. papers carrying good reports of Páez to circulate in Venezuela. In turn, as noted above, Páez took umbrage not at the official refusal to recognize his government but at the public announcement of that insult in U.S. papers in 1863.

If the State Department was innocent of manipulating the press in the cases cited, U.S. diplomats nonetheless did use the press to strengthen their positions; they frequently sent communications to be published in the Caracas papers in hopes of affecting Venezuelan sentiment. Vespasian Ellis, chargé in 1844–45, sent copies to the Caracas newspapers of all his communications to the Ministry of Foreign Affairs. The foreign minister complained of that practice to Ellis's successor, observing that the goal seemed to be to embarrass the Venezuelan government.[37] Later, Culver watched carefully how the Venezuelan press portrayed the U.S. Civil War. He grumbled that the British Legation encouraged the Venezuelan papers to show preference for the southern cause. Believing that the *National Intelligencer*, which he received, seemed weak in its defense of the Union, Culver applauded when the State Department replaced it with the *Daily Chronicle*. Since he circulated the North American newspapers among his Venezuelan friends, he judged the *Chronicle* to be a more useful vehicle for his public diplomacy.[38]

Nor did Americans overlook unfavorable press articles by Venezuelans. Culver protested to the Venezuelan government that its consul in New York, Simón Camacho, had published articles in Venezuelan papers that were too sympathetic to the South. Caracas relieved Camacho of his consular position in late 1863 "in deference to our wishes," Culver reported.

By October 1864, altered domestic and international contexts prompted Washington to extend recognition to the Venezuelan government. The North had gained control in the Civil War, and congressional elections in Venezuela legitimized Juan Crisostomo Falcón's claim to the presidency. Moreover, the French occupation of Mexico caused Seward enough concern that he even instructed his minister in Caracas to suspend the pressure on Venezuela about outstanding claims. In January 1865, the State Department justified the new flexibility: "Not only the United States, but Venezuela and all the other American States, are struggling with reactionary agencies that threaten the very existence of the republican situation itself. . . . Let us have political harmony and international sympathy, at least until the common dangers of the contest have passed."[39]

A month later, Antonio Guzmán Blanco, son of the founder of the Liberal party, reiterated the thesis of a defensive inter-American alliance against European aggression in the Americas. Guzmán Blanco told Culver that he believed that France had designs on South America as well as on Mexico and had encouraged Spain's aggression toward Peru. Secretary of State Seward responded that he was concerned about the threat but would not challenge the Europeans by making formal alliances with South American countries. He preferred to directly urge the French to withdraw their troops from Mexico and let the Spanish threat in the Pacific collapse of its own weakness.

Claims and Guano Filibustering

Washington's brief suspension of pressure with regard to U.S. citizens' claims against the Venezuelan government indicated how serious the United States considered the French threat to be. U.S. agents in Caracas had maintained a dogged insistence on recognition of the claims, even those they tacitly acknowledged to be exaggerated or fraudulent. Although many of the claims were trivial, they accounted for a great deal of nineteenth-century diplomatic activity. Latin Americans' failure to treat them seriously sometimes served as a pretext for foreign invasion, as in the case of the French attacks on Mexico in 1838 and again in 1862. Venezuela escaped such indignity until 1902 but generally held a reputation for being recalictrant in the face of foreign demands.

Many claims arose from damages suffered because of acts of omission or commission by the Venezuelan government, some dating from the conflicts over privateers in the independence era. U.S. citizens whose property had been seized or destroyed by rebels argued that the Venezuelan government owed them compensation because it could not provide protection and did not punish the rebels. The claimants, of course, said they were innocent bystanders, but the records suggest that both profit and political sympathies sometimes tempted U.S. citizens to take an active role in Venezuelan conflicts. Vespasian Ellis, for example, purchased a vessel in the United States to sell to *paecistas* who rebelled against the Monagas government in 1848. When the Monagas forces captured the vessel, Ellis demanded compensation for "his" property and blustered that his wealthy and influential friends would all help the rebels if he were not paid. In 1865 the Orinoco Steamship Line contracted to carry government soldiers along the Orinoco River. Rebels attacked the ship and killed several Americans, and the company demanded reparations from the government.

Hustlers, adventurers, and diplomats all tried to wring funds from the Venezuelan government. U.S. officials were not supposed to benefit from pressing official claims, but they could charge a commission for any claims they collected by acting privately and unofficially before the Venezuelan government. The emissaries noted that their salaries barely covered their living expenses in Caracas, so they had ample incentive to act as private intermediaries for U.S. citizens who wanted some concession from the Venezuelan government. Some of these negotiations doubtless contributed to the unsavory reputation held by U.S. officials in Caracas.

Occasionally, claims were so patently trivial or fraudulent that diplomats hesitated to act on them even unofficially. One scoundrel, Seth Driggs, was imprisoned for falsifying an affidavit he had registered in support of a claim. He then sued the Venezuelan government for illegal imprisonment and mistreatment in jail. Venezuelan jails did not provide meals, and Driggs charged that that practice constituted mistreatment. Driggs's antics proved too much for Chargé Vespasian Ellis, who wrote in June 1845 that Driggs was "probably the most artful and reckless villain who has ever come to this country from the United States," and recommended against aggressively supporting Driggs's claim.[40] Other diplomats were not so fastidious, and Driggs's case continued to appear in subsequent claims negotiations.

Many of the complaints after 1848 derived from the Liberals' financial laws. In April 1849 the Venezuelan government passed the Ley de Espera, a respite law that allowed debtors, with the consent of a certain percentage of their creditors, to postpone repayment of their debts for six to nine years. The law was intended to provide relief for hard-pressed hacendados who found themselves in hock to merchants and moneylenders. As it turned out, however, many of the creditors were foreigners. Foreign governments interpreted the law as being hostile to their interests and threatened the Venezuelan government until it agreed to assume most of the foreign creditors' losses.

A significant portion of the claimants to whom the United States offered protection were Venezuelans by birth. Some were adult children of U.S. citizens who had moved to Venezuela but had not given up their U.S. citizenship. Over several generations they claimed exemption from Venezuelan military service and forced loans, and they demanded U.S. government intervention if their business interests suffered. Others were Venezuelans who became naturalized U.S. citizens but continued to do business, and sometimes to reside, in Venezuela.

For example, José Antonio Mosquera went to the United States in 1846 to attend school. While he was there—and just before the respite law was passed—his father transferred the family business to his name. Mosquera became a naturalized U.S. citizen in July 1853, shortly after Mosquera y Compañía had been liquidated because of debts. As an American citizen, Mosquera asserted his right to the Venezuelan bonds that compensated foreigners who had lost property from the execution of the Ley de Espera. U.S. minister Charles Eames urged the State Department to protect Mosquera's rights.

The Venezuelan government offered various defenses to refute the foreign claims: foreigners should not be privileged over nationals in receiving indemnities; claimants should exhaust the remedy provided by the Venezuelan courts before turning to diplomatic intervention; many claims were inflated, fraudulent, or inadequately documented; some claimants were not really U.S. citizens; the Venezuelan government could not be held responsible for the actions of rebels. Venezuelan jurists cited Venezuelan law, Spanish legal tradition, and the Napoleonic Code to support their arguments, but they sometimes also cited U.S. legal precedents. They pointed out, for example, that the U.S. Supreme Court had rejected French claims for property lost in the New Orleans riots of 1866, holding that the government was not responsible for the rioters' actions. Venezuela's most effective defense, however, lay in delays and its generally impenetrable bureaucracy. Caracas acknowledged one series of claims in the Convention of 1853 and agreed by the Convention of 1866 to established a mixed commission to review and make awards in other cases. Decades would pass, however, before U.S. diplomats actually collected even the claims that had been recognized.

Venezuela suffered only one minor filibustering effort, but the Aves Island controversy inspired more claims. The island, no more than three quarters of a mile long, uninhabited, and uninhabitable, lay far from the Venezuelan coast just west of Dominica in the Windward Islands. Boston guano speculator Philo Shelton sent Captain Nathan Gibbs on an exploratory expedition, and the captain landed on and claimed Aves Island in April 1854. Gibbs confided to another Shelton employee, James Wheeler, that Aves looked like a promising guano deposit. Wheeler tried unsuccessfully to get Shelton to finance him rather than Gibbs in the great guano hunt. When Shelton favored Gibbs, Wheeler secured funding for his own Aves expedition from Shelton's rival firm, John H. B. Lang and William W. Delano. Both Gibbs and Wheeler, heavily armed, arrived at Aves with their crews in July 1854. They decided to divide the spoils and raised the U.S. flag over the new addition to empire. In December, Captain Domingo Díaz of Venezuela disembarked with armed soldiers to investigate the activities. The Americans convinced him that they were negotiating the appropriate permissions from the Venezuelan government. Díaz allowed Gibbs and Lang to continue their work until he could check with Caracas. This peaceful coexistence ended on 30 December when soldiers from another Venezuelan ship landed, lowered the U.S. flag, raised the Venezuelan flag, and ordered the U.S. citizens to leave immediately, abandoning their equipment, provisions, and guano.

These events, inspired by the bird droppings on a tiny Caribbean rock, led to nearly forty years of litigation. Representatives of Shelton and of Lang and Delano challenged each other's rights to the deposits—not the last time rival U.S. investors would fight over Venezuelan spoils. The United States asserted its sovereignty over the island, a claim contested by Venezuela and separately by the Low Countries. After Queen Isabela II of Spain affirmed Venezuela's sovereignty in an 1865 arbitration decision, the dispute was reduced to the issue of compensation for the U.S. guano merchants for their abandoned property. Venezuela agreed to make compensation in the 1859 Convention on Aves Island, but did not make the final payment until 19 February 1904.

The claims against the Venezuelan government were not exclusively about legal rights and arguments, of course. U.S. representatives, disgusted with a Venezuelan political culture that differed so markedly from their own traditions, wanted to teach Venezuelans to be more responsible citizens. Fines, humiliating treaties, and incessant diplomatic pressure punished behavior that fell short of the ideal. Like John Williamson's preference for hanging rebels and A. A. Hall's belief in the salutary influence of gunboats, the claims records show the same self-satisfaction of men certain that they have come from a superior culture with a mission to instruct Venezuelans in acceptable behavior.

Of course, France and Great Britain also insisted on compensation for their citizens. Some U.S. diplomats believed that the United States would suffer a loss of face if it submitted to "outrages" that the European powers would not tolerate. Venezuela, threatened more by Great Britain than by the United States, could ill afford to push its potential protector into open alienation.

Arguably, Venezuelans and North Americans knew little more of each other by 1866 than they knew in 1830. Lamentably, many of their experiences with the other were negative. Venezuelans resented the self-righteousness, racism, perceived corruption, and dislike of change they found in U.S. diplomats. Wary of U.S. filibustering and meddling in their domestic affairs, they nonetheless sometimes acknowledged an American destiny when they pressed Washington for a formal alliance against the European nations.

For their part, U.S. citizens distrusted the unpredictability of Venezuelan politics after 1848, the corruption and inefficacy of the courts, and the apparent disregard for the sanctity of property and contracts. They were uncomfortable with the potential volatility of the Venezuelan people of color and suspicious of the British influence. They desired the advantage of trade with Venezuela, but they wanted to remain aloof otherwise from people who did not appear to share their customs, values, or goals.

3 Rogues and Heroes, 1866–1896

No country in South America is richer in such natural products as cocoa, coffee, and sugar-cane. And in the interior there is a vast undiscovered and untouched territory waiting for the mining engineer, the professional hunter, and the breeder of cattle.

—Richard Harding Davis

The withdrawal of the French from Mexico in 1867 at least temporarily freed the Western Hemisphere from the active threat of European territorial colonization. Venezuela and the United States had survived their most threatening domestic civil wars. A new era of American destiny beckoned, driven by technology and trade rather than republican ideals. Material progress and development became the goal of all the American nations. Individuals avidly sought to prove their worth by accumulating fortunes, by fair means or foul.

During the last third of the century, the United States expanded territorially into the trans-Mississippi West and economically toward the South American republics, initiating what some would call the "new empire." Venezuela's coffee and cacao, forest products, coal and asphalt deposits, and rumored gold mines brought increased attention from its northern neighbor. Journalist James R. O'Beirne in 1890 praised the Venezuelans as the Yankees of the Southern Hemisphere and predicted that the country "has to be the key to all South America" for the future of U.S. commerce in that region.[1] Some Americans "sought opportunity" in Venezuela, as historian Walter LaFeber would have it, but ultimately found O'Beirne's view to be exaggerated. Nonetheless, pressure from the United States for markets, concessions, and other privileges did contribute to political disorder in Venezuela.[2]

Washington's diplomatic and consular officials still seemed to be rank amateurs in this age of robber barons. One minister alarmed *caraqueños* when he began "acting like a maniac."[3] The men of La Guaira stoned and nearly killed the U.S. consul there in 1872 for wandering around nude and exposing himself to their wives and sisters.[4] William Pile and William Scruggs had to resign because of improper business dealings, and Thomas Russell was expelled for insulting the Venezuelan president.

In spite of such peccadillos, Venezuelan leaders were impressed by the expanding power and wealth of the United States. Steamship travel and the telegraph provided the links that brought the Caribbean into the U.S. orbit. Venezuelans remained skeptical about the applicability of U.S. political institutions to their society, but they craved the economic and scientific progress they saw in the northern republic.

Venezuelans and U.S. citizens also shared the new faith of the day: social Darwinism, or positivism. They believed that nations, like individuals, struggled to survive and that science and technology would allow the strongest to dominate both nature and the weaker nations. To the United States, of course, the Latin American republics were the weaker and less capable nations. But to Venezuelans like President Antonio Guzmán Blanco, the weaker neighbors were the insular colonies of European powers, especially Curaçao and Trinidad.

Social Darwinist philosophy permeated the views of Venezuelans and U.S. citizens. Optimism became the mood of the day as all assumed that Venezuela was going through a transition that would give rise to a higher stage of civilization, order, and progress. Venezuelan engineer and first minister of public works Jesús Múñoz Tébar drew an analogy with the physical sciences when he wrote in 1890 that "the zero of each curve represents the completely barbarous state of a nation. As its government and its people implement measures that bring it closer to a legalist regime, the curve ascends; when personalist measures are imposed, the curve descends again."[5] U.S. observers, although still harshly critical of Venezuelan foibles, sometimes shared the confidence that Venezuela was ascending on the thermometer of progress.

The emphasis on struggle and competition both between nations and within nations intensified a blustery concept of national honor. Symbols of nationhood and republicanism demanded respect. As U.S. citizen J. W. Hancox said in 1871 when submitting a claim against the

Venezuelan government: "If the stars and stripes, our pride and glory are no guarantee to Americans in any or every clime, I say for one let me hoist a piece of calico in its stead."[6] Similarly, Venezuelans felt dishonored when their weakness forced them to bow to the shameful demands of another nation, and they became more proficient at protecting their own interests. A sensationalistic press in both countries wooed a public that responded to a perception of national triumphs and insults.

Individuals of both nations strove to put themselves into the company of the elect, or fittest—or as Venezuelans put it, *los vivos*. Corruption was rife both north and south; critics attacked the blight—and often participated in it. U.S. minister William Scruggs asserted that "there has not been an honest and clean administration of government in Venezuela for thirty years. . . . The moral sense of the country seems hopelessly debauched."[7] Venezuelan and U.S. citizens alike used their connections to secure favors and concessions from the Caracas government. Scruggs himself had to resign because of a charge that he had pocketed half of a claim that he had bribed the Venezuelan president to recognize. The Venezuelan press frequently pointed out that influence trafficking was common in the United States as well. *La Opinión Nacional* in 8 October 1890 reported that speculators had given President Benjamin Harrison a house in Cape May in order to boost sales of other houses in the area.

The "Illustrious American" and the Cult of Bolívar

In the mid-1860s, Venezuela still appeared to be "an organized anarchy."[8] Minister Thomas Stilwell reported in 1867 that it was "a republic in name only" and that some Venezuelans hoped "that the great Republic of the north, in extending its domain and power may someday not far distant, add Venezuela to the galaxy of States which constitute the great Union."[9] By the 1870s, however, the Yellow Liberals had emerged victorious from Venezuela's Federal War. Yellow Liberals traced their origin to the Liberals of the 1840s, but their old firebrand,

Antonio Leocadio Guzmán, had surrendered leadership to his son, Antonio Guzmán Blanco, the self-proclaimed "Illustrious American." Like most of their contemporaries in Latin America, the Venezuelan Liberals aspired to economic progress and development. Guzmán Blanco added a Ministry of Development, a Ministry of Public Works, an Office of Statistics, and a national post office to the public administration. The new Banco de Venezuela (there had been a short-lived one in the 1840s) and the Banco de Maracaibo facilitated credit operations. Urban construction, new highways, railroads, port modernization, and a transatlantic cable eroded the isolation of the country and its hinterland. The Liberals attacked an already weak Catholic church, decreed (but did not fund) free public education in 1870, and encouraged foreign immigration and colonization.

Professing a strong commitment to provincial rights, the new Liberals delighted the Caracas elite by sealing the dominance of the capital over the hinterlands. Despite the brief two-year presidential terms, from 1870 to 1888 Guzmán Blanco proved equal to the challenge of dominating the system he had invented. When he retired to Paris for extended vacations between his presidential terms, U.S. ministers sometimes complained that they could secure nothing without his assent. Although his colleagues rebelled against him when he left in 1888, Guzmán continued to influence Venezuelan politics from his Parisian exile until his death in 1899.

As in the halcyon days of Páez, there was no effective political movement to challenge the Liberals. Washington saw no alternative to Guzmán except local caudillos or personalist malcontents. U.S. ministers railed at Guzmán's arrogance and vanity, his public challenges and insults, and his excesses. Begrudgingly, however, they recognized that he did control the nation and that, despite his bluster, he ultimately accepted the realities of international power politics. In 1873, Minister William Pile wrote that Guzmán "will go just as far to meet the views of the Government of the United States in this matter as he can without producing a dangerous popular movement against him in Venezuela and among his own supporters."[10] Pile further acknowledged that Guzmán's troublesome traits included "a want of practical judgment in matters of finances, commerce and kindred matters of civil administration. I judge him to be wholly destitute of earnest and profound convictions."[11]

The U.S. mission to teach the benefits of North American republicanism and values to foreigners became a private tutorial for the president. As the fear of racial war in the 1840s gave way to an assessment of the masses as relatively inert, few were troubled by the modest uprisings that occurred. Guzmán, a well-traveled and educated man, ruled "over an uneducated and ignorant people,"[12] and "the low and ignorant persons were kept in their proper place."[13] Minister Scruggs explained that when he referred to "revolution," he did "not mean anything more than a change of officials, violently brought about. It seldom works any essential change in the form of government. . . . [T]he masses usually feel little or no concern in the dispute between the 'outs' and the 'ins.'"[14]

It was the age of the great man in history, and Guzmán sagely encouraged the cult of Bolívar among his compatriots and North Americans. In 1874, he converted the Church of the Holy Trinity into the National Pantheon of heroes, with Simón Bolívar's remains receiving the place of honor in 1876. Guzmán publicly annointed his father as a patriot when he had him buried in the Pantheon in 1884. A U.S. warship returned the remains of the rough-hewn *llanero* José Antonio Páez for interment with the other civic saints in 1888, but Guzmán characterized Páez as a reactionary caudillo—hardly a symbol for the new modern age.

The newly sanctified Bolívar, his reputation resurrected, represented national unity (under Caracas control), American republicanism, and glorification of the educated and racially pure elite hero (both Guzmán and Bolívar). Guzmán's rewriting of history overlooked Bolívar's megalomania, his later leanings toward dictatorship, and the abject failure of both the Gran Colombian state and the Pan-American movement. Guzmán Blanco also embraced the symbolic heroism of George Washington, encouraging the popular view of the historical parallels between the two American liberators. During the international exposition commemorating the centennial of Bolívar's birth, in July 1883, Guzmán sponsored the erection of a statue of George Washington in a prominent Caracas plaza.

U.S. minister resident Jehu Baker acknowledged the importance of the twin symbols when he recommended in October 1883 that the United States place a statue of Bolívar in Washington to "commemorate those great men and those great deeds of the past whose influence has been extraordinary in establishing, promoting or maintaining republican government." The statue would encourage friendship from South Americans and would focus attention on the United States as a model of republicanism.[15] Guzmán Blanco further associated the Liberator with U.S. secretary of state James G. Blaine's first invitation to a pan-American conference in 1881. Blaine's departure from office postponed the conference until 1889, but Bolívar's "wise and prescient vision" became linked with the initiative.[16]

Guzmán Blanco in fact shared both Bolívar's arrogance and his wider American vocation. His mighty ego led him to treat the diplomatic corps, and more powerful nations, as if they were equals, if not inferiors. He launched the most aggressive foreign policy Venezuela had seen since the era of Bolívar, especially in the Caribbean region. He could not be termed a nationalist or a populist in the modern sense of those terms, but Guzmán understood that an inchoate and popular xenophobia could work to his advantage both at home and abroad. In 1872 Guzmán became irate when President Ulysses S. Grant did not respond to a personal letter from him regarding the disputed claims commission. While he harried the U.S. Legation over Grant's lack of courtesy, Guzmán also had his unanswered letter printed and widely distributed. Minister Pile observed that Guzmán wanted "to increase his chances of election as President in case a general election is called; or if he attempts to continue his personal rule (as many believe he proposes) the effect of the letter will probably add to his prestige for the time being at least."[17] Guzmán, as expected, ultimately did act reasonably, no doubt guided by the thought that he would probably suffer more from stirring the masses to political life than the United States would.

Guzmán's successors from 1888 to 1899 lacked the wily Liberal's political acumen and ability to dominate the nation. U.S. ministers found them "narrow and unstatesmanlike," "stupid and ungrateful," and, at times, illegitimate rulers. Guzmán's most credible successor, Joaquín Crespo, was killed in April 1898, signaling the exhaustion of the Yellow Liberal party. New and untested groups began to cast their eyes on the Caracas seat of power, and U.S. observers wistfully recalled the Guzmán Blanco era as a time of order and prosperity, or at least predictability.

Material Goals in a Material Age

The United States emerged from the Civil War eager to continue its interrupted expansion and development. Many believed that the country could solve its domestic economic problems by constructing a new commercial empire encompassing South America. Thomas Russell concluded in 1876 "that one way to relieve business distress in the United States is to make better use of the South American market."[18] The U.S. consul in Maracaibo, Eugene Plumacher, agreed that influence in South America fell to the United States "by geographical and political right," and he was delighted when U.S. entrepreneurs and adventurers turned South America into "a commercial battleground" as they fought to secure their "right."[19] Venezuela's proximity to the United States made it a significant battleground.

The U.S. shipping industry had not kept up with the British in the construction of steamships and had declined considerably since the glory days of the 1830s. With Ferdinand de Lesseps's French canal company hard at work in Panama, a lucrative South American and Caribbean trade beckoned again. Venezuela's coastal harbors and Orinoco ports would be valuable in this new age, and even more so if the United States acquired some Caribbean islands to use as trade depots, as some advised. Venezuela imported coal from the United States, but its underexploited Tocuyo coal mines lay well within reach of all the major

Caribbean ports. The modest gold rush of the 1860s drew foreign eyes to Venezuela's Orinoco River and its tributaries. Some visionaries predicted that the future would see the continent's heartland linked by river transport from the Orinoco through the Amazon and down to the Río de la Plata. U.S. merchants, economists, and naval strategists were more intrigued with Venezuela than colonists were, for future glories could not overcome the hard realities of daily life for farmers, cattlemen, artisans, and small traders.

Venezuela continued to exchange sugar, cacao, coffee, and hides for United States flour, lard, and kerosene. Occasionally more exotic products like hams, oysters, and some industrial and farming equipment showed up on customs lists, as did orchids, tropical woods, asphalt, and egret plumes. Venezuela eagerly exhibited its natural and industrial products at international fairs and expositions in the United States. Delegations went to the St. Louis Fair, the 1876 Philadelphia Exposition, the 1883 Boston Fair, the 1884 New Orleans Fair, and the 1893 World's Fair held in Chicago to commemorate the four hundredth anniversary of Columbus's landing in America. The United States in turn sent products to Venezuela's 1883 exposition to commemorate the centennial of Bolívar's birth, and in 1896 Rudolf Dolge opened a permanent exposition of American manufactured goods in Caracas for the National Association of Manufacturers (NAM).

The trade balance between the two nations favored Venezuela. Venezuelans exported more to the United States than they purchased there, since they continued to prefer European manufactured goods. In fact, the United States experienced a negative trade balance with most countries that exported tropical products, but Venezuela's proximity to both the United States and Europe gave it a particularly advantageous position. Among Latin American nations, Venezuela's total trade value with the United States was relatively modest, but the differential between exports and imports was third in 1880 (after Brazil and Cuba) and continued to grow (see Table 1).

The bulk of U.S. trade was with Europe, but agricultural and industrial expansion encouraged a push to secure larger markets in South America. Washington courted Venezuelan markets with boosterism

Table 1

The balance of trade between the United States and Cuba, Brazil, Mexico, Colombia, Argentina, and Venezuela in 1880

	U.S. Exports	U.S. Imports
Cuba	$11,429,902	$57,738,239
Brazil	$8,282,768	$46,585,720
Mexico	$5,671,134	$6,090,574
Colombia	$5,256,879	$6,908,206
Argentina	$2,163,820	$3,892,865
Venezuela	$2,130,503	$5,312,076

Source: U.S. minister resident Jehu Baker to State Department, 28 September 1880, Diplomatic Despatches to the Department of State, 1835–1906, Venezuela (Microfilm Publication M79).

and proposals for new commercial agreements. Consul Eugene Plumacher urged Americans to perform their patriotic duty and sell more goods in Venezuela. In 1888 he wrote that "every distinctive American enterprise which may take root in this country does its part in bringing about the ultimate paramount supremacy of the United States."[20] He touted investment prospects in butcher shops, fresh vegetables, ice machines, transportation, trade, engineering, mining, railroads, and steam transport, among other possibilities. Plumacher frequently pointed out that U.S. commercial agents would never seize the advantage over European salesmen so long as they continued to ignore consumer preferences, send substandard or spoiled goods, and speak only English.

The advent of steam-powered travel contributed modestly to increased trade. Venezuela was the only South American country served directly by steamships from the United States, through the Red D Line, owned by the Boulton commercial house and its Philadelphia partner, Dallett and Company. Shipping routes contributed to Venezuela's trade profile and also accentuated regional differences within the country. The Red D Line principally served Maracaibo, and Andean coffee reached the United States through that route. In contrast, the vessels that touched at La Guaira carried the European trade, taking on central coastal coffee and cacao in exchange for European manufactures. Since

La Guaira served the more populous and affluent capital, Caracas, it was not surprising that European imports prevailed there.

Obsolete transportation and communication networks hindered the development of a national market but provided opportunities for foreign engineering firms with the capital and technology that Venezuelans lacked. U.S. diplomats and consuls frequently used their contacts to secure a good position at the public trough. In 1883 the first railroad from La Guaira to Caracas (23 miles) opened, built by former U.S. minister William Pile with British and U.S. capital. Pile also secured the concession for the Táchira railroad, promising to open up western Venezuela by bringing Andean products to Lake Maracaibo.

Some projects faced obstacles that were more political than technical. The sandbar at the entry to Lake Maracaibo limited direct access to that port, and merchandise and produce headed for the United States had to be first transshipped in smaller vessels to the Dutch island of Curaçao. Plumacher pleaded for some U.S. company to bid on the concession to drag the bar. Maracaibo residents, he asserted, favored the Monroe Doctrine and American enterprise and would welcome such an endeavor. Moreover, the project would draw attention to United States engineering, which was currently overshadowed by the French Suez and Panama Canal enterprises.[21]

Dragging the bar would help both U.S. trade and Maracaibo's commercial interests, but President Guzmán Blanco saw no benefit to encouraging Maracaibo's development as an autonomous port tied to U.S. interests. The rebellious western state of Zulia, whose capital city Maracaibo was, had secessionist tendencies, and Guzmán sometimes punished the *maracuchos,* and incidentally their U.S. trading partners, by closing their port.

Guzmán's usual treatment of foreign investments fell somewhere between the old Spanish monopoly practice and an open door policy. He had an untidy habit of granting exclusive concessions, in exchange for kickbacks, to several different investors, which consequently inspired a new wave of claims against the government. For example, in 1883 he granted the International Telephone Company of the United States an exclusive concession. Ostensibly because that company refused to lower its rates, the president subsequently granted another "exclusive" contract to a second U.S. firm. Challenged by the competing claims of two U.S. firms, the State Department refused to intervene, suggesting instead that the ministers use their "good offices" to secure some relief for the concessionaires.

The most famous, complex, and prolonged snarl of concessions and politics involved the asphalt fields. An Irish-American cookie salesman named Horatio Hamilton had ingratiated himself with Guzmán when he peddled Vanderveer & Holmes biscuits for tea parties. In 1883, Hamilton married a friend of the Guzmán family and secured a large concession in eastern Venezuela. Although Hamilton hoped to market tropical woods and other products as well, the major wealth of his claim lay in the Guanoco asphalt lake. With the paving of Pennsylvania Avenue in Washington in 1876, a paving mania swept U.S. cities. In 1885, while he was serving as Venezuelan consul in New York, Hamilton and his business associates, Ambrose H. Carner and William and Thomas W. Thomas, transferred his contract to the New York and Bermúdez Company. Rocked by poor management and inadequate capital in the depression of 1892, Hamilton's group sold their company to the Barber Asphalt Paving Company, one of the building blocks of the giant asphalt trust that would form in 1900. The trust was drawn into a decade of intrigue, revolution, chicanery, and lawsuits because four Venezuelans, for murky reasons of their own, in 1897 challenged the validity of Hamilton's original concession. Their *Felicidad* mine overlapped the claims of the New York and Bermúdez Company, and in 1898 President Joaquín Crespo sided with the Venezuelans and declared that Hamilton's concession had lapsed. The intricate story continues in Chapter 4; suffice it to say here that Guzmán's cavalier attitude toward government concessions played havoc on both shores of the Caribbean.

Doubtless such arbitrary and irregular government treatment discouraged U.S. investors when the rewards were minimal. Better opportunities existed elsewhere, except, perhaps, for men like William Pile, who used their friendship with politically prominent Venezuelans to secure and protect their concessions.

Both Venezuela and the United States used import licensing and tariffs to protect their trade position and punish their rivals. Guzmán Blanco, keenly aware of the interdependency of Venezuelan and Caribbean trade, decreed in 1881 that any goods coming through the Antilles should pay an additional 30 percent tariff. Guzmán wanted to retaliate against neighboring islands that shipped arms to his domestic enemies and sheltered them in exile. The tariff, however, also struck at U.S. interests, since U.S. goods usually were transshipped from Trinidad or Curaçao. Larger vessels could navigate neither the Maracaibo sandbar nor the silting channels of the Orinoco River. In response to Washington's protests, Guzmán retreated and exempted U.S. goods destined for Venezuela from the tariff.

The situation again highlighted the need, from Washington's point of view, for a new trade treaty with Venezuela to replace the old 1861 document, which had lapsed in 1870. Guzmán and his successors, on the other hand, saw no reason to change a situation that allowed their products to enter the United States relatively freely while they purchased cheaply the European goods they preferred. As British interest in the Guayana gold fields increased, Guzmán did occasionally revive the idea of linking a commercial treaty with a more general one of protection and alliance. Through the 1870s and early 1880s, the United States balked at an alliance and insisted on a more limited commercial treaty.

The mood became nastier in the United States when economic depression gave the Republicans the support to pass the high McKinley tariff in 1890. The executive had the authority to lower or rescind tariffs on certain items, and the State Department used this leverage to try to force reciprocal trade treaties on South American producers of tropical products. From late 1890 until the Venezuelan revolution of 1892, Minister William Scruggs pressed Venezuela to sign a reciprocity treaty that would give an advantage to U.S. manufactures, lard, flour, and wheat. If Venezuela did not sign, high duties would be levied on Venezuelan coffee and cacao.

President Raimundo Andueza Palacio responded that if Venezuela agreed, European countries would demand the same tariff reductions, causing the government to lose much of its principal source of revenue. Scruggs sulked that Andueza had "an almost incredibly narrow and unstatesmanlike view of the case" and predicted that the increased volume of trade would make up for any lost revenue.[22] He reiterated the U.S. thesis that Venezuela had no legal obligation to extend the same concessions to European goods—a thesis that European nations generally rejected.

On 16 November 1891, guided by a confidential memo from Secretary of State James G. Blaine, Scruggs proposed to Andueza that the United States was ready to take an "advanced and decisive step" in supporting Venezuela's claim in Guayana against the British if Venezuela would settle all outstanding differences with Washington and sign the proposed reciprocity treaty.[23] Otherwise, the retaliatory tariffs would be imposed on Venezuelan goods in January. Andueza Palacios promised to study the matter, but his counterproposal to consider a treaty that would treat only agricultural goods was deemed "absolutely unacceptable" by Blaine.

Walter LaFeber argued that tariff pressure in the 1890s triggered the Hawaiian and Cuban revolutions and hastened the coming of revolution in the Philippines.[24] Similarly, when the United States imposed an additional duty on Venezuelan coffee and cacao on 15 March 1892, the nation collapsed into another civil war that lasted until October of that year. After the civil war wrecked the Venezuelan economy and finally brought Joaquín Crespo to power, the tariff issue lost some of its urgency for Washington. Moreover, U.S. shippers and merchants complained that the tariff actually hurt them because it undermined their foothold in western Venezuela. Europeans discovered the high quality of Andean coffee and were willing to pay the expensive freight costs. The competition caused the Red D Line to suffer losses. If the Red D Line folded, there would be no direct steamer and mail service to the United States. Finally, the 1892 election in the United States brought in Democrat Grover Cleveland, who favored lower tariffs, and many of the punitive rates were rolled back in 1894.

Washington's efforts to negotiate reciprocity treaties generally met with little success in South America. Only Brazil signed one, and even that treaty was short-lived. Reluctant to reject European trading partners for closer economic dependence on the United States, Venezuela did not sign a formal trade treaty with the United States until 1939.

Uncle Rabbit Challenges Uncle Sam

Twentieth-century Venezuelan essayist Arturo Uslar Pietri says that the nation's traditional myths and legends reveal "the Venezuelan conception of the world, its spirit, its life, and its morality." From Venezuelan folk-tales we learn "that equality is worth more than liberty, and that justice does not mean to give one what is due him, but to punish and to harry the powerful, who never are good. . . . Fortune and wealth never come from methodical and enterprising work, but from an unexpected treasure, from a magic gift, or from violent plunder." In the Venezuelan version of Brer Rabbit, Tío Conejo (Uncle Rabbit) always wins out over Tío Tigre (Uncle Tiger). The rabbit defeats the more powerful tiger with "*astucia,* tinged with a little hypocrisy, deceit and fraud, the weapons of the weak against the strong in primitive societies."[25]

In defending Venezuela against the multiple claims lodged against it by the great powers, Guzmán Blanco and his compatriots displayed more than a little of the rabbit's *astucia.* They advanced legal arguments similar to the principles later associated with Argentine foreign ministers Carlos Calvo and Luis M. Drago; that is, foreigners should enjoy no more protection than nationals when their businesses or persons suffer damage, and nations should renounce force as a means of collecting debts. But just as the tiger would not accept the rabbit's view of the world, so the great powers objected that they intended, with force if necessary, to see that their citizens were treated as well abroad as they were at home, perhaps even better. By the 1920s, the threat of force generally had secured the legal interpretations favored by the powerful nations, but the nineteenth-century disputes had different meanings to the different participants. The contending parties all considered national honor to be at stake and wanted to force their principles on the opposing nation. At the same time, the cagy and the dishonest considered honor to be fully compatible with tweaking the powerful or demanding an undeserved windfall.

For nearly twenty years, Venezuela and the United States disputed the decision of the 1868 Mixed Venezuelan-American Claims Commission. The Venezuelan government charged that the decision was tainted because U.S. commissioner David Talmage, in collaboration with legation lawyer William Murray and Minister Thomas N. Stilwell, had named the third commissioner over Venezuelan protests. On controversial cases, the third judge usually sided with the United States. Moreover, Talmage, Murray, and Stilwell required claimants to sign over one-third of their judgments to them. Their obvious interest in the outcome of the complaints had contributed to inflate the claims from a 1863–64 maximum of about 200,000 pesos to an astounding 1.5 million pesos.[26] The Venezuelan government demanded that the 1868 decision be nullified.

The Venezuelan protest had some merit. In 1869, U.S. minister James Partridge wrote that the State Department "was prostituted openly and publicly for the purpose of extortion and private gain."[27] The State Department replied that Venezuela had inadequately documented its charges and that a bad precedent would be set if Caracas was allowed unilaterally to reject the commission's decision.[28] Venezuela could afford to pay the awards, and Washington wanted to teach Guzmán Blanco that the United States would uphold its rights, with force if necessary. Other U.S. ministers asserted that Guzmán's own reputation for taking "commissions" on claims and foreign loans lessened his credibility as a critic of corruption.[29]

In 1873, the U.S. Congress directed Venezuela to pay the claims. President Guzmán publicly accepted the dictate, but he demonstrated his *astucia* in 1875 by hiring his friend and business associate William Pile to act as his paid lobbyist in Washington. In 1874, Pile had been forced to resign as U.S. minister to Venezuela when the State Department discovered that he had purchased the steamships that the Venezuelan government had impounded from another U.S. citizen, J. W. Hancox. Hancox had demanded that the Venezuelan government compensate him for his lost property and presumably did not appreciate Pile's role in the business.

In 1875, Pile and the Venezuelan ministers to the United States began to work on the U.S. public and the Congress. The campaign took time and patience. Letters appeared in newspapers decrying the disgraceful bullying of a poverty-stricken, miserable sister republic. Finally, in 1882, Congress set aside the decision of the Mixed Claims Commission and directed that a new commission be appointed to settle the outstanding issues.

While the issue of old claims remained suspended, new ones arose from the spurt of U.S. citizens who came to Venezuela after the Civil War. Some of the more hardened fortune seekers, like clever Venezuelans, figuratively mined their gold in the national treasury, confident of receiving at least the "good offices" of the U.S. Legation. A certain Mr. Torrey prudently asked the U.S. minister how to register a claim—long before he found any suit to bring against the Venezuelan government.[30] Whaling vessels from the United States sometimes landed illegally in lightly inhabited areas and killed or carried off livestock or attacked the local inhabitants. If the hapless Venezuelans defended themselves or had the sailors arrested, then the shipowner might register a claim, as happened in the case of the *Hannah Grant*.[31] U.S. minister Jehu Baker concluded in 1883 that "Venezuela has been sinned against as well as sinning."[32]

Different notions of what constituted just reparations intensified the disputes. Guzmán Blanco's arbitrary regime usually took pragmatic care not to arrest or harass U.S. citizens. Most mistakenly jailed *yanquis* obtained quick releases and apologies. When some offended Americans demanded reparations in cash for their arrests, Venezuelans were puzzled. Neither their legal code nor their own highly developed sense of honor could conceive of placing a monetary value on an insult to human dignity. Venezuela usually resisted paying such claims. U.S. minister Russell reported "the utter inability of this people to understand our idea of the value of personal liberty."[33]

U.S. officials believed that the reparations had a moralizing effect on Venezuela by teaching the cost of arbitrary government and lack of order. Suspicious that the "frivolous and unfounded charges against foreigners" reflected the "antipathy to them notorious in all countries ruled by the Spanish race including Venezuela," the State Department consistently instructed ministers to press the claims even of notorious scoundrels. In the 1882 *Libro Amarillo*, Venezuelan foreign minister Rafael Seijas commented that the exaggerated and undocumented claims had been a "calamity . . . not only calling upon us the ire of powerful states, but also forcing us to accept humiliations and immense financial sacrifices."[34]

In 1873 Venezuela passed a series of laws that resembled the Calvo Clause and the Drago Doctrine. First, foreigners must exhaust all possible judicial remedies in Venezuela before they could ask for diplomatic help. Second, the Venezuelan state would accept responsibility only for actions taken by public officials acting in an official capacity, and not for rebel actions. Finally, a false or exaggerated claim would make the claimant liable to a fine.

Although the State Department disputed the legitimacy of these laws, they were in line—as Venezuelans well knew—with United States precedents. U.S. courts imposed penalties for perjury and false witness, and the U.S. government paid no indemnities to people who had suffered losses at the hands of the Confederate rebels. When rowdies attacked Chinese nationals in Wyoming in the mid-1880s, President Grover Cleveland directed Congress to offer some compensation out of benevolence, but not because there was a legal obligation to do so. The Venezuelan minister to Washington informed Caracas that the U.S. government's treatment of the Chinese vindicated Venezuela's arguments with respect to damages suffered in civil disorders.[35] Of course, Venezuelan politicians recognized that even the most elegant legal arguments could not sink a foreign warship. Uncle Rabbit's *astucia* dictated that he avoid a direct fight with Uncle Tiger.

Some other legal issues reflected deep philosophical differences between the United States and Venezuelan positions. In the 1890s, as travel to the Caribbean became easier, a few American fugitives took refuge in Venezuela. The U.S. State Department proposed an extradition treaty to Venezuela in 1893. Caracas was generally receptive but refused to agree to surrender Venezuelan citizens or anyone who would be subject to capital punishment in the United States. Venezuela had abolished the death penalty for political crimes in 1849 and for all crimes in 1863. U.S. minister Frank Partridge conceded that Venezuela need not surrender its own citizens, but he considered the retention of the death penalty to be "of the utmost importance."[36] Both nations held to their positions, and no extradition treaty was signed until 1922. That treaty provided that neither party would be required to surrender its own citizens, and Venezuela had no obligation to surrender someone who could be subject to the death penalty or life imprisonment.

Domestic Manners and Myths, North and South

The mythological Bolívar and Washington might have represented their countrymen to many, but flesh-and-blood humans also contributed to reciprocal views of the other society. Guzmán Blanco, claimants, consuls, diplomats, and entrepreneurs aired their views in the press, in books and pamphlets, and in the U.S. and Venezuelan Congresses. Scientists, engineers, geographers, cartographers, economists, journalists, and naval strategists added to the information—or misinformation—flow. Newspapers, in Spanish and English, avidly chased new scandals for their ever growing public.

Venezuela's modest efforts to attract immigrants from the United States met with little success. Venezuela needed labor but had neither money nor industry nor a viable transportation network to support settlers. Before the 1890s, most of what U.S. citizens knew of Venezuela was probably negative. Only a handful of U.S. citizens, like William Pile and William Scruggs, had forged the ties with the wealthy and powerful that guaranteed success in Venezuelan society.

The few North Americans who tried to settle in Venezuela directly following the Civil War met with bitter disappointment. In 1865, a Confederate soldier and doctor, Henry M. Price of Virginia, secured a land grant of 240,000 square miles to the southeast of the Orinoco River. With other investors and some Venezuelan contacts, he founded a colonization society that sent several groups to Venezuela between 1866 and 1868. Some of Price's associates tried to recruit British colonists with the publication of *The Emigrant's Vade-Mecum, or Guide to the "Price Grant" in Venezuelan Guyana.* Only a few British came, and the Confederate immigrant families found the land unattractive and isolated, with none of the amenities promised. The Venezuelan government added insult to injury by disputing the location and validity of the Price grant. Many of the immigrants died or returned home, and only a few of the would-be colonists remained to prospect for gold or adventure. Following the 1873 depression, a few U.S. workers and mechanics came to seek work or fortune. Few African Americans came, for the Venezuelan government discouraged their immigration. Some immigrants were sadly misinformed, like the printer who did not think his ignorance of Spanish would affect his employment opportunities. Entrepreneurs without political clout resented having to pay forced loans to the government, the insecurity of contracts and concessions, and the ravages of civil disorder. One of the most successful cotton planters in Aragua gave up and returned home to the United States when he lost his estate to rebels in the 1870s. Most had little to show for their dreams, often having to depend on the bounty of the U.S. Legation or a generous sea captain even for their return passage. Other nationalities who may have had fewer opportunities in their home countries proved more resilient residents of Venezuela than North Americans. In 1891, for example, foreign residents in Venezuela included 13,223 Spaniards, many from the Canary Islands; 10,929 Colombians; 6,116 English, 2,409 French, and 3,566 Dutch, many of them from the Antilles; 3,030 Italians; 917 Germans; but only 201 North Americans.[37]

Some renewed, and more systematic, interest in South America accompanied the closing of the American frontier and the conviction that exports to new markets would insulate the U.S. economy from depression. The U.S. Congress sent a commission to Central and South America in 1885 to report on trade possibilities. In January of that year, William Curtis, Thomas C. Reynolds, and Solon O. Thacher arrived in Venezuela, where the citizens generally welcomed them, especially impressed that Reynolds spoke Spanish—still an oddity for U.S. emissaries to Latin America. The commission's report, published in 1889, provided general background for merchants and the public and for the 1889 Inter-American Conference.

Curtis's work on the commission and as secretary of the Inter-American Conference made him acutely aware of the dearth of information on Venezuela in English. He helped to remedy that lack with two books: *The Capitals of Spanish America* (1888) and *Venezuela: A Land Where It's Always Summer* (1896). Travelers and entrepreneurs from the United States might have been encouraged—or misled—at Curtis's generally favorable account of Venezuela. Among other projects, Curtis urged U.S. architects, carpenters, and masons to hurry to Venezuela to construct modern hotels along the seafront at Macuto. "The natives," he wrote, "appreciate and enjoy comforts as much as anybody, and spend their money lavishly for the luxuries of life, but lack the experience and enterprise necessary to undertake such things."[38] He characterized Venezuelans as quick to absorb modern technology, asserting that the telephone was used more in Caracas than in any city of similar size in the United States. Upper-class Venezuelans traveled widely and had broken down many of the more rigid Spanish customs, including the social isolation of women.

Curtis also reported that academics and government officials were materialists who welcomed Protestantism as a way to fight the reactionary aspects of Catholicism. Venezuelans may have been tolerant, but the American Bible Society and the Southern Methodist church found few ready converts when they arrived in the 1880s. The policies of José Antonio Páez and especially of Antonio Guzmán Blanco had given Venezuela a culture of religious tolerance, but many *caraqueños* had no more use for Protestants than they had for the Catholic church. The poor transportation system made it difficult to minister to the scattered rural population, so the country did not become an active mission field for U.S. evangelists.

Richard Harding Davis's *Three Gringos in Venezuela and Central America* also appeared in 1896 and presented a similarly attractive picture. Davis drew on the George Washington–Simón Bolívar mythology to

assert that "the histories of the two countries of which they are the re-
spective fathers are so much alike, that they might be written in parallel columns."[39] Davis lauded the beauty of Venezuela and Caracas,
which he considered quite civilized, "a Spanish-American city of the
first class." The author optimistically predicted that Venezuela's easy
accessibility would tempt New Yorkers to abandon southern Europe
and the Mediterranean as winter vacation spots.

Davis also appealed to those who longed to escape from civilization
into idealized frontiers, "green mansions" of Edenic purity, or the di-
nosaurs' "lost world."[40] This romanticized Venezuela challenged the
sordid images of corrupt politicians who mistreated foreigners. Like
some of the Caribbean islands that the United States had considered
buying for entrepôts, however, Venezuela's attraction lay partially in
its small population spread over a vast expanse of territory. "To a
sportsman," Davis wrote, "it is a paradise. You can shoot deer within
six miles of the Opera-house, and in six hours beyond Macuto you can
kill panthers, and as many wild boars as you wish. No country in
South America is richer in such natural products as cocoa, coffee, and
sugar-cane. And in the interior there is a vast undiscovered and untouched territory waiting for the mining engineer, the professional
hunter, and the breeder of cattle."[41]

The scientific spirit of the age further encouraged the search for
practical, and profitable, applications for Venezuelan resources. In September 1875, U.S. minister Russell sent a shipment of Venezuelan orchids to the United States, initiating a modestly profitable trade. In
1881, Minister Baker offered to send a selection of Venezuela's woods
to be displayed at the Smithsonian Institution for the information of
businessmen.[42] U.S. physicians should visit the Venezuelan lepers' colony and study leprosy, Baker advised, because more frequent travel
to tropical countries might result in increased spread of the disease in
the United States.[43] U.S. naval missions charted and mapped Venezuelan coastal waters and rivers.

Social science remained flavored by social Darwinist attitudes about
inferior races and the debilitating effects of the tropics. Jehu Baker
pointed out that Venezuela received few immigrants from Europe, and

considering the "natural tendency of the greatly larger to invade and absorb the greatly less race element, I suspect that the proportion of the completely unmixed white stock is growing less, and that, under existing conditions, it will continue to do so." Venezuelan Indians, concentrated in Amazonas and the Goajira, illustrated the "universal law of savage life" that the "early stage of human development" was tribal organization. The "race instinct and climate" in Venezuela meant that the Venezuelan indigenous peoples had a greater chance of survival than the "nearly extinct" Native Americans in the United States.[44]

Venezuelans in the United States showed an equal interest in their host's society, if less fervor to civilize and convert it. To the contrary, they often shared the North American's urge to remake Venezuela in the model of the northern republic. For example, Venezuelan engineer Jesús Múñoz Tébar wrote that neither climate, geography, nor race accounted for differences in civilization and national success. Humans adapt to all climates, and an Australian raised in Berlin would be as German as the Germans. Lunatics and imbeciles showed up in all races and climates. Customs and traditions distinguished successful societies from failed ones. Múñoz Tébar advised his countrymen to work harder, to construct responsible and independent municipalities, courts, and congress, and to root out corruption and personalism, not only to achieve national happiness but to avoid absorption by the United States. The growing population of the United States would naturally require space in which to expand in the near future. If Spanish Americans "did not take charge of their future; if they did not improve their political and social condition by a bold and well-directed effort; if they did not prepare themselves to join the triumphal march of the new civilization with dignity, they will be absorbed or annihilated," he presciently warned. It would not be a violent absorption, he qualified, but rather a "peaceful work of nature, like the changing phases of the moon."[45]

Two other well-known Venezuelans published their observations on U.S. society: Simón Camacho (*Cosas de los Estados Unidos* [1864], discussed earlier) and Ramón Páez, favorite son of the old caudillo. Páez dedicated his book to the Argentine Domingo F. Sarmiento, who shared his commitment to education. Páez believed that the mixture of science and industry, a diverse population, and a strong education system had made the United States great. Like Múñoz Tébar, Ramón Páez lamented that the Spanish-American countries had fallen far behind the United States in progress. We have silver, gold, iron, coal, salt, and sulphur, and have done nothing with our resources, he wrote. We should compare the vigor of the Anglo-Americans who dominated their vast deserts and mountains and mined the gold of California.[46] Páez shared his father's fondness for the United States and achieved some renown there with an earlier book, written and published in English. *Wild Scenes in South America; or, Life in the Llanos of Venezuela* (New York, 1862) went through several editions in the United States and was translated into Spanish, French, and other languages. Influenced by the naturalist writings of Alexander von Humboldt and Charles Waterton, young Páez introduced North American readers to the flora and fauna of his native *llanos*, and incidentally treated them to a defense of his father's career.

At Guzmán Blanco's direction, Venezuelan consuls and diplomats reported on U.S. customs and commerce while they kept an eye on their compatriots in exile. The 1882 *Libro Amarillo* carried reports from consuls in New Orleans, St. Louis, San Francisco, Savannah, and Chicago in addition to New York, Philadelphia, Boston, and Baltimore. Most Venezuelans lived in the eastern seaboard cities, although Caracas knew of only twenty-seven Venezuelans who resided in New York in 1881. (Dual citizenship may have obscured an accurate count.) Venezuelan consuls found much to admire in the United States. Julio González attended a number of agricultural fairs and urged the Venezuelan government to emulate the scientific work of the U.S. Department of Agriculture. One consul recommended the U.S. educational philosophy of actively encouraging the use of logic and intelligence rather than rote learning. Another admired the clean, modern prisons and the goal of rehabilitating the prisoners rather than simply punishing them. González even commented on organized labor's participation in the New York mayoral campaign and hoped that Venezuela's political evolution would someday allow its own workers to play such a positive political role.[47]

Like Uruguayan José Enrique Rodó in *Ariel*, Venezuelans also showed ambivalence toward some aspects of progress in the United States, especially the rampant materialism and—to their eyes—uncultured and unethical behavior. On 28 January 1890 *La Opinión Nacional* (Caracas) featured a long article on the theme. In the United States, it said, "you will see the God of money in all his grandeur; but don't expect to find an impressive civilization, nor good manners, nor even mediocre education. There one goes to work, not to live. There is no art nor anything that approaches it."[48] A guide would tell a visitor how much a building cost, not about its aesthetic value. Since Yankees believed that time was money, they displayed "efficient" but boorish table manners and tolerated terrible food and rude waiters. Salesmen smoothly showed a product in a catalog but did not inform the customer that he would not receive all the parts shown. Even the priesthood had been tainted by materialism. "The priesthood there is a profession," an earlier article averred. "No pastor, priest or clergyman embraces a sect for reasons of faith; he will take his word and his art where he sees the greatest prospect of gain." Only the profitable sects survived among the many that arose, the writer asserted.[49]

America was a land of colossal fortunes, *La Opinión Nacional* conceded, many of them built in the last thirty years, but it was also a corrupt society with millions of poor. Workers and farmers were organizing against the capitalists. Young women went to Europe to trade their liberty and honor for European titles. Electoral practices had become so dishonest that new registration laws had to be passed to correct the situation. Perhaps the young republic had reached the stage of the fabled Roman Empire, the Caracas newspaper speculated.[50]

Nor did U.S. attitudes toward race escape criticism. Reacting to an account in the U.S. press that referred to the "impudent, filthy negroes" who had entered the theater box of a U.S. Legation official in Caracas, *La Opinión Nacional* retorted: "The Africans of Venezuela and even those of the Congo could give lessons of civility to the greater part of the pretentious whites of the United States of America."[51]

Journalists on both sides of the Caribbean delighted in fanning the flames of prejudice and suspicion, both on their own initiative and at the urging of politicians and lobbyists. Much of the debate on the meaning of the Monroe Doctrine and Pan-Americanism occurred in the popular press, providing an opportunity for the literate public to interject themselves more fully into the development of foreign policy.

A New Pan-Americanism

Venezuela, having revived the internationalist legacy of Bolívar, began to take a more active approach to hemispheric, and especially Caribbean, affairs. Up to 1898, Venezuela sometimes urged a reading of the Monroe Doctrine that required U.S. intervention in South America, both with respect to the British Guiana dispute and on other South American issues. Guzmán Blanco shared Simón Bolívar's interest in forcing Spain out of Cuba, and he surreptitiously aided the Cuban rebels between 1870 and 1873. Venezuelans were disappointed when U.S. secretary of state Hamilton Fish's caution won out over the hotheads in Congress who wanted to force Spain out of Cuba. Guzmán later pressed the United States to be watchful of Britain's endorsement of Chile's Pacific ambitions, predicting that Chile might even seize Panama and turn it over to British engineers to finish the canal.

At other times, Venezuelans criticized the heavy hand of Uncle Sam. *La Opinión Nacional* on 20 August 1870 charged that "Monroe's compatriots" were misinterpreting his doctrine of "America for Americans." "Far from protecting *Americans* (if those of the *South* are even Americans)," the writer complained, "they [the United States] believe that a scandalous fraud can be converted into a legal claim, even to the point of supporting it with the logical arguments of gunboats." A decade later, in the same newspaper, Simón Camacho referred to U.S. unhappiness about French capital in Venezuela: "To pretend that we would refuse French or any other capital we can get cheaply to bring out the natural resources of this country and that we could shut our door to progress *because it happens not to suit your "Monroe Doctrine" or any other idea of a protection you wish to exercise at a distance of two thousand miles would be the height of folly on our part.*[52]

These reservations aside, Caracas continued to urge the United States to apply Monroe Doctrine principles to British encroachment on Venezuela's eastern border. But Washington espoused a more conservative view of Monroe's proclamation and remained aloof from the dispute. In 1889, Venezuela determined to use the Inter-American Conference to garner American support against the British, challenging Secretary of State James G. Blaine's insistence on restricting the conference's agenda to commercial matters. Venezuela's Nicolás Bolet Peraza succeeded in having the conference consider Venezuela's request for peaceful arbitration of the British boundary issues, over the objections of U.S. delegate William E. Trescott, who explained Blaine's view that the American nations would be disqualified as arbiters if they took a position. Venezuelans criticized the U.S. delegation's apparent preference for parties and commercial agreements over action to protect the hemisphere against European aggression.[53] *La Opinión Nacional* advised North Americans to pay more attention to Latin America in general and repeated the Argentine view that "America for the Americans" seemed to signify "América para los Estados Unidos."[54]

Only six years later, in July 1896, U.S. secretary of state Richard Olney did an about-face and urged Great Britain to submit the boundary dispute to arbitration. Why had Washington changed its traditional policy? Public opinion, and the yellow press, had grown more favorable to expansionism in the 1890s, and some strategists wanted to ensure that the United States, and not Great Britain, would control the Orinoco River with its potential access to the heart of the continent. Venezuela's adroit lobbying also played a role in the changing climate of U.S. opinion.

Guzmán Blanco had employed William Pile to advance the Venezuelan position on the 1868 Claims Commission before the U.S. Congress and public. In 1894, President Joaquín Crespo followed his predecessor's successful strategy when he engaged William Scruggs to take the Venezuelan case on the boundary dispute to Washington. Scruggs, an experienced journalist and diplomat who had been minister plenipotentiary to Venezuela from 1889 to 1892, had—like Pile—been forced to resign his diplomatic post because of charges of corruption. Prior to 1894, some U.S. newspapers had run articles sympathetic to Venezuela's case, although few argued that the Monroe Doctrine was at stake. Scruggs set to work on his educational mission with the October 1894 publication of a pamphlet, titled *British Aggressions in Venezuela, or the Monroe Doctrine on Trial,* which he distributed to the president, the cabinet, members of Congress, and newspaper editors. Spokesmen for the State Department referred to Scruggs's "gross distortion of the Monroe Doctrine,"[55] but Scruggs's interpretation would prevail after May 1895 when Richard Olney replaced the more conservative Walter Gresham as secretary of state. President Grover Cleveland endorsed Olney's famous assertion that the United States was "practically sovereign" in the Western hemisphere. Olney, however, snubbed Scruggs and Venezuela when he decided to negotiate directly with Great Britain. The British and U.S. governments chose the judges for the international arbitration commission, and Olney persuaded the Venezuelan government to undercut Scruggs by employing another counsel to assist him. Scruggs continued to serve as legal adviser to the Venezuelans until March 1899, although in a weaker position. He poured his experience and knowledge of Venezuelan history into *The Colombian and Venezuelan Republics,* published in 1900.

Venezuelans initially welcomed Cleveland's and Olney's messages as victories for their cause. A crowd of six thousand gathered at George Washington's statue in Caracas on 18 December 1895 to hear an orator praise Cleveland's message to Congress and predict that his name would rank with those of Washington and Lincoln. *Vivas* for the United States and Cleveland rang through the air. The next day *El Tiempo* (Caracas) announced that "the Monroe principle . . . unites the North with the South; it establishes a diplomacy of law and guarantees institutions."[56]

Not too long after the fireworks stopped, some Venezuelans looked more critically at what had been gained. The mixed blessing of an interventionist United States became more apparent when the arbitration decision in 1899 preserved the Orinoco delta and the Guayana territory south of the Orinoco for Venezuela, but awarded Great Britain much of the originally contested territory between the Orinoco and the Essequibo Rivers. Eventually, Venezuela would challenge the decision of the arbitration tribunal, whose judges, like those of the Mixed Claims Commission of 1868, had favored the great powers over Venezuela.

Venezuela's importance grew in proportion to U.S. interest in the strategic and commercial value of the Caribbean and South America. Both nations shared the exalted republicanism of Bolívar and Washington alongside the more prosaic corruption of Guzmán Blanco, U. S. Grant, and Boss Tweed. Both wanted an "America for Americans," but one was inspired by Bolívar's Pan-Americanism and the other by Blaine's commercial expansionism.

The period from 1866 to 1896 represented a period of balance in the relations between the two nations. The United States had not yet assumed the full mantle of the new imperialism. Nor had European nations withdrawn from competition with the United States in the hemisphere. An astute Venezuelan leader could still resist U.S. entreaties by delay, subterfuge, denial, and enlisting U.S. allies in critical cases.

After 1898, Venezuelans still employed the tactics of Tío Conejo, but the changes in hemispheric power relations required a more circumspect style than that of Guzmán Blanco.

4   Venezuela Dodges the Big Stick, 1897–1912

I have never gotten them [the U.S. public] up to the point of taking even a tepid interest in Castro's outrageous iniquity in treating American interests in Venezuela; and this is all where the Monroe Doctrine applies.

—Theodore Roosevelt

Venezuelans at first thought that the Olney Corollary to the Monroe Doctrine marked a triumph in their relations with the United States. They had succeeded, they thought, in convincing the United States to act as their protector against the European powers. The tensions that had accompanied the debt and tariff controversies of the last quarter century seemed forgotten. The period just before 1898, however, proved to be the lull before several storms that would affect United States–Venezuelan relations.

A more aggressive interpretation of the Monroe Doctrine along with the Spanish-American War and Theodore Roosevelt's rise to the presidency in 1901 ushered in a new U.S. empire, especially in the Caribbean. That region, and Venezuela, acquired new importance with the advent of protectorates, with the Panama revolt, with the expansion of U.S. seapower, and with the imminent completion of the Panama Canal. Like Great Britain, Germany and the other European powers withdrew from the region after the blockade of Venezuela in 1902–3. U.S. presidents from Cleveland through Woodrow Wilson gave the Caribbean a higher diplomatic priority than had previous presidents. The stronger presidential involvement also was reflected in the more influential, if not necessarily more perceptive, ministers posted to Venezuela. Francis Loomis and Herbert Bowen, who served between 1897 and 1905, were prominent Republican activists.

Two very different political movements in Venezuela's hinterlands tacitly or openly threatened the U.S. formula for control of the country. The first, a brief populist political campaign and civil war in 1897–98, could have shaken Washington's comfortable alliance with the Caracas commercial and social elite. The second movement brought to power a military caste from the Andean region of Táchira in 1899. The irascible Cipriano Castro initially proved to be one of Roosevelt's most frustrating challenges, but Castro's successor, Juan Vicente Gómez, took on the role of the surrogate policeman who maintained order in Venezuela so that the U.S. Marines did not have to. Castro, like his contemporary Nicaraguan José Santos Zelaya, did not fully appreciate how much the Spanish-American War had changed the power equation in the Caribbean. In contrast, Gómez did understand that the new imperialism required a more cautious approach, an approach that continued to allow the Caracas elite to direct the nation's destinies and discouraged autonomous political activity by the masses.

Washington and the Venezuelan intellectual elites elaborated the ideology that rationalized the political formula. The cults of George Washington and Simón Bolívar continued in rhetoric, but the "democratic caesar" dominated reality. Venezuela was still in an early stage of political development, the argument went, and the best government was one that maintained order until the masses should be ready for full political participation. If the caesar to whom the nation's destinies were entrusted was democratic, that quality revealed itself best in his interactions with the Venezuelan and foreign elite.

In the important transitional period between the Spanish-American War and the inauguration of Woodrow Wilson, political and strategic issues affected Venezuelan relations more than trade and commerce. Still, Venezuela played a role in one chapter of the struggle in the United States between the trusts and the trustbusters, as the Asphalt Trust struggled to gain and retain its monopoly over the exploitation and marketing of the black goo. The other black goo, the "devil's excrement" as Venezuelan phrasemakers called petroleum, would not become a factor until after World War I, although the first foreign oil concession was awarded in 1909.

As in much of Latin America, a reactionary nationalism (and anti-Americanism) took form in Venezuela as U.S. interventionism increased. Or, better put, two separate nationalisms, not always compatible, began to develop. An unformed popular xenophobia railed at foreign blockades, racism, arrogance, and labor practices but was silenced during the Gómez dictatorship. Intellectuals such as César Zumeta took a more complex position that preferred Hispanic culture to Anglo-Saxon materialism and criticized the rising tide of U.S. hegemony. Venezuelan nationalism included both an assertion of a unique Venezuelan identity and a reactive distrust of the foreign. Still, the vulnerability of the long coastline to foreign attack, the eclectic tradition of the port-capital complex of La Guaira–Caracas, and the generally successful history of balancing foreign powers against each other developed in Venezuela a relatively mild and defensive form of nationalism.

Francis Loomis and Venezuelan Populism

Francis B. Loomis, U.S. minister to Venezuela from October 1897 to April 1901, presided over the transition from the relatively adaptable Yellow Liberals to the more volatile Cipriano Castro. He witnessed the change in attitude toward the United States from the euphoric praise that followed Secretary of State Olney's intercession to a more critical, if sporadic, anti-Americanism. The extra typewriter Loomis requested in September 1897 to respond to American adventurers and gold-hunters clicked furiously to combat press accounts hostile to the occupation of Cuba by the United States.

Loomis's stature indicated Venezuela's higher priority to Washington. A journalist (like Scruggs before him), Loomis had worked with the *New York Tribune* and the *Philadelphia Express*, and had been in charge of the publications of the Republican National Committee in New York City during the 1881 presidential campaign. He gave up a brief diplomatic career in Europe to become the first editor in chief of the *Cincinnati Daily Tribune*, in 1893, and then served as William McKinley's publicity adviser in 1896. After he left Venezuela in 1901, he assumed the office of assistant secretary of state and briefly became secretary of state ad interim in 1905. Loomis ultimately left the diplomatic service to become a foreign trade adviser to the Standard Oil Company of California in 1914. Both the Republican party and the State Department held him in high regard.

As minister to Venezuela, Loomis confronted an uncertain political situation. Loomis, President Joaquín Crespo, and most of the Caracas business class favored Ignacio Andrade in the 1897 election. For the first time since the 1840s, however, a viable rival political party arose to challenge the Yellow Liberals. The Partido Liberal Nacionalista, rather like the contemporaneous Unión Cívica Radical in Argentina, included many groups that had little in common except for their dislike of Guzmán Blanco's party and clique. Dissident intellectuals, orthodox liberals, young provincial elites, rural folk, and artisans carried the party banners, giving it a populist flavor in spite of its inherent conservatism. They all rallied around José Manuel ("El Mocho") Hernández,[1] who had fought against Guzmán in 1870 and for Joaquín Crespo in 1892. He became a member of Crespo's Congress, although he opposed Crespo's granting amnesty to his 1892 opponents. Wildly popular, Hernández defended republican principles and civil government and put together the first national political organization while he ran the first modern political campaign. El Mocho copied his campaign strategy from what he knew of political campaigning in the United States. He spoke at public meetings all over the country and publicized his platform through a network of forty-two local newspapers. Venezuelans responded to his national campaign in much the same way that U.S. voters responded to William Jennings Bryan in 1896 and Mexicans would greet Francisco Madero in 1910. The national enthusiasm for Hernández may have been even stronger because the official candidate, Andrade, was a mediocre man with little prestige and less talent for leadership.[2] Although Hernández was the national favorite, the election boasted a total of twenty-seven presidential candidates, including twenty generals and seven *doctores*. Fraud and bribery prevailed, and the official count showed Andrade receiving an overwhelming vote of 406,610 to Hernández's 2,203; five other candidates earned generous totals ranging from 11 to 203 votes. El Mocho, outraged, called for revolution. Although Crespo's death in battle effectively marked the end of the Yellow Liberal party, the government forces did defeat Hernández, who took some comfort in pointing out that even the soldiers who captured him carried his picture under the lining of their caps. Well into the twentieth century, malcontents and politically frustrated Venezuelans could be heard to shout "Viva El Mocho Hernández!"

Much of Hernández's appeal was personal, but his program also represented a populist attack on the centralized power and corruption of the Caracas elite. He called for greater municipal and provincial autonomy; the end of forced military recruitment; free, direct, proportional, and secret ballots for all males over age of eighteen; effective free public education; punishment of corrupt and irresponsible officials; construction of a national road system; the establishment of a professional army, navy, and diplomatic service; and both respect for the Catholic church and freedom of worship.

Hernández's uprising was the first occasion since the 1840s that gave the United States the opportunity to endorse a more participatory form of politics. Blinded by the alliance with the Caracas elite and deploring revolution more than fraud, however, Loomis favored the predictable Andrade, whom he characterized as "a man of high character and class." He dismissed Hernández's chances of success "unless the growing financial distress in the country brings to his support very large numbers of discontented and idle persons."[3] If Hernández should spark a serious threat to the government, Loomis advised that the United States should put on a strong naval demonstration in Venezuelan waters for the "moral effect it would have as well as for the protection of the property interests of American citizens."[4] Clearly, neither Loomis nor the U.S. government saw any need for political reform in Venezuela and preferred to stick with the devil they knew over the unknown and untested.

Concern over Hernández's short-lived revolt soon gave way in any case to a more pressing issue: the effect that the Spanish-American War was having on U.S. relations with Latin America.

The Spanish-American War and Anti-Americanism

When the Cuban revolt broke out in 1895, many Venezuelans favored independence for the island, as they had in 1825 and during the Ten Years' War. At the same time, Caracas's many Canary Islands immigrants—one-eighth of the city's population and "hot-headed, violent, and revengeful" by Loomis's account—contributed to some sympathy for Spain. The resident Spanish minister, many of the clergy, and the French Cable Company further bolstered support for Spain and fostered suspicion of U.S. motives after Washington entered the fray in 1898. Venezuelan newspapers published articles hostile to the United States. *El Pregonero* printed Colombian Ricardo Becerra's prediction that by taking Cuba, the United States would fulfill its ambition to make the Caribbean Sea an "internal lake," or *mare clausum*. The nations surrounding the Caribbean would soon see U.S. ships apply the modern Monroe Doctrine to them.[5] Andrade's government remained friendly to the United States, but Francis Loomis struggled to counter the Venezuelans' anti-Americanism, which the State Department considered more marked than in the rest of Latin America.

Loomis considered the situation serious because he thought that the Spanish had bribed the Cable Company and the Venezuelan newspapers "to create in the minds of the South Americans deep jealousy of the United States for the purpose of making our commercial expansion in this direction more difficult."[6] The U.S. minister then declared his own "splendid little war" of propaganda. He tried to fan President Andrade's hostility toward Spain by telling him that the Spaniards in Venezuela sympathized with the rebellious El Mocho. At Loomis's insistence, Andrade told Venezuelan editors that their papers would be fined or suppressed if they published false news. The State Department mildly cautioned Loomis that the U.S. tradition of freedom of the press made it "a matter of some delicacy" to insist that other governments try to manage the news.[7] Undaunted, Loomis persuaded advertisers to join him in reminding the editor of Venezuela's major newspaper how much business they gave him. The editor pragmatically agreed to publish anything that Loomis should send him, and Loomis enlisted the help of a respected lawyer and judge to prepare a series of articles to be distributed throughout Latin America.[8] Finally, Loomis undercut the French Cable Company's effort by issuing news reports from the embassy before the company could receive and distribute its version of events. He begged the State Department to assist his efforts by sending him more frequent cables.

Reflecting his concern about opinion in the region generally, Loomis also asked some resident Cubans and Puerto Ricans to reassure their compatriots that there was no need to resist U.S. occupation. One of his allies sent to Puerto Rico an address that praised the United States as the "first to chant the hymn of liberty in America." The writer further asserted that Washington was completing Bolívar's dream of breaking Spain's hold on America and urged his countrymen to join the soldiers of "the great Republic" who fought "to redeem our country from its perpetual servility."[9]

Satisfied with his efforts and those of the U.S. armed forces, Loomis exalted that victory had a good effect "upon an impressionable people." He claimed that U.S. prestige had risen with the victory and he reported that "a very considerable number of persons of real importance in a financial, political, and social way express with fervor the wish that Venezuela might one day pass under the control of the United States."[10] Unfortunately for Loomis's peace of mind, such luminaries did not constitute the entire Venezuelan population. Only nine months later, the minister complained that anti-Americanism was spreading among the "unenlightened" in Venezuela.[11] Loomis, like most of his predecessors, considered the popular classes and rural folk to be unworthy of serious consideration, or perhaps they were less susceptible to the kind of bribery and persuasion that worked with the "better sort" in Caracas. He and his allies underestimated the appeal of El Mocho in the interior, and they would soon be even more surprised by a new threat from the hinterlands.

The Scourge from the Andes: Cipriano Castro

In Venezuela the winds of change blew not only from the north but also from the west. Cipriano Castro launched his assault on Caracas from his Andean homeland of Táchira State in 1899. The Andrade government dissolved, giving way to Castro, a man who frustrated and angered the United States more than any other leader in the history of binational relations. President from 1899 to 1908, the *tachirense* became, like his contemporary Zelaya of Nicaragua, one of the "little dark men" who thumbed his nose at Washington. Castro's megalomania, his ambition, his inexperience, and his outrage at the excesses of foreign companies and their governments made him a volatile antagonist of the Caracas merchants and diplomats. In 1899, Loomis described Castro as "a very small, dark man who seems to have a considerable admixture of Indian blood" and who had "slight acquaintance with public men and with the details of Governmental business."[12]

Although Castro was not one of the enlightened *caraqueños* accustomed to seeking the advice and company of the U.S. minister, he was hardly a barbarian. Forty-one years old in 1899, Castro was a lawyer, journalist, former congressional deputy, and military leader. His Causa Liberal Restauradora was composed not of illiterate peasants but of young, high school–educated, urban middle-class men. The state from which they came, Táchira, had enjoyed the greatest population surge of the nineteenth century (growing from 68,819 to 161,709 between the 1873 and 1891 censuses) and the highest per capita income and meat consumption in Venezuela in 1900.[13] Small cattle farms and coffee plantations, often worked by wage labor, fueled the prosperity, and the railroad and steam navigation across Lake Maracaibo linked the region to its external market. Its proximity to Colombia imbued Táchira's politics with some of that nation's developmentalist liberalism, and the vagaries of international coffee prices frequently rocked the local economy. Coffee represented about 74.2 percent of the nation's total exports in the 1890s, but new production in Java, Brazil, and Colombia contributed to an oversupply and a consequent drop in the market price.[14] After 1898, the price drop was extreme, and the price remained low through most of the first decade of the twentieth century, wrecking Táchira's prosperity. Like the Mexican northerners whose more aggressive view of economic development and nationalism drove the Revolution of 1910, Castro's *tachirenses* had grown impatient with the tired and self-serving liberalism of the Caracas politicians. Their political slogan called for "new men, new ideals, and new methods."

Castro had received much of his education in neighboring Cúcuta, Colombia, the site of the 1821 Congress that established the union of Gran Colombia and became its capital. Like Guzmán Blanco, Castro considered himself an heir of Simón Bolívar and aspired to unite Latin America. Unlike Guzmán, Castro had developed a strong hostility toward the Anglo-Saxon imperialism he saw in Great Britain's encroachments in Guayana and in the occupation of Cuba by the United States. A Venezuelan historian characterized Castro's attitude as "petit bourgeois anti-imperialism, of the Latin against the Saxon, of Rome against Carthage, but strong enough to awaken the conscience of the continent in the face of the Yankee danger."[15] Indeed, this was a mentality that frustrated and puzzled U.S. officials accustomed to the erratic trickery of Guzmán Blanco and his Yellow Liberals.

His U.S. adversaries took Castro's recalcitrance personally and did their best to demonize him. They considered him anti-American, vain, corrupt, irrational, and unappreciative of all the United States had done for him. U.S. minister Herbert Bowen reported in 1904 that Castro "passes his time in the country drinking brandy and consorting with low women, and his head has been turned to such an extent by flattery and the apparent success of his nefarious schemes that he has become a very dangerous ruler."[16] Theodore Roosevelt called the Venezuelan president "an unspeakably villainous little monkey."[17] Secretary of State Elihu Root called him a "crazy brute."[18] U.S. consul James Weldon Johnson considered him "volatile, arrogant, cantankerous," and boorish.[19]

Editorial cartoonists in the United States invariably portrayed Castro as a petulant and destructive child—often with negroid features and sometimes wearing a Mexican sombrero—badly in need of a spanking by Uncle Sam.

By 1905, U.S. chargé d'affaires Norman Hutchinson argued that the prestige of the Monroe Doctrine in the hemisphere required the United States to remove Castro from power: "If we fight Castro, it will not be war against Venezuela, but for it, just as Castro himself fought for it, ostensibly, in his Revolución Libertadora [sic]. I believe we can found a stable and honorable government here and leave the country in peace with the world and itself. England has done this sort of thing on less provocation and with good results for civilization and humanity."[20]

Foreign Intrigue and the Blockade of 1902–1903

Castro's Venezuela provided numerous instances of chronic wrong-doing and misbehavior in U.S. eyes. Valid judgments these may have been, but the *andino* had not come to power at an auspicious moment. The civil conflicts since 1896, sinking coffee prices after 1898, general fiscal mismanagement, and new loans contracted in London in 1881 and Berlin in 1896 had driven the country nearly to bankruptcy. Castro, perhaps unskilled in the oily evasions of Guzmán Blanco, defied the foreign creditors and instructed them to seek remedy through the Venezuelan courts, in accord with the Calvo Doctrine, rather than through diplomatic channels. Although Venezuela had no choice but to default in 1901, Castro's belligerence alienated foreign governments, resident investors, and the Caracas business community. For the United States, the complex controversy involving the New York and Bermúdez Company, a subsidiary of General Asphalt of Philadelphia, revealed Castro at his worst and most recalcitrant.

As described in Chapter 3, four Venezuelans in 1897 contested the rights of the New York and Bermúdez Company to the rich Guanoco Lake asphalt concession. In 1900, this Venezuelan group sold their rights to Warner and Quinlan of New York, who wanted to challenge the monopoly of the Asphalt Trust. Litigation between the two U.S. asphalt groups proceeded through the Venezuelan courts, closely watched by the U.S. press. The State Department usually instructed the legation not to take sides in conflicts between rival U.S. investors in Venezuela. In the asphalt controversy, however, the legation sided with the New York and Bermúdez Company, in part because the second vice president, General Avery D. Andrews, was a friend and associate of William McKinley and Theodore Roosevelt. Reports from the U.S. Legation denigrated the claims of Warner and Quinlan and charged that Cipriano Castro favored them because he held a share in their business. Warner and Quinlan countered by enlisting a few U.S. congressmen to counsel the State Department to avoid taking sides in the conflict. In August 1901 Castro became so angry at Francis Loomis's insistent pressure regarding the matter that he demanded the minister's recall. Washington did recall Loomis, but only to name him an assistant secretary of state. Herbert Bowen replaced Loomis in Caracas.[21]

In the midst of the asphalt controversy, Castro had other problems to deal with. He had alienated the Caracas elite by parading them—including the wealthiest man in Venezuela, Manuel Antonio Matos—through the streets of Caracas to jail when they refused to make loans to the government. Castro had already weathered a brief revolt by the indefatigable El Mocho Hernández, but Matos proved a more formidable foe. Matos financed and spearheaded the so-called Liberating Revolution (la Revolución Libertadora) that invaded Venezuela from Colombia in January 1901. Foreign companies in Venezuela, including the French Cable Company and the New York and Bermúdez Company, surreptitiously contributed money and resources to the Matos revolution. The well-financed revolution lasted nearly two years, cost more than fifty million bolivares to put down, and resulted in twenty thousand deaths before Castro triumphed in November 1902.[22] Castro had little time to enjoy his victory.

Still rankling over their economic losses, the European creditor nations decided to teach Castro a lesson. Germany, Italy, and Great Britain withdrew their representatives, seized Venezuelan warships, and blockaded the Venezuelan coast in December 1902, demanding immediate payment of their debts. The Europeans had informed President Theodore Roosevelt beforehand, and he agreed that civilized nations could not condone Castro's irresponsible behavior, but he warned them not to use the situation to seize American territory. Castro chose U.S. minister Herbert Bowen to be Venezuela's arbiter, immediately agreed to all demands, and authorized Bowen to sign protocols to that effect on 13 February 1903. In defiance of Bowen's urging, the Europeans maintained the blockade and the detention of Venezuelan warships even after the signing of the protocol. The one-two punch of domestic conflict and foreign blockade damaged both Venezuela's economy and Castro's mercurial humor.

The blockade and its aftermath had several consequences. Castro fumed at the humiliation, and he still needed funds. Although scrupulous in meeting the foreign protocol obligations—to be paid by a 30 percent levy on the customs revenues of La Guaira and Puerto Cabello—Castro reduced the revenues of those two ports by diverting trade to two newly opened ones, Tucacas and Cristóbal Colón. He passed new laws to govern the activities of foreigners in Venezuela, taking care to tighten up the mining legislation. In 1904, agents of the Warner and Quinlan asphalt interests helpfully gave Castro evidence of the support that the New York and Bermúdez Company had given Matos's Revolución Libertadora. Castro seized the properties of the company (as well as those of the French Cable Company) and began actions against them in Venezuelan courts. Outraged by critical and allegedly false press accounts in November, Castro ordered the publisher of the English-language Venezuelan Herald to leave the country within twenty-four hours. The editor, Albert F. Jaurett, who was born in France but had acquired U.S. nationality after some dubious activities in Mexico and Central America, had come to Venezuela in 1896. His paper boosted U.S. businesses and investment, and Jaurett also reported for the New York Herald, which had been printing unfavorable articles on Venezuela. Complaining that his hasty departure left him no time to put his business affairs in order, Jaurett promptly filed a claim against the Venezuelan government.

Castro's Chronic Wrongdoing and the Roosevelt Corollary

Theodore Roosevelt and U.S. diplomats worried that Castro dared to harass his European creditors because he believed that the United States would defend him against another intervention. In June 1904, Herbert Bowen argued that

> the fear of losing territory and sovereignty is, and always has been, a wholesome fear to every nation. We, by our Monroe Doctrine, relieve Venezuela of that fear. In exchange, she gives us nothing. That is the weak point of the Monroe doctrine, and it is a very irritating point to European nations. They naturally believe that if our sister American republics are to be protected by our Monroe Doctrine from the usual punishments inflicted on disorderly and dishonest nations, we should see that they conduct themselves with even greater propriety than other nations do that are unprotected.[23]

Bowen urged Washington to put a stop to Castro's blackmail so that foreign capital would be safe to contribute to Venezuela's prosperity.

United States officials observed that the "better class of people," such as Enrique L. Boulton, did not support Castro. Bolton told the U.S. chargé in November 1904, "I can assure you that they [Boulton's business colleagues] are looking forward to the United States coming down here and setting things right." In early 1905, Bowen outlined a plan by which the United States could please Europeans and the Venezuelan elite by removing Castro from power. Captain Frank Parker, the U.S. military attaché, had drawn up plans for a U.S. force to scare Castro into yielding, seize him, and send him into exile on a U.S. warship. U.S. agents could then take over the customs houses, and a force of fifteen hundred U.S. troops would keep peace in Caracas while a provisional government formed from Caracas's leading men would "act by and with the advice of an American Counsellor." Bowen did not advise the establishment of a U.S. military government, "for it would soon be very unpopular, and we should need a force of at least 25,000 soldiers with which to keep the interior of the country in order."[24] Bowen's plans tacitly acknowledged that the small Caracas economic elite who might welcome U.S. intervention did not represent the majority of Venezuelans.

With the plans all made, and the provocation so clear, why did the United States *not* invade Venezuela? There were several reasons. By 1905, it was difficult to argue that the United States had to intervene in order to check European ambitions. After the 1902–3 blockade, the United States had warned that it would not again condone such actions. Moreover, both Germany and Great Britain had lost interest in pressing their advantage in the Caribbean, effectively accepting U.S. hegemony there. Other arguments for intervention proved less persuasive to the American people.

Throughout his presidency Theodore Roosevelt wanted to take military action against Castro. Public and congressional criticism of his Caribbean policy, however, made him cautious. Roosevelt wrote to Secretary of State John Hay in September 1904, "Of course we do not want to act in the closing weeks of the campaign, but I think we should make up our minds ourselves to take the initiative and give Castro a sharp lesson, . . . it will show those Dagos that they will have to behave decently."[25] After the election, in December 1904, Roosevelt made his "chronic wrongdoing" speech to Congress, announcing that the United States would assume the role of policeman toward irresponsible Latin American governments on behalf of the great powers. The president's declaration came to be known as the Roosevelt Corollary to the Monroe Doctrine. Wanting to take action somewhere to make his point, Roosevelt decided that the case for intervention was more clear-cut in the Dominican Republic. Even the Dominican intervention caused more trouble than Roosevelt had anticipated, however, for the Senate balked at giving approval for the customs receivership there for two years.

Roosevelt may also have believed that intervention in Venezuela would be costlier than similar action in the Dominican Republic. After all, the hated Castro had mustered support from his worst enemies (including El Mocho and Manuel Antonio Matos) during the 1903 European blockade. Unlike the Dominican Republic or Cuba in 1906, there was no organized opposition party in Venezuela to invite U.S. intervention and assume a cloak of political legitimacy. In January 1906, Roosevelt cautiously queried the General Staff of the War Department: "Is there a plan developed for the campaign against Venezuela, including the transports, and so forth? Any such campaign should be undertaken with a force so large as to minimize the chance of effective resistance."[26]

Roosevelt had to acknowledge that the general public did not share his outrage at Castro. Although he ordered a new intervention in Cuba in September 1906, he complained to William Howard Taft: "I have never gotten them [the U.S. public] up to the point of taking even a tepid interest in Castro's outrageous iniquity in treating American interests in Venezuela; and this is all where the Monroe Doctrine applies and where in consequence the average American has something in the way of traditional national action to which appeal can be made as a precedent."[27]

Castro had few defenders in the United States, but the trustbusters may have helped to generate an impression of Venezuela as an underdog. William Scruggs's book on Venezuela, which appeared in 1901, reminded the public of British threats against Venezuela in the 1890s. The 1902–3 European blockade again placed the United States in the role of saving the country from rapacious Europeans. In 1907, Orray E. Thurber's *The Venezuelan Question: Castro and the Asphalt Trust* highlighted another predator. The muckraking history depicted Cipriano Castro as a victim of the greed and corruption of the trust. The accumulated effect of these publications and events may have had some part in frustrating Roosevelt's plans.

Angered afresh at Castro in June 1908, Roosevelt still dared go no further than to sever diplomatic relations. Four months later, Roosevelt lamented that his hands had been tied with Castro: "How I wish I could get the American people to take the least interest in Castro. It is literally true that if I started to deal with him as he deserves, the enormous majority of my countrymen would be so absolutely amazed and so absolutely out of sympathy with me as if I undertook personally to run down and chastise some small street urchin who yelled some epithet of derision at me while I was driving."[28]

Intervention in Venezuela became even harder to sell when a smoldering feud between Minister Herbert Bowen and Assistant Secretary of State and former U.S. minister to Venezuela Francis Loomis became public knowledge. In April 1905, Bowen accused Loomis of having accepted bribes from the New York and Bermúdez Company. Secretary of War William Howard Taft, acting for Secretary of State John Hay, who was ill, investigated the charge and ruled that Loomis may have been indiscreet, but he was not guilty of bribery. Roosevelt became furious when Bowen leaked his evidence of Loomis's corruption to the press while the investigation was still being conducted. Roosevelt fumed, "In Venezuela I am tempted to wish that Castro would execute Bowen and thereby give us good reason for smashing Castro. This, however, is merely an iridescent dream."[29] Roosevelt concluded that the now-public feud had further tied his hands with respect to moving against Venezuela and had harmed U.S. interests in South America generally, where the United States had "not merely to act courteously, justly and generously, but to make it evident that we are thus acting." Such public allegations, even if they remained unsubstantiated, discredited the U.S. government "not only in the newspapers of our own country, but in the newspapers of the various Latin American republics."[30] Bowen was dismissed from the foreign service, and Loomis quietly disappeared from State soon afterward, although he took on occasional official missions before he went to work for Standard Oil of California in 1914. Thus, a "conceited, arrogant, and by no means too well bred" U.S. diplomat (Bowen) may inadvertently have saved Cipriano Castro from suffering the effects of the Big Stick.[31]

As it turned out, the United States only had to wait for Castro to remove himself from the scene. Castro's drinking bouts and venereal disease, aggravated by aphrodisiacs containing strychnine, intensified his health problems and his bouts of irrationality. In December 1908 he boarded a ship to seek medical treatment in Europe, leaving his loyal subordinate, Juan Vicente Gómez, in charge, as he had during a brief bogus retirement in 1906.

This time, however, Gómez moved quickly to ensure that Castro did not change his mind. Gómez sent word to Washington that he would immediately settle all claims, and Washington gratefully sent warships to assist him in consolidating his power. Unexpectedly, the *yanquis* and the Venezuelan elite had found the democratic caesar for whom they had searched for nearly a century. Gómez came to power in December 1908, and there he remained until he died of old age in December 1935.

Venezuelan Nationalism

Before turning to a discussion of Venezuela under Gómez, it is useful to examine Venezuelan attitudes in this jingoistic age. Much has been written about the expansionist nationalism of the United States, driven by Spencerian views of the white man's burden as well as by more concrete economic, military, and security goals. At the same time, many U.S. citizens feared that expansionism and the "burden" of absorbing people of color would destroy the very nature of U.S. democracy. Venezuela's nationalism, that of a weak and vulnerable country, was even more complex.

Venezuelans slowly acquired a conscious national identity that arose from their own history, geography, and circumstances, but was further shaped by the new international interest in the Caribbean. Venezuelan literary historian Maurice Belrose has written that "the Venezuelan nation was not born when the Caracas aristocracy proclaimed independence in 1811, nor when the Congress of Valencia consecrated the withdrawal from the Republic of Gran Colombia in 1830. . . . [T]he first time that Venezuela forcefully affirmed the will to make itself respected as a nation was under Cipriano Castro's dictatorship when German, English and Dutch imperialism tried to make the nation hang its head by blockading the coasts and bombarding the ports."[32] If the invasions by France, Spain, and the United States put steel into Mexican nationalism in the nineteenth century, Venezuela's experience with British, European, and U.S. expansionism after 1890 contributed to a reflexive national spirit in that Caribbean country.

The late nineteenth century also saw a cultural awakening in Venezuela. The popular classes continued to sing their *llanero* songs; dance the *joropo*; play the *cuatro* (four-string guitar), harp, and African-inspired *tambores* (drums); reinact popular festivals and traditions like the dancing devils of Yare and the burning of Judas; and give devotion to the cult of María Lionza. Artists and writers depicted national themes, and folklorists like Arístides Rojas linked the popular and the elite with books and articles on creole traditions and tales like those of Tío Conejo and Tío Tigre. In 1888, the National Academy of History was founded to encourage research and teaching of Venezuela's national past.

Logically, patriotism and ideas of the nation varied with region and social classes. It is especially difficult to document expressions of popular nationalism. There are some scattered hints that the Venezuelan popular classes resented foreigners and that racial and class tensions influenced their attitudes. On occasion they identified the excesses of foreigners with those of the Caracas white elite who ruled over them. In the 1840s, rebel Ezequiel Zamora and his followers adopted the battle cry "Death to the whites and to those who can read," a slogan that applied equally to members of the Caracas elite and their foreign allies. The masses responded both to El Mocho's nationalism and to Cipriano Castro's xenophobia. Venezuelans had no *mambisa* tradition like the Cubans, but Castro received wide popular support in his struggle against Matos and the foreign blockade between 1901 and 1903.

U.S. citizens living in Venezuela reported scattered hostility over the years. Archaeologist Hiram Bingham wrote that a cattleman in rural Venezuela charged him with being a spy or an army officer during his 1906–7 trip. Bingham commented, "To suspect travellers of being emissaries of their governments is an Oriental and also a Spanish trait."[33] A mob attacked the U.S. consul in La Guaira in the 1870s because of his indecent behavior. Villagers sometimes harassed Protestant ministers and Bible salesmen who ventured away from the major cities. James Weldon Johnson, an African-American writer and the U.S. consul at

Puerto Cabello, characterized the members of the Puerto Cabello Club in 1908 as anti-American, although they welcomed him as a member.[34] United States–owned businesses often preferred foreign to Venezuelan workers, but that preference may have made a virtue of necessity. During a trip to visit the asphalt works in 1901, the commander of the USS *Scorpion* remarked that Venezuelans refused to work for the American owners of the Orinoco Company Limited.[35] He concluded that Venezuelan workers were lazy, and numerous observers from the United States commented on the anti-Americanism of the poor, or "unenlightened," classes. Foreign ownership of basic services like electricity, telephones, railroads, or steamships may have exacerbated popular feelings of hostility.

By and large, the elite saw no advantage, and some danger, to encouraging nationalism and political participation among the lower classes. The masses could easily, like Ezequiel Zamora, turn on their wealthy compatriots along with their foreign associates. The poor, moreover, would have a more logical interest in issues of land and labor than in more abstract topics like the tariff. Especially after 1898, Venezuelan leaders worried that an activist population could contribute to a disorder that would discourage investment and prompt U.S. intervention. The Venezuelan elite then espoused the positivist dogma that the masses should remain quiescent until they acquired the necessary culture. They had not yet discovered that forceful popular support strengthens rather than weakens a president in his dealings with foreigners.

The educated elite shared some of Guzmán Blanco's and Castro's outrage at the constant, and frequently fraudulent, foreign claims and the appearance of foreign warships along the coast. They resented the hypocritical "America for Americans" initiative of Blaine, his pressure for a commercial open door treaty, and the retaliatory tariff on Venezuelan coffee. Their Bolivarian heritage of Hispanic unity contributed to a distaste for Anglo-Saxon imperialism in Guayana and Cuba. Their education and intellectual sympathies often lay with France, further accentuating a Mediterranean perspective over a northern one in cultural terms.

César Zumeta's Sick Continent

One of the most articulate spokesmen for Venezuela's creole nationalism was César Zumeta, born in Caracas on 19 March 1864. Zumeta wrote for Venezuelan, New York, and European newspapers between 1883 and 1908. Believing that his writings could help to develop an informed democratic electorate, Zumeta, like Francisco Madero of Mexico, deplored violence and attributed Venezuela's backwardness to *caudillismo* and civil conflicts. He criticized the vices of the tropical nations, but he hoped that education combined with Mediterranean creativity would eventually overcome them.

Since he angered both Guzmán Blanco and his successors, Zumeta spent much of his time in exile. Like the Cuban José Martí, with whom he was associated in New York, Zumeta argued that the Latino-Mediterranean civilizations had to block the northern onslaught.[36] Zumeta also supported Bolívar's prescription that Hispanic nations had to unite in order to survive. As a positivist and an apologist for dictatorship, Zumeta has over the years acquired a reputation for accommodation rather than resistance. Yet, his passion to preserve Venezuelan sovereignty in a dangerous age sets him apart.

Much of Zumeta's writing reflected the tension between his realistic appraisal of U.S. power and his own assertive patriotism. Weak nations needed strong rulers, he believed, to confront the Anglo-Saxon threat. In April 1899, President Andrade dismissed Zumeta as Venezuelan consul in New York because he feared the United States would take offense at Zumeta's acerbic essays. At first, Zumeta collaborated with Cipriano Castro, hoping that Castro would, like Porfirio Díaz of Mexico, be "a dictatorial temperament with the soul of a republican."[37] He broke with Castro in 1903, however, when Castro first brashly provoked the humiliating blockade and then meekly allowed Herbert Bowen to negotiate his capitulation. Zumeta counseled accommodation to avoid threats to national sovereignty, but resistance to the last man once intervention became inevitable.[38]

Zumeta further argued that a strong leader could minimize the damage done to the nation by the coveted, and necessary, foreign capital. When foreigners brought their money into the unstable and chaotic political climate of Venezuela, it became "ruinous in the economic realm, corrupting in politics, and dangerous for our international relations."[39] A weak nation also had to be sensitive to rivalries among the great powers. Zumeta feared that the United States might intervene to nullify Manuel Antonio Matos's deal with the German Disconto Gesellschafft to establish a bank in Caracas. He advised instead seeking Mediterranean capital, both because Venezuela had cultural ties there and because it would cause fewer problems with the United States. Finally, although Zumeta endorsed the Calvo Doctrine, he thought it wiser to surrender the doctrine than to surrender the nation. Zumeta feared that if Venezuela did not settle differences with the United States by arbitration, Washington would take over the nation as it had Panama.[40]

Zumeta wanted to see strong leadership in Venezuela, but he reacted angrily to an editorial in the *New York Sun* that praised Castro for squelching a nascent rebellion with force after he had Antonio Paredes and seventeen companions assassinated in 1907. Zumeta raged that the *Sun* endorsed lynch mobs as a convenience to the imperialists. "To them," he added, "the only good Hispanic American, like the only good Indian, is a dead one."[41]

In the wake of the U.S. occupation of Cuba, Zumeta published his most famous work, "The Sick Continent," in New York in 1899. The continent was sick, he said, because the United States had renounced the moral force of its democratic tradition and had conquered Cuba and the Philippines. Like the other great industrial states, the United States ignored international law in its mission to expand southward in search of raw materials and markets. The tropical Caribbean, especially Panama, Nicaragua, and Venezuela, stood in danger so long as the great powers thought that they were incapable of developing their own lands. Zumeta concluded, "The strong conspire against our independence, and the continent is sick with weakness. Iron fortifies. Let's arm ourselves."[42] The advocate of civilian power felt impelled to call for a military buildup in Latin America.

Like his contemporary José Enrique Rodó of Uruguay, Zumeta vividly contrasted an idealized Hispanic culture with a materialistic Anglo-Saxon one.

Sons of the tropics, we should love our region as it is, more than any other on the globe, and be capable of guarding it against these civilizations of the golden calf, where hundreds of men oppress millions of salaried slaves, and people live in an agitated hell of perpetual covetous misery, driven by the fear of hunger; a civilization under the sway of bank, church, and barracks, saved only by the handful of wise men, artists and dreamers who cover so much nakedness with the vestment of the light of an ideal.[43]

Zumeta did acknowledge that the Yankees held no monopoly on crass materialism. Latin Americans—and Venezuelans, he added—bore some of the blame for U.S. expansionism when greedy and corrupt men like Guzmán Blanco and Cipriano Castro pillaged their nations for their own profit.

At heart, though, Zumeta shared the optimism of the positivists. Venezuela would pass through its weak and vulnerable stage, he predicted, and the United States would go beyond its imperialist stage to recover its idealism. "The eclipse, even though it is total, will be transitory."[44]

For all of Zumeta's patriotism, of course, the tragic flaw in his vision paralleled that of the Cuban liberals. Distressed at the poverty and weakness of his country, he placed a high premium on stability, order, and good relations with foreign governments. Like José Antonio Páez, he spoke primarily for the "nation" of the wealthy and educated. That class, after all, had the most to lose from foreign blockades, invasions, seizures of customs houses, and disruption of trade. But few of the elite could honestly claim that they were husbanding the nation's resources for their less fortunate compatriots.

Zumeta became Castro's implacable enemy, but he welcomed Juan Vicente Gómez as the "republican dictator" who would deal cautiously with foreigners but not enslave himself to them. Zumeta served Gómez faithfully from the latter's accession in 1908 until his death in 1935. One of the generation of positivists—like José Gil Fortoul, Pedro Manuel Arcaya, and Laureano Vallenilla Lanz—who provided Gómez with his aura of legitimacy as a democratic caesar, Zumeta was ostracized and attacked after 1935. He lived until 1955, but he wrote almost nothing after Gómez's death.

The Advent of the Democratic Caesar:
Juan Vicente Gómez

When Cipriano Castro left Venezuela in November 1908 to seek medical treatment in Europe, the Venezuelan elite and the U.S. government hoped that his successor would prove to be a Venezuelan Porfirio Díaz. Barely a month after Castro's departure, Juan Vicente Gómez announced that he was in charge. On 14 December, he informed the State Department that he was willing to settle all outstanding disagreements and requested that U.S. warships be sent to maintain order. By 21 December, the USS *North Carolina*, USS *Maine*, and USS *Dolphin* were steaming to the Venezuelan coast, where they hovered for three months. While the ships' crewmen polished Venezuelans' baseball skills, Judge William I. Buchanan negotiated a protocol with Gómez. Theodore Roosevelt, the lame-duck president, would have the satisfaction of certifying the victory over his old nemesis, Castro.

The Buchanan Protocol, signed in February 1909, recognized all outstanding U.S. claims against Venezuela and restored diplomatic relations between the two nations. Venezuela agreed to exempt the New York and Bermúdez Company from paying damages for financing the revolt against Castro and even restored the company's Guanoco Lake properties with a new fifty-year contract. Journalist Albert Jaurett got twelve thousand dollars compensation for being deported so quickly, half the sum he had requested. Caracas submitted the long-standing Orinoco Steamship Company dispute to The Hague for arbitration, an arbitration that went against Venezuela. In 1910, U.S. chargé Sheldon Whitehouse wrote approvingly of Gómez's foreign minister, Dr. Francisco González Guinán, who had negotiated the protocol: "He is a man of wide intelligence and has no anti-American feeling and sees that the natural country to assist in the development of Venezuela is the United States."[45] The attitude that inspired these pragmatic agreements with the sole hegemonic power in the region allowed Gómez to predict, quite accurately, "God is the only One who will cast me from power." God allowed Gómez to rule for twenty-seven years before he removed the wily Venezuelan from power—and the earth—in December 1935.

The U.S. Navy and diplomatic service assisted God in protecting Gómez. Venezuelan and U.S. agents reported Castro's movements, and the navy several times intercepted Castro on his way home to Venezuela and turned him back. On one occasion, the harassment extended to a brief detention on Ellis Island when Castro touched in New York on his way to the Caribbean. The former president was allowed to get no closer to his homeland than Puerto Rico, where he died in 1924.

Gómez's intellectuals labored to suppress any residual anti-Americanism in their country and to convince their compatriots of the good intentions of the United States. Manuel Antonio Matos, in his turn as foreign minister in 1910, assured Venezuelans that statements made by U.S. government spokesmen at the Inter-American Conference in Rio in 1906 and later "show clearly that U.S. policy has no aggressive intentions against the republics of our continent or their territorial integrity."[46] Matos hoped to discourage any embarrassing Venezuelan criticism of U.S. actions and accusations that Gómez was an unpatriotic *vendepatria.*

In spite of Gómez's censorship, some Maracaibo newspapers did censure the United States for its role in overthrowing Nicaraguan president José Santos Zelaya in 1909. The Táchira newspaper *Horizontes* also denounced the U.S. military intervention in Nicaragua and the aggressive application of the Monroe Doctrine. The editors characterized the *yanquis* as the "new Roman Empire," accused them of bad faith, and pessimistically predicted invasions of Cuba and Mexico in 1911 and 1912.[47] The paper tempered its hostility somewhat after the flattering visit to Venezuela of U.S. secretary of state Philander Knox in 1912, but attacked again after the United States invaded Haiti in 1914.

U.S. and Venezuelan spokesmen constantly invoked the cult of Bolívar, hoping a flurry of symbolic patriotism would distract their critics. Venezuela's centennial celebration of independence in 1911 provided the occasion for numerous U.S. diplomats and journalists to praise the nation's new order and "democracy." The approaching opening of the Panama Canal inspired another celebration of hemispheric unity in general and Venezuela's importance in particular. Secretary of State

Knox addressed Venezuelans in Caracas in 1912: "The Saxon of the North and the Hispanic of the South are joined as associates in the common cause of progress and peace, consecrated equally to the common duty of promoting the good will and mutual confidence and esteem that create relations of true fraternity among the democratic republics of America."[48] Knox took care to associate Bolívar's 1826 Panama Congress with the symbolic union of the Americas that the imminent opening of the Panama Canal would forge.

Gómez's strong hand obviously precluded public criticism of his dictatorship. Yet, the old *andino* did share much of Zumeta's brand of nationalism. He intended at all costs to avoid foreign intervention that would diminish Venezuelan sovereignty. That goal required him to maintain order, settle foreign claims, welcome and protect foreign business and capital, and put national finances on a sound basis. Like Zumeta, however, he did not relish the prospect of having northerners overrun his nation at will. Gómez organized and built up a national army, principally to deal with domestic foes but also as a veiled warning to foreigners; he chose a West Point graduate, General Francisco Linares Alcántara, to direct the reorganization of the military.

The semiliterate president emulated Páez's formula by surrounding himself with respected intellectuals like Francisco González Guinán, César Zumeta, Laureano Vallenilla Lanz, José Gil Fourtoul, and Pedro Manuel Arcaya. He placated the economic elite by bringing Manuel Antonio Matos into the government and placing Vicente Lecuna in charge of finances and the central bank. Gómez's mandarins ensured domestic harmony and the avoidance of any disturbing "chronic wrongdoing." They slavishly flattered and supported the dictator and enriched themselves through his favor, but their sophistication equipped them to deal effectively with foreign emissaries.

Gómez's opponents, like those of Mexico's Porfirio Díaz, received no *pan* and many tastes of the *palo*. Obviously, they could not publicly find fault with the dictator. Under certain circumstances, however, they could criticize the United States or reassert the superiority of the Hispanic culture over the Anglo-Saxon. As Gómez's regime wore on, some Venezuelan nationalists trod this delicate line, suppressing the guilty secret that the United States they criticized maintained the dictator they dared not attack.

By 1912, on the eve of the great petroleum finds, Venezuela had clearly fallen into the orbit of the United States. The elite had decided that Castro's type of belligerance placed the nation at risk. With only one hegemon left in the Caribbean, the traditional strategy of playing the foreign powers off against each other was no longer an option.

Nor could the nation afford to dissolve into civil war, inviting the marines to come in to restore order. *Caraqueños* effectively accepted a deal by which the Táchira strongmen kept the peace but allowed the merchants and *doctores* to display the external trappings of power. *Tachirenses, caraqueños*, and Yankees concurred that the majority of Venezuelans should best remain silent until they had acquired the necessary civic culture. The United States preferred the predictable formula of the democratic caesar. Many Venezuelans, like César Zumeta, also found the formula beneficial, but in any case, they saw no alternative.

The next quarter of a century would bring unrivaled order and prosperity to Venezuela while the United States rose to become an international power of the first rank. Venezuela's new wealth and stability, driven by the foreign-controlled petroleum industry, laid the bases for the emergence of a new populist nationalism. Ironically, king petroleum simultaneously created new areas of common interest and interdependency between the two nations.

5   Oil and the Democratic Caesar, 1912–1935

> The advent of great numbers of Americans connected with the oil industry has had a decided effect and Venezuela looks towards the United States much more than ever before.
>
> —Jordan H. Stabler

The troubled first decade of the twentieth century marked a major change in United States–Venezuelan relations. Venezuelan affairs had served as an impetus to the formulation of the new U.S. doctrines toward the Caribbean and Latin America; the Olney Corollary and the Roosevelt Corollary. The United States fully intended to be the policeman of the Western Hemisphere and to squash would-be nationalists like Cipriano Castro and José Santos Zelaya. Issues of national security, including the first glimmers of anticommunism, and commercial advantage drove U.S. policy toward hegemony. Venezuelans had a more defensive, but critical, objective: to preserve Venezuelan sovereignty and autonomy.

By 1913 Juan Vicente Gómez had already outlasted two U.S. presidents. He would survive four more and live into the era of Franklin Delano Roosevelt. Despite evidence of the brutality and corruption of his de facto regime, with every year official U.S. views of this democratic caesar grew more mellow. The dictator with "blundering cunning" (1913) became a "scoundrel" (1918) during World War I, but by 1927 his "kindliness of manner and benignity of countenance" accompanied a "bold and sagacious leadership" (1928). From a necessary evil Gómez had evolved into a positive good in official U.S. opinion. Some unofficial views were less sanguine about Gómez and what he represented.

Gómez was both the last of the caudillos on the Porfirio Díaz model and the first of the 1930s policemen like Rafael Trujillo and Anastasio Somoza. Yet he was not simply a puppet of the *yanquis* and their oil

117

companies. Like César Zumeta, Gómez wanted to guard Venezuelan sovereignty, to avoid invasion by the United States, and, within those strictures, to construct a new Venezuela whose order and prosperity would make it less vulnerable to attack. He employed a number of tactics, some old and some new, to achieve his goal and remain in power. If he usually acceded to the *yanquis'* "suggestions," Gómez still retained the power to grant or refuse those requests.

The United States treated Gómez with a certain wariness. Venezuela's increasing prosperity and the economic elite's support of the dictator gave little pretext to intercede. Moreover, Gómez allowed no political parties to operate and no contested elections from his accession in 1908 to his death in 1935. During the same era, disputed elections in Cuba, Nicaragua, the Dominican Republic, and Haiti sometimes gave Washington a reason to intervene. A government that effectively intimidated any viable opposition could survive indefinitely, especially after Theodore Roosevelt's and Woodrow Wilson's Caribbean activism gave way to the more pragmatic policies of Warren G. Harding, Calvin Coolidge, and Herbert Hoover.

Relations between the two nations became more complex during the quarter of a century of Gómez's rule, for there were more players to lobby the State Department and the Venezuelan government: oil companies, missionary boards, human rights groups, labor organizations, chambers of commerce, universities, scholars, adventurers, scientists, and businessmen. The advent of the United Press and the Associated Press, radio, and the aviation age brought new experiences with other cultures. Most of the "Americanization" that occured during this period was confined to Caracas and the oil zones, principally Maracaibo. Still, increased contact with U.S. citizens and businesses, added to Gómez's authoritarian centralization, contributed to a stronger sense of Venezuelan national identity.

Washington Embraces a Dictator, 1912–1935

Woodrow Wilson's most critical problem in Latin America was dealing with the chaos that followed the overthrow of Porfirio Díaz and the murder of Francisco Madero in Mexico. His 1913 Mobile address, which warned that illegal seizure of power would be interpreted as "chronic wrongdoing," encouraged Gómez's enemies. Gómez's presidential term was due to expire in 1914, and there was a constitutional prohibition on reelection, but Chargé Jefferson Caffrey chose not to press Gómez to hold an authentic election. In 1914, Gómez illegally extended his presidential term, but then cautiously refused to take office until 1922. How could the U.S. Marines come in and overthrow someone who was not in office? Dr. Victorino Márquez Bustillos served as provisional president, but U.S. diplomats and businessmen complained that he could not or would not act on their requests. Wilson's State Department clung to the view that "a moderate soft-shell despotism" was necessary in Venezuela, and Minister Preston McGoodwin received instructions in April 1914 to refrain from encouraging Gómez's enemies.

The *andino* survived round 1 of the campaign against de facto governments. In 1917, round 2 began because Venezuela was feared to be a wartime security threat. Gómez had maintained Venezuela's neutrality during the war, but he was known to favor Germany.[1] Rumors flew that he planned to transfer Margarita Island to the Germans for a submarine base and that the funds he had deposited in German banks gave him a stake in a German victory. In a cockamamy story reminiscent of the Zimmerman telegraph hoax, one U.S. consul reported that Gómez had secretly agreed to help the kaiser re-create the sixteenth-century Hapsburg empire in exchange for a promise that Gómez should be king of the tributary state of Venezuela.[2] Gómez, like Castro before him, benefited from Washington's judgment that the effort to remove him and keep peace over an outraged population would require too great a diversion of military resources. The State Department's Division of Latin American Affairs even decided to suppress news of Gómez's crimes so that the American public would not demand his removal.[3]

If Gómez and many of the *andinos* favored Germany, most of Venezuela's intellectuals favored France and the Allies. Minister McGoodwin reported widespread appreciation for the United States and democratic values. As the war drew to a close in 1918, Gómez's enemies hoped the United States would seize the democratic moment to assist them in expelling the dictator. In early 1918, President Woodrow Wilson did ask his secretary of state if "this scoundrel" could be put out without upsetting "the peace of Latin America more than letting him alone will?"[4] Alas for democratic hopes, the massive Caracas demonstrations planned by the anti-*gomecistas* for 28 October 1918 fizzled out. The influenza epidemic, Gómez's ruthless use of force, the lack of a coherent organized opposition, and the quiescence of the United States allowed Gómez to survive. Washington apparently decided to stick with the devil they knew rather than gamble on one of Gómez's little-known and unpredictable opponents.

Washington even opted cautiously to ensure order and the status quo. Minister McGoodwin telegraphed that the warship he had requested (the *Salem*) had contributed to "dampening the ardor of the leaders of the movement and they seem to have abandoned their plans at least for the present."[5] In May 1919 the State Department cabled the U.S. Legation in Bogotá, Colombia, that it should "discretely intimate" to the Colombian government that the United States would frown on armed expeditions from Colombian territory into Venezuela.[6]

In October 1920 another group of Venezuelan rebels requested assurance that the United States would not help Gómez if they launched an attack. Chargé d'affaires John C. Wiley, distressed at Gómez's torture and murder of the young military men who had framed a plot in January 1919, warned that if Gómez survived another revolt, he "will consider himself installed in perpetuity and, being already difficult to treat with will become, it is feared, intolerant like Castro of foreign interests."[7] Moreover, Wiley added, anti-Americanism was on the rise, and most Venezuelans would oppose intervention on Gómez's behalf. The distraction of the presidential elections in the United States and the weakness of his opposition once again worked to Gómez's advantage.

Warren G. Harding's administration gave new consideration to Gómez's rule, initiating a dialogue over U.S. policy toward Venezuela that would continue throughout the twentieth century. U.S. oilmen in Venezuela placed a high priority on order and appreciated a leader who deferred to their interests, while some academics argued that the United States should encourage democracy in Latin America. William

Sherwell, a professor of languages at Georgetown University, the author of a book on Bolívar, and an official in the Pan-American Union, prepared a report on Venezuela for the State Department in May 1921. The United States, he wrote, ran a risk whether it backed the rebels or Gómez, since violence and repression would ensue in either case. Sherwell advised the United States to try to broker a deal to bring to power an authentic democrat, preferably one "who would have witnessed democratic practices long enough in this country and lived here among us long enough to get a thorough knowledge and understanding of our practices and sympathy with them."[8] Sherwell had just the man: the Venezuelan ambassador to the United States, Santos Dominici, whom Sherwell had come to know in Washington. Foreshadowing the tactics that Ambassador Sumner Welles would use in Cuba in 1933, Sherwell advised replacing Minister Preston McGoodwin with someone who would encourage Gómez to leave, arrange the candidacy of Dominici, and guarantee free elections.

Sherwell's report confirmed that McGoodwin, a Wilson appointee in 1913, had abandoned his early criticism of Gómez and had become a fast friend, ally, and sometime business partner of the dictator. "I can say positively that we are very poorly represented in Venezuela," Sherwell wrote. McGoodwin and his cronies in the legation drank, gambled, bribed officials, caused social commotions, and failed to pay their bills. Venezuelans believed that McGoodwin's very presence warned against a challenge to Gómez. Sherwell concluded with an uncharacteristically optimistic prediction about Venezuelans' capacity for democracy. "As soon as the power can be transferred in Venezuela two successive times without disturbance, I am certain that Venezuela will not stop in a most brilliant political and economic life."[9]

The State Department passed up the opportunity to advance Santos Dominici's political ambitions but did remove McGoodwin, who subsequently returned to Venezuela as a local representative of Pan American Airways. McGoodwin, however, was not Gómez's only American friend. The new minister, W. C. Cook, noted that most of the U.S. citizens in Venezuela—now including the powerful oilmen—favored Gómez. The dictator had won over the oilmen by allowing them to dictate new oil legislation in 1921 and by dismissing a development minister whom they disliked. In 1927, a former U.S. diplomat, Jordan Herbert Stabler, reported with satisfaction to the State Department, "The advent of great numbers of Americans connected with the oil industry has had a decided effect and Venezuela looks towards the United States much more than ever before for imports and any financial needs it might have." Stabler thought the human rights situation had improved and expressed concern only about what might happen on Gómez's death. He believed the peace-loving and malleable Venezuelan lower classes to be less troublesome than those of Mexico or Guatemala, but he warned that foreign radicals might take advantage of disorder.[10]

Gómez's alliance with the oil companies, the death of his enemies (Castro in 1924 and El Mocho Hernández in 1921), and the spreading prosperity allowed him to remain in power. His tenure was ensured in the late 1920s when the State Department began to espouse a policy of nonintervention. The Venezuelan ambassador in Washington informed Gómez in April 1926 that Secretary of State Frank B. Kellogg had announced that the United States would renounce imperialism and intervention in Latin American domestic affairs. A year later, Kellogg telegraphed Cook in Caracas to deny the rumor that the United States intended to oppose Gómez's reelection: "The United States will express no opinion and will take no part, directly or indirectly, in the choice of a President. This is purely a matter for the sovereign State of Venezuela and under no circumstances will the United States interfere in this matter."[11] A few months later, on 28 February 1929, Kellogg proclaimed that "the [Monroe] Doctrine is not a lance; it is a shield." Landing U.S. troops to restore order, he continued, was not part of the Monroe Doctrine, but a police action to protect American lives and property. The United States would not interfere in the internal affairs of American states.[12]

The nonintervention policy and the general approval of Gómez precluded any action against him, but U.S. observers were concerned about who might rise to the top after Gómez's death. Describing the now legendary student revolt in Caracas in 1928,[13] U.S. chargé d'affaires

C. Van H. Engert first reported that Gómez had overreacted to an insignificant student demonstration and had foolishly angered elite families by jailing their sons. Engert saw no signs of bolshevism. A few weeks later, however, the chargé thought he might have been too quick to dismiss Jóvito Villaba's "anti-American" speech and Pío Tamayo's poem, which was "somewhat Bolshevistic in tone." Gómez should have sought public sympathy by publicizing the subversive elements in the demonstration, the chargé thought.[14]

Gómez's death, Engert predicted in 1929, would unleash a class war in Venezuela. In that event, Washington could only hope for the emergence of a strong man who would check communism and radicalism in the country. Engert considered the passive Venezuelan masses still "too easy-going and too inexperienced" to appreciate democracy: "This backwardness of the masses, due not only to political immaturity but also to racial inferiority, made progress toward a popular form of government next to impossible, especially as very little was done for education and nothing for social betterment."[15]

Other observers minimized the prospect of class war and bolshevism but still feared that disorder could harm U.S. interests. One chargé pointed out that the workers had little incentive to initiate a rebellion against Gómez since the elite view of freedom included the "right" to exploit the masses "under the cloak of democratic institutions." A brief post-Gómez disorder probably would not harm U.S. interests, but a prolonged civil war would be dangerous.[16] As it had done in Gerardo Machado's Cuba in 1933, Washington wanted to dictate who would succeed the unpopular dictator and avoid the emergence of a truly popular movement. The whirlwind that had followed Porfirio Díaz's ouster in Mexico in 1911 exemplified the radicalism that could arise during prolonged civil conflict.

Why did the United States government not try to nudge Gómez out as it had done to Machado in 1933? The answer lies in the difference between the Cuban and Venezuelan situations. Machado's multiclass opposition caused the political situation to degenerate quickly in Cuba in 1933. Venezuela remained calm in the 1930s, and Gómez's opponents seemed content to await his death. Gómez, unlike Machado, had influential advocates in the U.S. oil companies who aided Venezuelan ambassador Pedro Manuel Arcaya's propaganda barrage. Finally, Sumner Welles's Cuban machinations had not been an unqualified success, leading as they did to six months of conflict and the near triumph of a government considered "bolshevist." Moreover, other Latin American concerns took precedence, including the inter-American meeting in Montevideo in 1933, the Chaco War from 1932 to 1935, and the threat of war between Peru and Colombia over Leticia.

In sum, U.S. policy toward Gómez remained fairly constant over the twenty-seven years of his government. From dollar diplomacy to Roosevelt's Good Neighbor policy, Gómez survived. Throughout the period, Gómez and the U.S. presidents employed the now hallowed symbols of republicanism, modernity, and binational friendship. President Harding attended a ceremony to install a new statue of Simón Bolívar in Central Park in 1921. When General John Pershing visited Venezuela, Gómez gave him a national treasure, a sword used by José Antonio Páez, an action that secretly dismayed many Venezuelans. Secretary of State Philander Knox visited Venezuela, as did aviator Charles Lindbergh. U.S. naval and commercial missions were lavishly entertained by the Caracas elite. These visible symbols of cooperation complemented the Venezuelan propaganda in the United States that portrayed Gómez's Venezuela as a model of progress, modernity, and order.

A Dictator's "Astucia"

Studies of U.S. policy toward Gómez often leave the impression that the interests of the United States entirely shaped the relationship. Gómez, however, played the role that Zumeta had outlined as the only possible one to guard national sovereignty: maintain order, build up the country, and avoid angering the great powers. Gómez well deserved the epithet "tyrant of the Andes," but his Táchira roots had formed a man who kept his own counsel and required foreigners to play by his rules. He maintained his residence not in cosmopolitan Caracas but in the small, dusty town of Maracay about ninety-eight kilometers away.

Foreigners came to Maracay to pay homage and make their requests. The symbolism was not lost on Venezuelans. Altogether, Gómez proved a master at delivering what the Americans wanted while leaving them doubtful that he would continue to do so.

After World War I and with the advent of the oil industry, U.S. hegemony in Venezuela was undisputed. Gómez accepted that reality but retained some modest European ties. Many of his intellectuals were considered "too European" in outlook by the U.S. Legation. Although the U.S. oil companies dominated the scene, Gómez encouraged British and Dutch concessions as well for competition. Gómez's improved army received training, matériel, and assistance from the United States, but the old dictator also contracted European training missions and matériel. In the 1920s, he chose a French aviation team to bring planes and train his new air force, to the chagrin of U.S. aviators. The army, of course, both reassured foreigners that the surrogate policeman could protect the oil fields and reminded them that an armed takeover of Venezuela would be more difficult than a battle against the ragged military forces in the rest of the Caribbean.

Gómez also found U.S. concerns about bolshevism convenient. Like many Latin American dictators, he tarred nearly all his opponents indiscriminately with the term, thus justifying to foreign eyes his abuses of human and civil rights. Pedro Manuel Arcaya, Gómez's ambassador to the United States from 1922 to 1924, and again in the 1930s, read up on communism in Washington. He surely could not have done so in Venezuelan libraries. When he became minister of interior relations, Arcaya included a clause condemning communism in the 1928 Constitution and consistently characterized Gómez's enemies as Communists. Some Venezuelan exiles in New York or Mexico were indeed Communists, but few could act with impunity under Gómez's nose in Venezuela. Ironically, a U.S. citizen, Joseph Kornfeder, organized the first underground communist party in Venezuela, in 1928. Thus, both communism and anticommunism came to Venezuela by way of the United States.

Gómez further strengthened his position by avoiding conflict with the United States over economic issues. He immediately cut national expenditures, methodically paid off the foreign debt, and organized banking and central finances. He was, in fact, so draconian in his early years that the U.S. Legation complained that his slashing bureaucratic salaries by 50 percent could cause an uprising and that his limit on government spending prevented foreigners (and nationals) from securing government contracts. In October 1915, Minister McGoodwin lamented that Gómez refused to approve a $2 million contract with a U.S. syndicate to build a modern water and sewage plant in Caracas.[17]

Wanting to link Venezuela's economy more tightly to that of the United States, McGoodwin attributed Venezuelan recalcitrance to ignorance of U.S. business practices. Minister of the Treasury Román Cardenas and the close associates who implemented Gómez's austerity measures, McGoodwin reported, had never visited the United States.

> In consequence the officials and individuals upon whom the President of Venezuela has depended for establishing and maintaining fiscal policies have been unfamiliar with our institutions, our methods, ideals and aspirations and frequently prejudiced against them. On the contrary, most of those who from time to time have constituted this element have been influenced by their more or less accurate knowledge of and favoritism for various countries in Europe. When this situation clears up, as I am confident it will early in the forthcoming return of General Gómez to the Constitutional Presidency, there can be no doubt of the vast advantage which will accrue to our commerce and American interests in general.[18]

McGoodwin was encouraged when Vicente Lecuna, who had visited the United States, took over the Banco de Venezuela in April 1916. Gómez, however, signaled Venezuela's eventual economic independence in 1930 when he paid off the entire foreign national debt in celebration of the centenary of Bolívar's death.

Gómez even introduced a more puritanical version of corruption, one less likely to attract foreign criticism. He and his cronies grew wealthy on the sale of oil concessions, but they honored their contracts with foreigners. Gómez plowed his own profits into land and cattle rather than the wild Bacchanalia and conspicuous consumption that Cipriano Castro had enjoyed. None of Gómez's subordinates dared to dip their hands into the treasury without his knowledge and approval, as witnessed by the almost pitiful letters from some of his most trusted aides—including Vallenilla Lanz, Zumeta, and Arcaya—asking for loans or favors. All in all, Gómez kept the gouging of foreigners to a predictable, and acceptable, level. The growing oil industry provided enough income for foreign and domestic elites to share comfortably.

Pan-American Eclipse and the Origins of Venezuelan Internationalism

Gómez had little interest in international politics and considerable suspicion of foreigners meddling in his affairs. He tolerated a modest multilateral activity as a counterweight to U.S. influence and a means of bolstering Venezuelan trade. Caracas sent no mission to the 1918 Versailles Peace Conference, because the United States insisted that neutrals should not be invited. Pedro Manuel Arcaya argued that Venezuela should refuse to join the League of Nations because the United States was not a member. The rest of Gómez's brain trust—José Gil Fourtoul, Esteban Gil Borges, and Diógenes Escalante—countered that the very absence of the United States made the league more attractive. Venezuela joined. Diógenes Escalante, who with César Zumeta formed part of the Venezuelan delegation from 1920 to 1936, wrote to Gómez from Paris in 1921:

> The League of Nations is gradually acquiring great importance and great authority, in spite of United States opposition, and we should not forget that, but become more involved because the League will serve us in the future to counterbalance the all-absorbing influence of the United States and to work with the Europeans to frame policies more in our interests. One of the reasons that the United States dislikes the League is because it removes the South American republics from Washington's tutelage, according us the international importance and the maturity that the United States prefers us not to have. I have always believed that small and weak countries like ours should cultivate the friendship of all and depend on

Europe against the United States and the United States against Europe, without throwing ourselves into the arms of one alone. This balancing game will allow us to have good relations with both, to frighten one with the other and to extract the greatest advantage from both.[19]

Escalante might have added that participation in the league also provided an education in multinational diplomacy, experience that proved valuable for later international activism.

Although the Pan-American Union was touted as the fulfillment of Bolívar's dream, the Washington-based association remained so subservient to the wishes of the United States that many Latin Americans considered it tainted. Delegates to the union also represented their nations in Washington, further limiting their independence. Venezuelans held high executive positions in the union, but they were not Gómez loyalists. Gómez distrusted Venezuelans who spent too much time in the United States, correctly counting many of them among his enemies. The dictator recognized that if the State Department planned to replace him, it would be with someone who had acquired a North American patina. When William Sherwell proposed that the State Department consider grooming Santos Dominici to succeed Gómez in the early 1920s, he confirmed Gómez's suspicion. Venezuelans in New York and Washington posed potential threats to the dictator because of their access to newspapers, human rights associations, and other Latin American exiles, but most importantly to U.S. politicians of both parties. Gómez had them carefully watched.

Gómez's Public Diplomacy

Gómez and his advisers surpassed all their predecessors in their campaign to control the news of Venezuela that appeared in the U.S. press. They paid publicists to promulgate a view of Venezuela as a stable, peaceful, progressive country. On 20 September 1923 Rafael Requena wrote from New York that Venezuelan exiles, with their "truly criminal propaganda" about Gómez's "tyranny," were affecting Venezuela's reputation.[20]

Venezuelan publicists took special care to place their material in the *Washington Post*, a newspaper they considered to be a State Department organ. In 1923 Ambassador Arcaya arranged for the *Post* to do two favorable articles a month on Venezuela for a period of three months and to have the articles distributed to other newspapers at a cost of $3,000.[21] A subsequent Venezuelan ambassador to Washington, Carlos Grisanti, recommended that Venezuela purchase two pages of text and one of photographs in the *Post*'s special Pan-American supplement for its fiftieth anniversary issue on 5 December 1927. The story would help Venezuela, and the $6,600 payment would purchase the goodwill of an influential newspaper that had treated Venezuela well. When the Spanish-language *La Prensa* of New York criticized Venezuela's political dictatorship in early 1928, the Venezuelan consul in New York responded by citing the *Post* articles—without, of course, revealing that Venezuelan spokesmen had written them and paid for the coverage.[22]

Gómez also tried to control the news that went out of Venezuela. The United Press correspondent in Venezuela, Pedro Moreno Garzon, let the Ministry of Foreign Relations review his innocuous dispatches before he sent them. His caution earned him the Order of the Liberator when he left in February 1929. In the traditional *pan o palo* approach, the *gomecistas* also rewarded their allies in other ways. Joseph L. Jones, the foreign editor of the United Press Association, asked the minister of foreign relations to get some of the Maracaibo newspapers to subscribe to United Press. "I certainly appreciate your interest," Jones wrote, "and hope that a Maracaibo connection can be made, because naturally the more business we can get in Venezuela, the more we shall be able to spend in improving the news service supplied to papers there."[23]

The *gomecistas* controlled the news of Venezuela that went abroad fairly effectively, but they had more difficulty controlling the world news that Venezuela received through international news services like Reuters, Wolf, and the Associated Press. Thus, the Venezuelan government had even more interest in seeing that the international press wrote favorably of Gómez. Radio, of course, intensified the challenge, although Gómez kept tight control of Caracas's first transmitter when it appeared in 1926. The real history of Venezuelan broadcasting began in 1930 when W. H. Phelps opened a commercial radio station, Radio Caracas, to advertise the products he sold: RCA radios, Underwood typewriters, Frigidaire appliances, and Ford automobiles. The first broadcast, on 9 December 1930, covered the ceremony to install a statue of Henry Clay in a public plaza near the Teatro Nacional. The dictatorship required domestic news to be read from the papers without comment, but international news enjoyed more latitude so long as it contained no criticism of Gómez.

The Advent of the Hydrocarbon Economy

World War I catapulted the United States to the status of world power and confirmed its hegemony in the Western Hemisphere. Gómez's fiscal responsibility solved Venezuela's nineteenth-century economic problems, but new times called for new strategies. The *gomecistas* acknowledged the United States as their natural trading partner, especially when U.S. shippers replaced European ones during World War I. After the war, Venezuelans did not want the United States to monopolize their trade, but the lack of a national merchant marine and the dependence on international shipping consortiums canceled much of the advantage of Venezuela's maritime proximity to both the United States and Europe. For example, Kansas wheat was considerably cheaper in New Orleans than in New York. Both cities were about the same distance from Venezuela, but Venezuela had to pay the higher New York prices because there was no direct shipping from New Orleans.

Venezuelans knew that they had to increase their agricultural production or find other exports to attract more frequent ships and better prices. Shippers wanted larger cargos than Venezuelan farmers could produce, but if production were increased first, before ships were available, the produce would rot on the docks. Venezuelan farmers tried halfheartedly to solve the conundrum by building on a modest regional trade. They had increased their food production during the war, but postwar efforts to expand trade to Cuba fell afoul of a U.S. law that forbade ships of less than thirty tons to trade in Cuban ports. Moreover, U.S. insurance companies refused to insure the smaller sailing vessels that Venezuela had available for regional trade.

Unfortunately for Venezuela's goals, the United States had all the advantages: credit and capital, shipping, insurance companies, communications networks, aggressive advertising and sales associations, de facto control over the lucrative Cuban market, and consumer goods that newly affluent Venezuelans wanted. The traditional Venezuelan preference for European products had begun to shift as the industrial capacity of the United States grew. European nations, still reeling from the effects of the war, had inadequate incentive to pursue their old economic position in South America.

Hoping to retain some prospect of reestablishing European trade, Caracas resisted granting the United States most favored nation status. In 1927, the State Department proposed that the 1923 treaty between the United States and Germany be a model for a new treaty with Venezuela. Advisers to the Venezuelan Ministry of Foreign Relations pointed out that the German treaty was more appropriate for two countries with similar populations, capital, and resources than it was for Venezuela and the United States. Reciprocal licensing of legal and medical professionals and right of airflight over the other's territory, for example, conceded privileges that conveyed no benefit to Venezuela. Moreover, Venezuela had to be able to offer trade concessions to European nations in order to maintain that market for the country's coffee and cacao.

President Woodrow Wilson had taken advantage of the war situation to ensure economic dominance in Latin America in a number of ways. Venezuela's geographical proximity to both New York and, through Panama, to the U.S. West Coast made it a more attractive trading target than its small market would suggest. In December 1913, the U.S. Federal Reserve Act for the first time authorized national banks to establish branches in foreign countries, allowing institutions like the National City Bank and the Mercantile Bank to edge out European competitors and encourage U.S. trade. The availability of credit was thought to be responsible for the more than 100 percent leap in U.S. trade with Latin America between 1914 and 1917. U.S. commercial groups pressed their advantage. The Pan-American Society of the United States (based in New York) grew from 130 members in 1912 to 500 in 1915 and undertook more frequent visits to Latin America.[24]

The war also heightened appreciation in the United States of the importance of transportation and communications networks. The U.S. Legation in Caracas pressed Gómez to allow an American company to succeed the old French Cable Company when the latter's concession ran out. Washington wanted to replace the European companies with direct cable and air communication with the United States. Always suspicious, Gómez stalled in awarding the mail contract, which would provide a subsidy to Pan American Airways. The airline's director, Juan Trippe, engaged former U.S. ambassador and Gómez crony Preston McGoodwin to act as the company's local representative in Venezuela. Shortly thereafter, Pan Am arranged a visit by famous aviator Charles Lindbergh. Lindbergh dutifully showed up in September 1929, attended a party at Maracay for Gómez, and Pan American got the mail contract.

Airplanes and cable networks arguably had less impact on Venezuela than the automobile. William Phelps sold nearly twenty thousand Ford autos to Venezuelans between 1909 and 1934. Phelps expanded his operation to form Almacen Americano, which peddled all manner of durable consumer goods, including refrigerators, typewriters, and appliances. As noted, he opened a radio station in 1930 to promote the U.S. products he sold. With the favor of both the U.S. and Venezuelan governments, Phelps parlayed these modest beginnings into an industrial and communications empire that made the Phelps family one of the wealthiest in Venezuela by the 1950s. In 1921, the State Department became alarmed when Phelps wrote them to say that Gómez erroneously believed that Phelps had been the source of a negative U.S. press article on Venezuela. Secretary of State Hughes ordered Minister McGoodwin immediately to try to repair the situation with Gómez lest Phelps lose his "work of a lifetime," which had made him the "bulwark of American trade in Venezuela."[25]

By the 1920s it had become clear that the petroleum industry would be the key to future Venezuelan economic relations with the United States. A subsidiary of a British-Dutch consortium (Royal Dutch–Shell Group) had drilled the first commercial well in 1914, but the United States became dominant in the industry after the war. President Warren Harding's administration gave high priority to promoting the expansion of U.S. oil companies overseas. In spite of the impressive productive capacity of the domestic oil producers, many strategists believed that the war had seriously depleted U.S. reserves. At the same time, the nationalistic Mexican Revolution of 1910–17 had made the nearby Mexican fields less attractive. Venezuela became a logical target area, but the entry of a few large companies, principally Standard and Gulf, originated a new tension in U.S.-Venezuelan relations. The independent oil producers in the United States resented the favoritism shown to the international producers and formed the Independent Petroleum Association of America, whose objective was to exclude Venezuelan oil from the U.S. trade.

Royal Dutch–Shell had no intention of surrendering its hold on Venezuela, but the company lacked the ready capital for the expensive exploitation, exploration, and infrastructure that Venezuela required. The oil regions around Lake Maracaibo had no roads, houses, hospitals, communities, or camps to support the petroleum industry.

The choice of former diplomats to act as agents for the oil companies in Venezuela highlighted the perception that a critical U.S. national interest was involved. Two former heads of the State Department's Division of Latin American Affairs represented oil companies in Venezuela: William T. S. Doyle became the resident manager of Shell interests in 1919–20, and Jordan Stabler represented Gulf Oil in the late 1920s. Another former high State Department official, Francis Loomis, also worked for Standard Oil.

Gómez dealt with the oil companies in a way consistent with his other international policy. He welcomed the U.S. companies, but he denied them an opportunity for monopoly control by granting concessions to the British-Dutch consortium and numerous small producers. The U.S. companies expanded rapidly, rising from 5 percent of the production in 1924 to more than 50 percent in 1929. The big three—Exxon, Gulf, and Shell—together controlled 99 percent of the production, but 120 other companies also obtained small shares.[26]

Gómez never quite solved the dilemma of the independent U.S. producers. He needed to award concessions to some of them, both as an implicit threat to the multinationals and to check their lobbying to exclude foreign oil from the U.S. market. On the other hand, the multinationals guaranteed the most orderly development in the country, and Gómez wanted to avoid the kind of contentious situation that Castro had faced with the asphalt companies. William F. Buckley's underhanded maneuvers with his Venezuelan allies to secure a monopoly on transshipping oil from Salinas became a case in point in 1927. Neither the State Department nor Standard Oil was amused. Jordan Stabler wrote of Buckley: "He has never been engaged in the legitimate producing business and has tried to make his money by parasitical methods, attempting to gain some advantage or monopoly and then make the companies pay him."[27] Gómez judiciously heeded the displeasure of the multinationals and their diplomatic allies and vetoed Buckley's transshipment monopoly.

At the same time, Gómez allowed the codification of generous mining legislation. If investors were attracted to Venezuela, Gómez could use the increased revenues to secure both his political power and his enormous personal fortune from resale of concessions. Still, Gómez did not give away the national store. He understood that legislation had to be attractive to the foreign companies but still guarantee the rights of the state. By appointing the mildly nationalistic Gumersindo Torres as development minister in 1917, Gómez signaled a warning to the companies. But then, in response to the oil companies' complaints, the dictator allowed the companies' lawyers to draft the 1921–22 petroleum legislation and compliantly dismissed Torres in 1922. Even so, the standard forty-year concessions were shorter than those granted in the Middle East, the tax structure discouraged inactive concessions with no investment or exploitation, and no one company or financial group could obtain a monopoly. The caution proved fortunate, for Gómez presided over astounding growth. By 1928 Venezuela was the second largest world oil producer and the leading world exporter.

Gómez allowed no one to doubt that he alone defined and enforced order in the nation—over both foreigners and Venezuelans. He limited the excesses of the companies and their employees. When the oil companies begged to be allowed to remove the sandbar at the entrance to Lake Maracaibo, Gómez refused. He would not allow the fiercely independent *maracuchos* to ally with American countries and declare a Panama-style "revolution." The Motilones Indians to the southwest of Lake Maracaibo frequently raided the oil camps, showering the foreigners with poison darts. Gómez sent a small army there to keep order, but he would not exterminate or move the Indians to please the companies. The companies preferred English-speaking workers from the Antilles for ease of communication and to discourage labor organization, but many Venezuelans found the West Indians as arrogant in their attitudes as the white American and English bosses. In 1929 Gómez forbade the entry of West Indian blacks, an action that reflected both racism and resentment at the foreigners who competed for scarce jobs at a time of industrial contraction. Gómez supressed all signs of autonomous labor organization, but his 1928 labor law established some standards for maximum working hours, accident compensation, death benefits, and employers' responsibility for sanitation, ventilation, and safety. There was no right to strike, and the government could dissolve unions at will. Government authorities remained the final arbiters in labor disputes. The weak legislation gave Gómez a powerful weapon if he should become displeased with the companies.

Gómez reappointed the unpopular Gumersindo Torres as minister of development from 1929 to 1931. Torres charged the companies with misrepresenting their costs, and thus reducing the royalties that they owed to the government. The Venezuelan press supported Torres and criticized the companies. The companies complained, and Torres again left office. The looming economic depression allowed the companies to respond to Gómez's mild threats with a veiled warning that they could leave Venezuela as suddenly as they had come. They cut back operations, reducing government revenues and creating a pool of unemployed workers who could cause trouble for Gómez.

The oil companies cared little about the pollution of Lake Maracaibo and the danger to the inhabitants of the region. The residents of Lagunillas, a small town built out over the lake, frequently complained about violation of their rights to communal land, dangers of fire from the petroleum exploitation, and the lack of good drinking water once the oil companies had polluted the lake. Since Gómez decided what issues his courts and local officials should address, his tolerance of Lagunillas's complaints in court indirectly harassed the oil companies.

Also indicative of Gómez's intention to retain control over Maracaibo was his appointment of General Vincencio Pérez Soto as president of Zulia State in July 1926. After his appointment Pérez Soto wrote to Gómez: "Here the doors have been opened too widely to the foreigner, and I, I don't know to what point these complications can carry us, especially with the Americans."[28] Pérez Soto kept Gómez closely informed of local events, including the brawling, drinking, gambling, and public disorder of the oil company employees. He reported that the companies refused to pay legal compensation to workers who were injured on the job. One man who had lost an arm should have received the equivalent of nine months' salary, or approximately 2,064 bolivares. The company at first refused to pay anything but ultimately paid him 1,600 bolivares, of which his lawyer took 1,000.[29] Pérez Soto's letter suggested that only Gómez's watchfulness compelled the companies to give some respect, however modest, to Venezuelan authority.

The Dictator's Friends and Foes

The war years, the oil industry, and the transportation and communications revolutions brought more Venezuelans and U.S. citizens into contact with each other. Although these people had myriad interests, they can all be arranged along two major axes: those allied with the dictator, the multinational oil companies, and the merchants engaged in U.S.-Venezuelan trade on one, and the U.S. State Department and those who opposed one or all of those groups on the other.

The most powerful interlocking alliance benefited from the democratic caesar's status quo.[30] Former State Department officials like Doyle, Stabler, McGoodwin, and Loomis became agents for U.S. enterprises in Venezuela and continued periodically to advise the State Department on Venezuelan issues. Venezuela's merchants and great families, and the professionals who worked for the companies knew that their own fortunes would rise or fall with the Venezuelan oil industry. Some of Venezuela's wealthiest and most influential families—De Capriles, Tinoco, Pietri, Mendoza, and De Armas—achieved their position directly or indirectly through oil concessions. Merchants and chambers of commerce, north and south, depended on the oil revenues that allowed Venezuelan consumers to purchase goods manufactured in the United States; they lobbied against Venezuelan protective tariffs and U.S. restrictions on the importation of foreign oil. All these groups feared that their interests would suffer when Gómez died.

By the mid-1920s a counteraxis had begun to take shape. Venezuelan exiles, some of them workers or Communists, joined U.S. groups to criticize Gómez's repression and Washington's support of him. New York, which had an estimated ten thousand Venezuelan exiles in 1929–30, was especially lively. The exiles disseminated information about Gómez's repression to the League of Nations, to other American nations, to the U.S. government, and to the pope. In 1933 the International Committee for Political Prisoners of New York sent a letter of protest about political prisoners to Venezuelan ambassador Pedro Manuel Arcaya and to the Venezuelan Ministry of Foreign Relations. The signers of the letter included Roger Baldwin, and the general committee included Clarence Darrow, W. E. B. DuBois, Waldo Frank, Sinclair Lewis, Luis Múñoz Marin, and Norman Thomas.[31] Venezuelan exiles also worked through the Pan-American Federation of Labor, the International Labor Organization, and the American Federation of Labor to protest Gómez's stifling of the Venezuelan labor movement. Church groups in the United States complained about Gómez's order to exclude foreign priests from the country and the occasional harassment of the Protestant ministers who did reside there. By and large, the State Department ignored the protests, taking refuge in a judgment that Venezuela's political prisoners were better off than Italy's or Russia's and that in Venezuela, "personal freedom is as great as in any country in the world, subject, of course, to certain observances essential to the Gómez system."[32]

In the late 1920s, however, a celebrated case of Gómez's highhandedness spurred a coalition of Gómez opponents that included U.S. Democrats, other critics of Republican Latin American policies, independent oil producers, and critics of the multinational oil companies. The depression and the growing oversupply of oil on the world market encouraged the independent producers to hope for some softening of Washington's favoritism toward the multinationals. At the center of the controversy was James Welch, a mining engineer who had had a daughter with a Venezuelan woman. On returning to Venezuela after a brief absence, he found that his daughter had been given to her maternal grandmother. In 1928, Welch legally recognized the child as his and petitioned the Venezuelan courts to have her returned to him. For his effrontery, he was thrown in jail. The engineer then asked the State Department for assistance in securing custody of his daughter and an indemnity for his jailing. When the State Department refused to help him, Welch took his case to the U.S. press and to Congress. One news photo depicted the American standing in front of the White House with shackles on, symbolic of Gómez's prisons. In 1930, both the Senate and the House of Representatives passed resolutions calling for an investigation of conditions in Venezuela. Democratic congressmen Allard Gasque of South Carolina and John Sandlin of Louisiana and Senator Joseph E. Randsdell of Louisiana led the attack. Governor Huey Long of Louisiana, an advocate of the independent oil producers and a legendary enemy of Standard Oil, also weighed in on Welch's side.[33]

Ambassador Arcaya, concerned because the criticism of Gómez had penetrated Venezuela through AP and UP reports, proposed a counterattack to the Ministry of Foreign Relations. They should discredit Congressman Gasque through a smear campaign that alleged that he approved of the lynching of blacks in his native South Carolina and that he would corruptly share Welch's reparations. Furthermore, Gasque would be said to be collaborating with Venezuelan revolutionaries to destabilize the Gómez government, a violation of Venezuelan sovereignty.[34] Pointing to the State Department's recent renunciation of intervention, Arcaya asserted that Venezuela would not tolerate meddling by the United States Congress in its domestic affairs. In December 1930 Arcaya published a book, *The Venezuelan Courts and the Welch Case*, which purported to give an objective account of the whole affair. Welch finally received custody of the child, but he and his allies insisted for several more years that the Venezuelan government should pay him compensation for his mistreatment.

Journalists, writers, scientists, and academics in the United States also contributed fuel to the campaign against Gómez. Some attacked Washington's Latin American policy while they fed the public's taste for the exotic. Spencer Dickey, a surgeon who had spent thirty-one years working and exploring in Latin America, led several expeditions between 1929 and 1931 to discover the source of the Orinoco River. He published a book on his experiences in 1932. Dickey had little good to say about either his own countrymen in Venezuela or the dictator. He judged oil company employees to be a total disgrace and asserted that the "drunken oil well drillers" who sang ribald songs while driving through the streets with "laps laden with prostitutes" did not represent the flower of American youth.[35] On Gómez's dictatorship and the State Department's role in supporting him, Dickey wrote: "For neither life nor property, not even thought, is safe in this republic of Venezuela, notwithstanding the frantic efforts of our own State Department to make it seem all that is good in progress, liberality and enlightenment."[36]

Dickey predicted that Gómez's death would spur such a revolution that a U.S. military force would be sent to restore order. Cynically, he expected that "a few youths from Iowa and Oklahoma" would have to "chase the bandits" who refused to accept the Washington-endorsed "former lawyer to one of the oil companies" who would follow Gómez in the presidency. Subsequently, "a crop of Sandinos—the aftermath of our peculiar type of pacification" would arise periodically, but futilely, to interrupt the domestic peace.

As Dickey foresaw, Gómez's last years laid the groundwork for the kind of popular release that followed his death. If the democratic caesar was associated with the American oil companies, then an attack on one implied criticism of the other. Without heeding the linkage, Gómez allowed no criticism of himself but tolerated some expressions of an anti-Americanism that encouraged the coagulation of a new form of nationalism in the country.

Some Venezuelans railed at the American influence that swept the country, especially in the oil enclaves like the Lake Maracaibo region. In 1925 the U.S. minister concluded that anti-American sentiment was growing in Maracaibo, "due to the conduct of many Americans there, who are acquiring generally the reputation of being a drunken and disorderly set, disrespectful to the local people and contemptuous of local law."[37]

Venezuelans in the oil zones objected to the segregation of Venezuelans and foreign employees, reminiscent of conditions in the Panama Canal Zone. Foreign workers were paid in dollars, lived in nicer houses, and did not permit Venezuelans to share their movie theaters and clubs. Venezuelans naturally resented the practices that marked them as racial and social inferiors. William T. Wallace, vice president of Venezuelan Gulf, confirmed the meaning of the segregation when he wrote, "It is impossible to expect the native mind to conform to the accepted method of living in highly developed countries after centuries of dirt and unsanitary living." If they demanded decent houses like those of the American workers, they simply wanted "to get something for nothing."[38] During a 4 July 1925 baseball game in the La Rosa petroleum camp, two Venezuelans rode their mules onto the playing field and disrupted the game. They were ordered to leave, but they replied that "they were Venezuelans, that this was their country, and they intended to ride where they pleased."[39] Many of the protests and demonstrations in the petroleum zone represented social tensions as much as articulated labor goals.[40]

Maracaibo's respected newspaper *Oriente* often printed laments about the changes that *maracuchos* saw happening around them. Fernando Mantilla deplored the arrival of American films "full of imperialist ambition and poisoned with scorn for all that is not puritan, Saxon and abolitionist." The Venezuelan public had no defense against this cultural invasion, he added: "The use of such a formidable weapon [as film] can inculcate a new ideology, a new system of customs, values, and ways of thinking in our society."[41] Another article on U.S. films argued that they glorified brute force and promulgated the stereotypes that Spaniards were "lazy, boastful, and cowardly beings"; Mexicans were "assassins, thieves, and traitors"; the English were "dandified, full of mannerisms, elegant and shameless"; and the Yankees were "strong, audacious, honorable, and valiant young men."[42]

U.S. officials also fretted about the negative impact of their films on impressionable Venezuelans, but from a different perspective. Chargé Warden Wilson wondered in 1933 whether the film *Washington Masquerade* left a subtle impression of anti-Americanism. U.S. lobbyists were portrayed in the film as sinister forces who employed an adventuress to destroy a French senator. Wilson also found negative messages in *Gabriel over the White House* and *Washington Merry-Go-Round*. He suggested that the State Department ask the Motion Picture Producers of America to remove any hint of anti-American sentiment before the films were exported.[43]

Oriente also worried about the cultural and economic impact when Venezuelans, through a misguided *snobismo*, aped the consumer habits of the foreigners. The foreign oil enclaves imported duty free nearly all their necessities, including fresh fruits and vegetables, and many of these products found their way into local markets. The editorialist charged that Venezuelans who preferred northern fruits and vegetables like California oranges, pineapples, apples, and tomatoes to those produced in Venezuela were simply sending national money "like the Catatumbo River flowing northward, to Yanquilandia."[44] Tito Rubio complained that the Venezuelan newspapers were full of "legs in all sizes and positions; legs, legs and legs. And they aren't even our legs, creole legs, but only Yankee legs, more Yankee than the Pan-American conferences."[45]

Venezuelan novelist, historian, and essayist Ramón Díaz Sánchez was an especially harsh critic. He blamed the oil companies for a careless oil spill on the lake near where the small wooden houses of Lagunillas had been built out over the water. In June 1928, a spark ignited the oil and burned more than three hundred of the houses. Several years earlier the companies had petitioned Governor Pérez Soto in vain to move the town because it interfered with their drilling. After the fire, Gómez and Pérez Soto defied the oil companies by allowing the town to be rebuilt in the same place. Of the event, Díaz Sánchez wrote in *Oriente* that the companies could have prevented the tragedy. But, he continued bitterly, modern scientific progress endorsed a hierarchy of human value:

> This classification principle finds it not only irrelevant but necessary that inferior races sacrifice themselves for the progress of superior races. . . . Then, we must be the inferior races, men without initiative, without the character of conquest, . . . slaves of the physiological weakness of the Indian and of the vain indolence of the Spaniard; . . . humiliated by the blood of slaves. . . . Isn't it tropical foolishness then to think that the representatives of those superior races would have any scruples of conscience toward a poor little wooden town that perhaps impeded the development of their activities, that is, their happiness?[46]

Díaz Sánchez's 1936 novel *Mene* further explores the personal tragedies of the people who suffered from the racism and disregard of the foreigners. A black Trinidadian worker is fired and blacklisted for using the bathroom reserved for whites. Unemployed, unemployable, and unable to support his wife, he commits suicide. A Venezuelan woman marries an American to please her social-climbing brother but is shunned by the American community. Her husband prepares to divorce her when he plans to return to the United States. Disgraced and isolated, she too commits suicide. The book concludes with Díaz Sánchez's apocalyptic vision that Venezuela will never be happy again until all the oil has been sucked from the ground, leaving in its place the sweet, clear waters of the verdant Eden that has been lost.

During the long Gómez dictatorship, new attitudes and coalitions developed both in the United States and in Venezuela. The rich petroleum fields altered most of Venezuela's social, political, and economic patterns and transformed the relationship between the two nations. Scholars, human rights organizations, Venezuelan exiles, and Democratic politicians in the United States questioned the State Department's uncritical support of the multinational oil companies and the dictator who appeared to serve their interests. No public criticism of Gómez was tolerated in Venezuela, but Venezuelans' impressions of the United States and its citizens became more complex. From the poorest black to the wealthiest *mantuano*, Venezuelans both resented and admired the blond Protestants who so confidently dominated their economy and influenced their culture.

The growing network of roads and radios also brought urban Venezuelans into more contact with their rural cousins and encouraged a spark of national spirit. Novelists such as Díaz Sánchez and Rómulo Gallegos accentuated the effect with their portrayal of rural Venezuela: the *llanos*, the Andes, Lake Maracaibo, the eastern coast, the most miserable and the most authentic, the most *venezolano* of the *patria*. The nation, it appeared, was indeed more than just the Caracas elite and an "uncultured," passive rural *pueblo*.

These developments, north and south, eventually required that Washington and the Venezuelan elite find a new political formula more inclusive and more popular than that of the democratic caesar. Juan Vicente Gómez's death in December 1935 opened the way for new alliances to form.

6 Good Neighbors and the Dismantling of Democracy, 1936–1958

> The probable truth of the entire matter is that the people of Venezuela are not yet ready nor adequately prepared for democracy.
> —Franklin W. Wolf

The period between 1936 and 1958 saw the greatest changes in U.S.-Venezuelan relations in more than a hundred years. Franklin Roosevelt's Good Neighbor policy, Juan Vicente Gómez's death, World War II, the increasing assertiveness of the Venezuelan masses, and the rush of oil wealth to Venezuela challenged the political role of the democratic caesar. Gómez had successfully eliminated chronic wrongdoing as a pretext for U.S. intervention in Venezuela, and his active public relations campaign in the United States had helped to counter his critics. After Gómez's death, Washington and the oil companies were willing to accept almost any government that would unequivocally guarantee them control over and access to the Venezuelan oil fields. Access to the oil required a peaceful and predictable political situation—neither a takeover by another great power nor a chaotic domestic conflict like that of the Spanish Civil War.

The Venezuelan political elite, enlarged by the growing middle sectors of professionals and military officers, generally concurred that their well-being for the moment remained tied to positive relationships with the United States and the international oil companies. Even so, they wanted to secure a larger share of the petroleum revenues for the nation and to exercise more influence over industry decisions and policies. Both U.S. analysts and Venezuelan politicians recognized that they could no longer leave the Venezuelan masses out of the political game, but all feared that including them would disturb the delicate

144

balance that they wanted to construct. What political formula could replace the democratic caesar and yet achieve all of these aims?

Between 1936 and 1958, the United States and the Venezuelan elites accepted a populist caesar, lost their nerve and endorsed an authoritarian leader, and finally returned to the populist formula. They still believed that the Venezuelan populace was underdeveloped and needed political tutelage. U.S. leaders during the height of the cold war in the 1950s feared that Communists would exploit the naive population to their own benefit and had nightmares about sabotage of the oil fields. After the McCarthy hearings in the United States, some analysts considered the alternative thesis that unconditional support of dictators by Washington could give the advantage to the Communists in the Americas. By 1958, Venezuelan and U.S. leaders gambled that a strong political organization coupled with some trickling down of petroleum wealth to the bottom ranks of society could channel popular aspirations into acceptable paths.

During this period of evolving U.S. policy toward Latin America, Venezuela became a proving ground for the debate over whether the United States should practice strict nonintervention, active support of democracy, or even favoritism toward dictatorships with their promise of stability. The issues were more clear-cut in Guatemala, but Venezuelan events continuously posed challenges to the State Department—and the oil companies: the 1945 revolution, the 1948 coup, the fraudulent 1952 election, the repression and the cynical plebiscite of 1957, the revolution of January 1958. The crises arose from Venezuelan factors, but acts of omission and commission by the United States affected their outcomes. As in the early 1930s, Democrats and Republicans in the United States used events in Venezuela as evidence to support their arguments for one Latin American policy or the other.

Underlying the Venezuelan political changes, of course, were economic and social changes. The revenues from petroleum altered the internal balance among classes and contributed to the rise of the middle sectors and a nascent labor organization. Immigrants from southern Europe and large numbers of U.S. citizens living in Venezuela, coupled with the growing ease of global travel, mass communications, and trade, altered Venezuelan consumption habits and outlooks. The "American way of life" became much admired and emulated among many Venezuelans. The social and economic changes in Venezuela during the post-Gómez period and their effect on U.S.-Venezuelan relations are examined in Chapter 7.

Ambivalent Endorsement of Democracy, 1936–1948

The model of U.S. democracy, as interpreted by Franklin Roosevelt and intensified by the universal struggle against totalitarianism, proved more attractive to Venezuelans than at any time since the age of Bolívar. For most of this period, Venezuelans and U.S. citizens agreed on the merits of liberal democracy and warily hoped that Venezuela too could be governed by such a fragile system.

Gómez's minister of war, Eleazar López Contreras, succeeded the old dictator in December 1935. Unexpectedly, López relaxed the rigidity of the dictatorship. He lifted press censorship and tolerated the organization and activities of labor unions and political opposition groups. In early 1936 López promised a series of reforms—known collectively as the February Program—that started the nation on a path toward securing a larger share of the oil revenues and investing them in the social welfare of Venezuelans. A new constitution in 1936 codified many of the promises and limited the presidential term to five years. Democrats in the United States welcomed the changes and launched a delayed barrage of invective at the fallen Gómez. Thomas Rourke's *Gómez: Tyrant of the Andes* (1941) was typical.

López's reformism and nationalism owed something both to the new activism of the masses and to an awareness of political currents in the United States. On 14 February 1936, a Caracas crowd of 40,000 (in a city of 250,000) took to the streets to protest a government measure. López reacted by proposing the mildly populist measures of the February Program, even attempting to calm the crowds with a radio speech. Many of López Contreras's measures paralleled those of the New Deal: an expanded role for labor, some modest social welfare measures, and government intervention in the economy. The Venezuelan Legation in Washington informed Caracas that the U.S. Supreme Court decision of 12 April 1937 that affirmed the right of workers to organize (the Wagner Labor Relations Act) had opened a new era of labor policy. The United States provided examples and assistance as Caracas inaugurated new social service agencies.[1] The U.S. Embassy in Caracas pointed out that Rómulo Betancourt's call for government intervention or takeover of public utilities to improve service and rates drew on U.S. and European precedents, not Soviet models.[2]

López lost his nerve in the face of labor and political protests in late 1936 and 1937, however, and again outlawed the political opposition, denouncing his enemies as Communists. A few groups in the United States protested López's renewed repression in 1937, but the Roosevelt administration—hounded by the oil companies and haunted by the Mexican petroleum expropriation in 1938—expressed more concern about López's mild economic nationalism than his domestic repression. The oil companies complained about the new tax legislation of 1938 while they generally ignored it, but welcomed the crackdowns that quieted the labor activism (see chapter 7).

In 1940, as López Contreras prepared to nominate his successor for congressional endorsement in early 1941, U.S. analysts viewed Venezuelan politics through an international prism. Believing López to represent the acceptable limits of democratization, Ambassador Frank Corrigan warned that Venezuela in 1941 resembled Spain in 1936 with its two political extremes, neither commanding a clear majority. López Contreras himself was moderate, but the populace lagged behind in political development, and the totalitarian (Corrigan's term) *andinos* might well make a pact with the Germans if war broke out.[3] López's choice of a candidate, his minister of war, Isaías Medina Angarita, initially concerned U.S. military attachés because of his allegedly pro-German sympathies, but he appealed to Venezuelan conservatives furious at López Contreras for opening the door to mass political participation. Former Gómez adviser Pedro Manuel Arcaya, for example, remained convinced that history "shows up to satiety that the system of popular elections, the basis of theoretical democracy, is foreign to

Venezuelan customs; . . . democracy has been a myth in Venezuela, and a dangerous myth because it has served as the banner for the revolutions which afflicted and ruined the country."[4]

As it turned out, both the *gomecistas* and the U.S. military mission guessed wrong on Medina Angarita. Medina combined an authentic populism with a perceptive unwillingness to challenge U.S. control of the oilfields. He realized that popular support could strengthen his hand in dealing with the foreigners but that he had to demonstrate his ability to control the masses. He used this knowledge most tellingly in imposing a new taxation policy on the oil companies, but he also employed his skills to solve other wartime problems.

Four wartime issues illustrate Medina's efforts to walk a path between U.S. demands and popular Venezuelan attitudes: the stationing of U.S. troops in Venezuela, Venezuela's import policy, the nature of the postwar inter-American community, and the postwar treatment of Venezuela's German population. The most significant issue—negotiating a new agreement with the petroleum companies—is discussed in Chapter 7.

Venezuela left no doubt of its Allied sympathies during the war, but Medina's government also recognized the appeal of Venezuelan nationalism and Pan-Americanism. In early 1941, Medina refused to allow U.S. troops to be stationed in Venezuela. A year later, after the attack at Pearl Harbor, he allowed the troops to enter the country but quieted the expected protest by explaining that they were in Venezuela only briefly to train Venezuelan troops in the installation and management of coastal artillery.[5] Medina took advantage of the wartime situation in 1943 to experiment with a modest industrial protection policy, but he exempted many U.S. products when the U.S. Embassy and Venezuelan importers complained about the import licenses. Looking toward postwar arrangements in the Americas, Medina, in line with Venezuelan sentiment, opposed isolating Argentina from the United Nations for its alleged pro-Axis synpathies and argued that an all-inclusive international community could best control aggressor states. Finally, responding to popular pressure, Medina agreed to restore full constitutional guarantees in Venezuela in 1945. As part of the constitutional initiative, he proposed eliminating the Proclaimed List, which had frozen the funds of Germans residing in Venezuela, including those of many German-Venezuelan nationals. The United States pressed Medina to maintain the restrictions, although Ambassador Corrigan recommended that the United States quickly reduce the list to the hard-core cases to lessen the effect of Venezuela's unilateral action.[6]

As the war ended, issues of popular democracy became prominent in Venezuela and elsewhere in the Americas. Medina promised free, popular presidential elections in 1951 but retained the practice of indirect election by Congress for his successor in 1945. Unfortunately, his nomination of Angel Biaggini displeased both the reformist civilians of Acción Democrática (AD) and the impatient young military officers who had formed a military lodge known as the Unión Patriótica Militar. Led by Carlos Delgado Chalbaud, Marcos Pérez Jiménez, and Luís Felipe Llovera Páez, the young officers invited the civilian opposition party to join a conspiracy to overthrow Medina.

The unexpected *golpe* of 18 October 1945 left the U.S. government scrambling for an appropriate policy. The coup occurred on the same day as the massive demonstrations in favor of Juan Perón in Argentina and at about the same time that U.S. ambassador Adolf Berle was trying to pressure Brazilian president Getulio Vargas to retire. Since there were no obviously fascist overtones to the new Venezuelan government, Washington was most concerned about the treatment of the oil companies and the junta's ability to maintain control.

Reformist civilian leader Rómulo Betancourt, aided by other AD activists, headed up the new governing junta because his military allies shared the goal of establishing a popular democratic government. On the oil issues, the news was reassuring to the United States. Ambassador Corrigan telegraphed, "anxiety of Junta to please almost pitiful. Their attitude to oil company representatives has been cordial and conciliatory."[7] The heads of the three major U.S. oil companies met with the junta shortly after the *golpe* and certified the new leaders as "realistic." J. Edgar Hoover's FBI intelligence reports had routinely characterized Rómulo Betancourt and the AD leaders as Communists, but embassy officials more accurately considered them to be pragmatic nationalists who realized that their reformist programs required an uninterrupted flow of oil revenues.[8]

Still, the new popular government prompted debates about U.S. policy. Should the United States help to strengthen Rómulo Betancourt's reformist junta by expressing unequivocal support, or should approval be tempered with warnings and pressure to encourage Betancourt to follow the U.S. line on all matters? Generally, Ambassador Corrigan favored keeping the pressure on, and embassy officer Allan Dawson advised stronger endorsement of Betancourt. On 27 October, Corrigan recommended delaying diplomatic recognition because the new government's objectives were more laudable than their methods.[9]

On 30 October the State Department decided to follow other American governments in a fairly rapid diplomatic recognition, concerned that delay could alienate the new leaders. At the same time, over Dawson's objections, Corrigan criticized Betancourt for delaying elections until October 1946. In early 1946 Corrigan opposed selling surplus war matériel to Venezuela. Withholding the arms, he believed, would highlight U.S. reservations about the junta and encourage the early scheduling of elections. Dawson countered that Betancourt deserved better treatment than the dictators had been given and that the arms sale could strengthen Betancourt's position and the morale of the Venezuelan armed forces. In this instance, Dawson's views corresponded to those of the War Department, which still feared a bloody civil war, and to those of Joseph Flack, chief of the State Department's Division of North and West Coast Affairs, who predicted that a disaffected Venezuelan military elite might fall under Soviet influence.[10] The policy debate continued in Washington for the three years that the popular government lasted in Venezuela. Ultimately, those in the State Department who argued for the encouragement of democratic institutions resigned, retired, or lost out to those who believed that continental unity and a pledge of nonintervention better secured U.S. interests."[11] In December 1947, Walter J. Donnelly replaced Ambassador Frank Corrigan in Caracas. Corrigan had been in Venezuela since August 1939 and had usually, if sometimes reluctantly, defended Betancourt. Donnelly was an experienced foreign service officer, but he was new to Venezuela and lacked the personal ties that Corrigan and Dawson had developed with the Acción Democrática leaders. Increasingly, the United States government viewed Latin America through a European lens, and many of the New Deal experts on Latin America drifted out of the circles of influence. Old suspicions about the volatility and immaturity of the Latin American masses again cast doubt on politicians who courted their own citizens.

Rómulo Betancourt, inspired in part by the democratic hemispheric unity during the war years, challenged Washington's tilt toward non-intervention and geopolitics. He advocated breaking relations with Latin American dictatorships and endorsing democratic governments regardless of their political coloration. The Venezuelan junta broke relations with the Dominican Republic, Spain, and Nicaragua because those countries were regimes of force, but in early 1946 Caracas recognized the popularly elected government of Juan Perón in Argentina. Betancourt remained suspicious of Perón's politics, but he would not cooperate with Washington and quarantine an elected government while the United States continued to do business with Latin American dictatorships.

Washington's willingness to help the Venezuelan government outflank its authoritarian enemies waned between 1946 and 1948. In mid-1946, at Betancourt's request, the State Department sent Allan Dawson to Colombia to try to persuade Eleazar López Contreras to stop conspiring against Betancourt's government. López privately denied that he was planning a *golpe*, but he refused to issue a public statement of support for the junta.[12]

By 1947, however, actions to discourage *golpismo* seemed unrealistic and in conflict with the objective of maintaining inter-American unity. In January 1947 Betancourt again asked the U.S. government to stop López Contreras from plotting, this time from U.S. territory. Betancourt challenged the United States to overlook its distaste for him and serve its own interests by averting a civil war in Venezuela. Secretary of State James Byrnes protested that the United States had "demonstrated every good will" toward Betancourt and desired to cooperate "in every appropriate manner," but "it is obvious that [the] ultimate solution [to]

Venezuela's exile problem is essentially [a] matter [of] Ven[ezuelan] internal politics."[13] Five months later, Secretary of State George Marshall refused to embargo arms to the Dominican Republic's Rafael Trujillo, despite independent confirmation of Betancourt's charge that Trujillo was helping the Venezuelan plotters. Marshall argued that the United States gained no political influence over Trujillo by withholding arms, which the dictator could secure elsewhere, and he refused to authorize an embargo "on pragmatic grounds."[14]

When Betancourt tried to take unilateral action to frustrate the plotters, he met with resistance from the United States. In late 1947 the State Department refused Betancourt's request to block a Brazilian arms sale to the Dominican Republic. The move would not prevent Trujillo from securing arms, it might alienate the Brazilian armed forces, and any resultant anti-Americanism in Brazil could weaken the civilian political sectors that State wanted to nurture. Betancourt, supported by Venezuelan popular sentiment, threatened to cut off shipments of Venezuelan oil to Brazil if the arms sale went through. The State Department and the oil companies viewed the threat to U.S. control over the Venezuelan oil industry with alarm.[15]

By late 1947, the State Department considered the Venezuelan situation volatile. The December 1947 elections that brought novelist Rómulo Gallegos to the presidency in January 1948 heightened the tension. Betancourt was combative, demagogic, and troublesome, but he knew the value of compromise and could control his followers. Gallegos's political ingenuousness and principled rigidity limited his ability to manipulate the conflicting forces swirling about him. Two days before the 24 November 1948 *golpe* that overthrew the president, State Department official Sheldon T. Mills reported that AD could either satisfy all of the military officers' demands or call a general strike to challenge the officers. The former solution would provoke instability by dividing power, Mills concluded, and the latter would lead to civil strife, which would destroy the economy. Washington apparently was prepared to accept a *golpe* as both inevitable and less harmful to U.S. interests than any measures to assist Gallegos would have been.[16]

Carlos Delgado Chalbaud, Marcos Pérez Jiménez, and Luís Felipe Llovera Páez led the military junta that replaced Gallegos on 24 November. The United States delayed formal recognition of the junta until January 1949 but quickly and privately signaled its acceptance of the new regime. On 29 November State Department spokesman Paul C. Daniels told Antonio Casas-Briceño, counselor of the Venezuelan Embassy in Washington, that the State Department endorsed Resolution 35 of the Bogotá Conference, which specified that diplomatic recognition of new governments should not involve judgments about their origins. Still, he temporized mildly, the Bogotá resolution made no mention of an appropriate time period, so Washington would not act immediately.

Some debate did ensue in Washington, dominated by the concern to protect U.S. interests in the oil fields. Ambassador Donnelly argued for quick recognition, although he acknowledged that an extremist dictatorship might allow the Communists to gain credibility by uniting with the liberal and socialist opposition. Donnelly cabled, "While I deplore overthrow constitutional government by force, I am of opinion that our national interests in Venezuela would on balance be best served by recognizing Junta."[17]

The U.S. secretary of the army, Kenneth Royall, also argued for quick recognition in order to maintain the flow of oil to the United States. The new Venezuelan government would provide better security for oil production than a restored Gallegos regime, which had relied on labor and Communists for support. Royall concluded, "Recognition of the new government of Venezuela would permit the continuance of the U.S. Army Mission in Venezuela, and the subsequent influencing of a generally pro-United States element thereby furthering Venezuelan orientation toward the United States."[18]

George Kennan, director of the State Department's Policy Planning Staff, summed up the prevailing realism. A few other American countries might stand with the United States in a nonrecognition policy, but inter-American division on such a complex issue served no purpose. Unless the United States wanted to use this situation to discourage all future changes of governments by force, it was preferable to recognize the junta. Kennan found no compelling consideration of national interest that warranted withholding recognition.[19]

The State Department's pragmatic acceptance of Gallegos's overthrow and the lack of any consistent public affirmation of support for democratic government in the Americas aroused suspicions in Venezuela. Washington did not press the new junta, as it had Betancourt in 1945 and 1946, to hold popular elections. From exile, Gallegos himself charged that Colonel Edward D. Adams, the U.S. military attaché, had advised the conspirators from the Venezuelan Ministry of Defense and the presidential palace during the *golpe*. President Harry S Truman and State Department spokesmen denied the charges, and Gallegos withdrew his bitter accusation. Many Venezuelans continued to believe, however, that U.S. agents had encouraged the *golpe*, either actively or tacitly.

Of course, some Venezuelans had also applauded the *golpe*. The Comité de Organización Política Electoral Independiente (COPEI, Christian Democratic) and the Unión Republicana Democrática (URD) were young, weak, and poorly organized compared with AD. Many of their activists welcomed the coup as a political opportunity that they could not have achieved on their own. They would not press for popular elections until AD had been effectively squelched. Like many American analysts, they had been wary of AD's hold over peasant and labor groups, and they considered AD's appeal to the masses to be irresponsible demagogy. In effect, they looked again to a democratic caesar to restore order and allow them to play a political role without endorsing mass political participation. The new junta immediately jailed and exiled the AD leaders and then moved to outlaw the party and the labor and peasant unions associated with it. As in the 1840s, the domestic and foreign elites concurred that popular activism endangered their interests.

The Security of Dictatorship, 1949–1957

The U.S. government recognized the junta headed by Carlos Delgado Chalbaud on 13 January 1949. Shortly thereafter, Venezuela restored relations with Somoza's Nicaragua, Franco's Spain, and Trujillo's Dominican Republic. The cold war revived the truism that authoritarian governments somehow prepared unsophisticated peoples for "real" democracy. Yet, the argument about the need for dictatorial tutelage had changed over the years. In the nineteenth century, after a frisson of fear about Afro-Venezuelan dominance, the elites usually agreed that the Venezuelan population was passive, inert, uneducated, and apathetic. By the 1950s the population appeared to be dangerously active but likely to make the "wrong" choices. In the first case, the dictator and his elite allies ruled on behalf of the masses. In the second, the dictator ruled in spite of the masses. The 1950s dictatorships logically required more aggressive measures of intimidation and sometimes an international public relations campaign to obscure and justify their repression. The U.S. State Department concurred with, and aided, that effort. For example, Dean Acheson in April 1949 let it be known that the United States opposed discussion of the Venezuelan human rights situation in the United Nations. Such discussion could only detract attention from Soviet abuses and would cause dissension among the American republics.

U.S. military officers tutored Venezuelan officers on their responsibilities during the cold war. The most immediate mission for the Venezuelan armed forces, of course, was to defend the country in general and the oil fields in particular from sabotage by communist subversives. In more general terms, continental security required that Venezuelan officers share the perception of a bipolar world of Communists and anticommunists. U.S. officers took pride in representing democracy and apolitical military professionalism, but they also accepted the erosion of traditional civil liberties and the semisecret wars fought against governments characterized as subversive. They also found it more difficult to suggest that military officers should remain apart from the political arena when General Dwight D. Eisenhower became president.

The new geopolitics of the cold war required that Venezuelans understand their subordinate role. Lieutenant Colonel John Kieffer lectured Venezuelans on the special vulnerability of oil-rich states such as Venezuela. If the Communists overran Western Europe or North Africa, they could launch bombs or missiles at Venezuela without even entering the Caribbean, Kieffer warned. Only the United States could save the Caribbean nation from such a threat. Kieffer accompanied his warnings with appeals to Venezuelan dreams of glory. He predicted that Venezuela had the opportunity to be a naval and air power in the "secondary space" of the Caribbean and encouraged Venezuelan officers to project their influence further into the Caribbean. Almost as an afterthought, Kieffer remarked that a state with popular democratic support could resist attack better than a dictatorship.[20]

The Venezuelan officers who shared Kieffer's cold war geopolitics demonstrated their distance from César Zumeta's Hispanic Catholic world struggling against the Protestant English one. The petroleum industry, the accompanying trade with the United States, investment and influence, and the experience of two world wars had reconfigured the global struggle for Venezuelans. Petroleum, not Hispanic culture, shaped Venezuelan national and strategic interests in the late twentieth century.

Like their Southern Cone counterparts, Venezuelan officers sometimes failed to recognize the approved limits of their dependent position. For example, Pérez Jiménez caused consternation in Washington in 1956 when he unilaterally extended Venezuela's territorial seas from three miles to twelve. The United States protested this geopolitical assertiveness and refused to recognize any territorial sea beyond the traditional three-mile limit. Venezuela's insistence on the extended maritime zone foreshadowed the coming controversy between developing and developed nations over control of maritime resources and boundaries in the 1970s.

Venezuelan officers turned their role as defenders of the hemisphere to their advantage in securing desired military matériel from the United States, but their oil wealth also allowed them to diversify their military purchases. They bought from the Belgians, the French, and the English. In fact, they may have favored European suppliers because of the latter's greater willingness to pay "commissions" on government purchases, a significant form of graft for Pérez Jiménez and his defense ministers. Some U.S. officials opposed awarding large military credits to Venezuela because military expenditures would divert funds that could be used for economic development and would also spur Brazil,

Colombia, and other nations to spend more. In 1955, Venezuelan defense minister Oscar Mazzei reminded Acting Secretary of State Herbert Hoover, Jr., of Venezuela's special responsibility for hemispheric defense and announced that Venezuela had placed orders for military jets in England. Shortly thereafter, the U.S. Air Force tentatively agreed to sell twenty-two F-86F Sabre jet fighters to Venezuela for eight million dollars.[21] A joint agreement on military cooperation followed in 1956, paving the way for the extension of more U.S. military credits to Venezuela.

Some effort went into trying to develop personal ties between U.S. and Venezuelan military officers. On several occasions, groups of officers studying at the U.S. War College visited Venezuela, where Seguridad Nacional director Pedro Estrada briefed them in English on the relationship between the Venezuelan situation and general U.S. security. There were a few joint military exercises, like the January 1957 antisubmarine maneuvers held in Venezuelan waters.

Venezuelan officers generally welcomed their closer relationship with the U.S. armed forces, but they also found friends and models in Latin America. Young officers studied in the Peruvian superior war school in the 1930s as well as in the United States. They admired Juan Perón's military nationalism. Like their colleagues to the south, officers such as Pérez Jiménez believed that their mission included directing national economic development. Pérez Jiménez's "New National Ideal" asserted that a nation with a weak economy, or one that was dominated by foreign investors, could not be strong militarily. Economic nationalism required the state to take a strong hand in the economy. The Corporación Venezolana de Fomento (Venezuelan Development Corporation, CVF) directed government funds into large projects such as electricity generating plants and irrigation facilities; the construction of roads, airfields, ports, and petrochemical facilities; and the iron and steel complex near Ciudad Guayana. A State Department memo reported in mid-1955 that senior oil executives were concerned about the Venezuelan government's economic activism. The memo warned that the Venezuelans were "starting to take pleasure in throwing their weight around." Pérez Jiménez's bombastic touting of his achievements had "begun to crystalize, on a materialistic and economic basis, the deep-seated and widespread nationalism of the Venezuelan people which has heretofore had to content itself largely with historical values (Bolivarianism) or transitory and somewhat illusory political process (the moves toward political democracy of the post-Gómez governments)."[22]

In sum, cold war ideology and their mission to protect the oil fields advanced the self-confidence and professionalism of Venezuelan military officers. Although they relied heavily on the United States for training and matériel, the very importance of their national mission to defend the oil fields and develop the economy encouraged some degree of independence. Unlike the armies of the Central American and other Caribbean republics, the Venezuelan armed forces were more than a praetorian guard to a dictator or a surrogate U.S. militia.

After 1948, both the Truman and the Eisenhower administrations had ample opportunities to criticize the repressive Venezuelan dictatorship and to urge reforms. The die, however, had been cast for nonintervention, for unequivocally anticommunist leaders, and perhaps for naive self-deception. In November 1950, Venezuelan Junta president Carlos Delgado Chalbaud was assassinated in a botched kidnapping attempt, possibly inspired by his promise to hold elections. Marcos Pérez Jiménez became the effective leader, legitimized by carefully orchestrated popular elections in December 1952.

With AD outlawed, URD leader Jóvito Villaba emerged as the civilian alternative to Pérez Jiménez. Pérez Jiménez, and the analysts in the U.S. Embassy, confidently expected an overwhelming victory for the military man. Ambassador Fletcher Warren, who became as famous as Gómez's Preston McGoodwin for his warm and uncritical relationship with the dictator, cabled Washington on 28 November: "Embassy inclined to believe elections will be held quietly, honestly and that government will win satisfactory majority delegates constituent assembly but no (repeat no) one can be sure hence this message."[23]

Unfortunately, Pérez Jiménez and Warren had miscalculated, and the dictatorship had to delay the announcement of the election results while the votes were clumsily reshuffled in Pérez's favor. Pérez advised the URD leaders responsible for his embarrassment to leave the country. The U.S. Embassy acknowledged the fraud when it reported that the URD probably had won 1,122,000 votes to Pérez's 525,000 and COPEI's 330,000. In effect, Venezuelans had voted nearly three to one to return to civilian government. What to do? In a 2 December telegram Ambassador Warren said that he could not "recommend too strongly" that the United States ignore the question of the legitimacy of the election and continue its relations with Venezuela. Pérez Jiménez and the army would not, he warned, surrender power to the URD, which was a front for AD and the Communists.

A modestly face-saving story emerged. Arthur Proudfit of Creole Petroleum Company commented to the U.S. chargé in Caracas that the URD had also engaged in chicanery during the election. Two wrongs, in American political wisdom, did not make a right, but they could make it possible to rationalize choosing among the wrongs. Chargé Franklin W. Wolf added the old shibboleths about "underdeveloped voters":

> The probable truth of the entire matter is that the people of Venezuela are not yet ready nor adequately prepared for democracy. Certainly they have had very little experience with it, and it is not to be wondered at that this most recent experiment so rapidly turned into such a fiasco. . . . The problem posed by the foregoing analysis is, in the first place, that the United States, believing in democracy must, however distasteful it may be, view with intense realism the particular situation in Venezuela.[24]

Wolf concluded by characterizing the Pérez Jiménez government as "relatively honest" and committed to economic development from which "all of the citizens of Venezuela must eventually derive benefits." Overlooking the dictator's electoral fraud and his "occasional deplorable ruthless methods" would help to preserve hemisphere solidarity, maintain law and order, fight communism, and would also contribute to "the battle against all evil manifestations of extreme nationalism." In spite of this flurry of praise, Wolf advised that it would be wise to postpone the date of the Tenth Pan-American Congress, tentatively set for Caracas in the final quarter of 1953, to 1954.

Ambassador Warren recommended that the U.S. government send a telegram of congratulations to Pérez Jiménez on his election, because he would bring "this people nearer normal democratic institutions and rule." He added, however, that "no (repeat no) regime is going to bring Venezuela full-fledged working democracy until her 5 million people travel on the democratic road much farther."[25]

The old democratic caesar arguments sounded hollow. And indeed, they were. Pérez Jiménez and the U.S. State Department placed a higher priority on their shared aversion to revolution and their shared intention of reaping the material benefits from their association than they did to building democracy. In the 1950s, the U.S. fear of communist revolution in the Caribbean paralleled Pérez Jiménez's concern that a revolution would unseat him. The interests of the United States and Venezuela converged in the effort to overthrow the reformist Guatemalan president Jacobo Arbenz. To Pérez's chagrin, however, the United States wavered when Pérez, Rafael Trujillo, and Anastasio Somoza proposed ridding the Caribbean, and perhaps the earth, of their other reformist enemies—Rómulo Betancourt, José Figueres of Costa Rica, Jesús de Galíndez of the Dominican Republic, and Luís Múñoz Marín of Puerto Rico.

Pérez Jiménez, Venezuelan military officers, and Pedro Estrada, the head of Pérez's brutal Seguridad Nacional police force, conspired actively with their counterparts in Peru and the Caribbean in May 1954 to plan the overthrow of Arbenz and Figueres. Secretary of State John Foster Dulles warned this "International of the Sword" that they should delay until a proposed OAS conference could review the situation.[26] Estrada protested that the United Fruit Company and the United States should acquiesce in Venezuela's plan to arm and support Costa Rican exiles. What good would another conference do?[27]

Pérez Jiménez became so incensed at the lack of support for his campaign against Figueres that the State Department recommended conciliatory action. The United States thus awarded the Venezuelan president the Legion of Merit in November 1954 for "special meritorious conduct in the fulfillment of his high functions, and anti-Communistic attitudes." Pérez Jiménez's favorite cheerleader, Ambassador Fletcher

Warren, reported that the conferral of the decoration "has proven to be the most popular event in Venezuela-American relations in many, many years." Warren expansively concluded, "As an American schooled in Texan politics, my guess would be that if an honest election were held today, he [Pérez] would be re-elected."[28]

Other observers of Latin America remained unimpressed with Venezuela's "Texas democracy." In a *New York Times* article economist Robert Alexander of Rutgers University protested the decoration of a repressive dictator who had gained office by force and fraud. Pérez Jiménez graciously ignored such minor insults when *Time* published a glowing feature article on him in the 28 February 1955 issue. State Department spokesmen later argued that flattering Pérez had served the national interest. The decoration encouraged the awarding of new petroleum concessions to U.S. investors in 1956, protected U.S. exports to its fourth largest market, and did not affect Venezuela's political situation since there was no viable organized opposition at the time. The elaborate justifications for embracing dictators proved less convincing in 1960, however, than they may have been at the height of the cold war.[29]

The Democratic Alternative

At critical moments, then, the State Department officially discouraged the development of democratic institutions in Venezuela in the 1950s. At the same time, U.S. officials maintained relatively cordial contact with some Venezuelan democratic exiles, influenced, perhaps, by the insistent lobbying campaign on their behalf. Eleanor Roosevelt, often encouraged by Robert Alexander, argued for the support of democratic institutions in early 1949 and protested some of the dictatorship's repression in 1951. Senator Herbert Lehman (D–New York) joined other petitioners between 1951 and 1953 to ask the State Department to secure the release from prison of AD activist Dr. Alberto Carnevali, who was seriously ill. Rómulo Betancourt orchestrated much of the campaign on Carnevali's behalf with his active correspondence to allies in the United States, Latin America, and the European Socialist International. The State Department, unmoved, responded that it could not intervene in Venezuelan affairs, and Carnevali died in jail in 1953 without having received adequate medical treatment.

The Inter-American Association for Democracy and Freedom lobbied strongly for Venezuelan democrats. Headed by Frances R. Grant, the association numbered among its members educators, labor leaders, Democrats, and intellectuals such as Robert Alexander, Dr. German Arciniegas, Roger Baldwin, Emanuel Demby, Francine A. Dunlavy, Jesús de Galíndez, Donald Harrington, James Loeb, John C. Mundt, Jr., Serafino Romauldi, Dr. Ernst Schwarz, Clarence Senior, and Norman Thomas. The association kept in close touch with Venezuelan exiles in the United States, Trinidad, Puerto Rico, and Mexico.

The State Department also maintained contact with Betancourt, Pérez Alfonzo, and some of the other Venezuelan leaders. Reminiscent of the surveillance of Cipriano Castro in the early twentieth century, U.S. diplomats around the Caribbean reported on the movements and actions of the *adecos* (AD members). In addition, State Department officials cautiously cultivated some of the Venezuelan exiles in an effort to influence them and to mitigate their hostility toward the United States if they should ever return to power. Rómulo Betancourt naturally received a good deal of attention. C. Allan Stewart, deputy director of State's Office of Middle American Affairs, frequently recorded his conversations with the AD leader. Betancourt wouldn't cooperate with the Communists, would he? He wouldn't cancel the new petroleum concessions awarded by Pérez Jiménez in 1956, would he? Betancourt assured Stewart that he would not cooperate with the Communists and that, although he considered the new petroleum concessions to have been made in bad faith, he might alter their terms but he would not cancel them. Betancourt further informed the State Department in 1956 that AD was not engaging in any clandestine violence or assassination plots to remove Pérez Jiménez from power. AD hoped to join with other civilian reformers to select a politically unaffiliated unity candidate, perhaps a well-respected businessman like Eugenio Mendoza.

Betancourt tried to wring some reciprocal pledges from State, but he usually came up emptyhanded. Why had no high U.S. officials recently reaffirmed an interest in Latin American democracy? the Venezuelan queried. Why hadn't the United States laid the groundwork for a return to democracy by urging Pérez Jiménez to end his reign of terror and hold elections in which some unity candidate might run? Stewart and other officials pressed Betancourt for guarantees but refused to give him any in return to avoid the impression that the discussions had any formal status.[30] The continuing conversations with Betancourt and oil maven Juan Pablo Pérez Alfonzo did, however, suggest that State was pursing a limited two-track approach to Venezuelan relations. Nonintervention and flattery placated Pérez Jiménez and his anticommunist supporters in the United States, and maintaining personal ties with Betancourt and instructing him on U.S. attitudes left the door open for a productive working relationship if Betancourt should return to power.

The events of 1957 showed the wisdom of retaining a Betancourt track in U.S. Venezuelan policy. The U.S. press stepped up its attacks on Latin American dictators, including Pérez Jiménez. From mid-1957, some muted criticism of the dictatorship also began to emerge in Venezuela from the church and from Venezuelan businessmen worried about the fiscal chaos within the administration. In late 1957, a clandestine group called the Patriotic Junta actively plotted the dictator's overthrow, and a group of notables issued a manifesto asking Pérez to leave. Obdurate, Pérez fueled more resistance with a new wave of arrests of eminent respectable citizens like COPEI's Rafael Caldera.

Stung by the criticism at home and abroad, Pérez and his allies scrambled to devise a formula with some democratic trappings to allow him to continue in office. His minister of the interior, Laureano Vallenilla Lanz, son of the Gómez adviser who had penned the famous *Césarismo democrático*, proposed a popular plebiscite in which Venezuelans would simply vote *yes* or *no*.

Although Pérez was still considered secure, the State Department's internal memos nonetheless revealed concern about the implications of continued uncritical support for him, including Betancourt's assertion that the warm embrace of dictators was creating anti–United States feelings in Latin America.[31] The policy also had political repercussions in the United States, as a petroleum consultant pointed out to the White House on the arrest of Rafael Caldera: "From a political standpoint we are losing to the Democrats all the votes of Americans of Latin origin."[32] Finally, State Department analysts considered the possibility that communism might be strengthened rather than weakened by authoritarian governments. A September Office of South America memo remarked of Rafael Caldera's arrest that his "continued exclusion from political activity would represent a serious long-range loss for the democratic forces combating the Communists in this strategic region."[33] Even the oilmen complained. Arthur Proudfit of Creole charged that Pérez Jiménez harmed his own cause when he chose such a crude and unsophisticated method of continuing in power. Proudfit thought that Pérez should have patterned his *continuismo* on the methods of Mexico's Partido Revolucionario Institucional.[34] Pérez Jiménez's supporters in the United States expressed doubt about the dictatorship but appeared to accept the Caracas embassy's judgment that "the Venezuelans are as monotonous as their weather." A memo from the U.S. Embassy in Caracas dated 16 December 1957 concluded that there was no effective resistance and no prospect of any in Venezuela.

About five weeks later, on 23 January 1958, military officers, civilian conspirators belonging to the Patriotic Junta, and Caracas urban mobs forced Pérez Jiménez to flee the country. The new governing junta, headed by Admiral Wolfgang Larrazábal, had representatives from the business community and the Patriotic Junta. As in 1945, 1948, and 1952, Venezuelan political events again challenged the United States to tip the balance toward a solution that would provide stability and continued access to oil. The State Department and many Venezuelan notables expressed concern at the active participation of the Caracas masses in the revolt and at the presence of members of the Communist party in the Patriotic Junta. The dilemma they addressed through 1958, and later, was how to put the genie back into the bottle. Clearly, neither the masses nor radical politicians could be allowed to seize control of the chaotic situation, but a fervent anti-Americanism heightened tensions. Proposals by Congress to place quotas on Venezuelan petroleum imports in 1957 had angered all sectors of Venezuela. Pérez Jiménez's ill-fated choice of Miami as his home in exile provided a constant reminder of U.S. support for the dictator. AD leaders pointed out that they, in contrast, had been refused visas to live in the United States in the 1950s. When a Caracas mob nearly killed Vice President Richard Nixon and his wife, Patricia, in May 1958, the proponents of a moderate solution realized that the situation was serious.

After the *golpe* the U.S. government extended diplomatic recognition fairly quickly to Larrazabal's new governing junta. Secretary of State Christian Herter was reassured by the participation of Eugenio Mendoza and other stalwarts of the Venezuelan business community on the junta. He hoped that diplomatic recognition might promote stability and strengthen Mendoza and his allies on the junta and in the presidential elections scheduled for December 1958. U.S. hopes of forging a political alliance with Venezuelan business leaders were shattered in late May, however, when popular pressure forced the oligarchs off the governing junta.

Somewhat warily, the State Department continued its grooming of Rómulo Betancourt. Just as assiduously, Betancourt worked to assure the U.S. government that he could deliver a system that was at the same time reformist, anticommunist, and stable. In exile, he had learned the same lesson that Che Guevara learned from the overthrow of Arbenz in Guatemala in 1954: no reformist government could prosper in the face of U.S. hostility. Both Betancourt and COPEI's Rafael Caldera also recognized the cost to Venezuelan civil society of their partisan feuds during the *trienio* (three-year period of AD rule). Before returning to Venezuela from the United States, Betancourt and Caldera determined to forge an alliance of all the Venezuelan democratic sectors, excluding only the Communists and any of the young partisans who refused to accept their moderate leadership. The U.S. State Department was a silent partner to this pact.

In late January, Caldera and Betancourt separately held conversations with State Department officials in Washington. Both Venezuelans lauded their country's unity in overthrowing the dictator and pledged to work toward finding a unity presidential candidate. Like the State Department, Caldera and Betancourt disliked the presence of Communists on the Patriotic Junta and agreed that they would welcome the dissolution of the heterodox junta. Their own "traditional" parties were preferable political organizations. Even so, the Venezuelans mildly challenged State Department spokesman Roy Rubottom when he continued to warn them about communist activity in Venezuela. Caldera replied that the Communists posed no threat and that he preferred that they function in the open as a legal party rather than as a clandestine threat.[35] When Rubottom "expressed his surprise" at the inclusion of the Communists in the Patriotic Junta and at Betancourt's willingness to work with the junta during the transition period, Betancourt retorted that renewed communist prestige in Venezuela was one of the unfortunate consequences of the Pérez Jiménez dictatorship. Betancourt himself had no intention of collaborating with the Communists in the future.[36]

U.S. politicians seized on Pérez Jiménez as a symbol of dictatorship and failed U.S. policy. For example, Congressman Charles O. Porter (D–Oregon) sent a letter of congratulations to the new Venezuelan junta and then wrote to President Eisenhower reiterating his belief that the United States should openly express disapproval of dictators like Pérez Jiménez, Fulgencio Batista, Anastasio Somoza, Alfredo Stroessner, and Rafael Trujillo: "We ought to stand up and be counted as deploring police states and favoring democracies."[37] Groups such as the Inter-American Association for Democracy and Freedom protested that issuing Pérez a visa to live in Miami bespoke a lingering sponsorship of him.

The Venezuelan presidential elections of December 1958 ushered in one of Latin America's most enduring contemporary democracies. AD's Rómulo Betancourt captured 49 percent of the vote, and Admiral Wolfgang Larrazábal and COPEI's Rafael Caldera won 35 percent and 16 percent, respectively. Ironically, U.S. officials in Washington had to embrace their old nemesis Betancourt with relief, since he had defeated Larrazabal's popular coalition that included the Communists.

The U.S. government and the multinational oil companies engineered no changes in the Venezuelan government between 1936 and 1958. Still, subtle signals and choices at critical junctures encouraged or stifled the forces for democracy. The evolution of U.S. policy toward Venezuelan governments exemplifies what Bryce Wood called "the dismantling of the Good Neighbor Policy."

Moreover, Venezuela's new hydrocarbon society spawned a more complex group of political actors. These new actors—business associations, labor unions, industrialists, professional military officers, and middle-class professionals—often chose alliances with their counterparts, or complementary interests, in the United States over making common cause with their compatriots. As U.S. economic and cultural forces penetrated Venezuela more deeply, these transnational alliances became more logical and effective. At the same time, many Venezuelans resisted and criticized what they perceived as the erosion of Venezuelan culture and the spread of the "American way of life."

7 The Hydrocarbon Economy and the American Way of Life, 1936–1958

> Why, anybody who came to Venezuela in 1950 and isn't a million-aire by 1970 ought to go to the Mayo Clinic and have his head ex-amined, we're thinking.
>
> —*Caracas Journal*, 23 July 1951

Petroleum altered the Venezuelan economy and society drastically between 1935 and 1959. The oil business dwarfed nearly all the traditional economic activities. As the multinational oil companies re-created the mythological El Dorado, foreign immigrants rushed to Venezuela. Confident *yanquis* in the process of seeking their own fortunes offered Venezuelans lessons on how to live and make money "the American way." If Venezuelan economic practices and consumer preferences would only become more synchronized with the business style and export market of the United States, the complementarity of the two economies would be accentuated. Popular American magazines, films, advertising, and television reiterated these lessons and introduced Venezuelans to a cornucopia of new consumer products and values from which they could choose. The hydrocarbon effect, or the "American style," drifted out of the enclaved oil camps to affect all ranks of Venezuelan society.

Some Venezuelans enjoyed the boom, with little thought of its long-range economic or cultural impact. Others, often aspiring industrialists, feared that the open economy favored the penetration of foreign entrepreneurs to the exclusion of Venezuelan investors. Writers and intellectuals struggled, as César Zumeta had, to identify and retain national authenticity and autonomy along with the new wealth.

Between 1936 and 1958, U.S.-Venezuelan relations felt the ripple effect of the increasingly global nature of the petroleum industry. Venezuelan policies affected investments and relations in other areas of the world and contributed to the domestic political debate in the United States. Independent and multinational oil companies, exporters, professional associations, chambers of commerce, and a growing number of academics, human rights advocates, and labor leaders watched Venezuelan events carefully. Pérez Jiménez's repression provided additional evidence for those who charged that Washington encouraged dictatorship over democracy in Latin America. Venezuelan petroleum and oil from new fields in the Middle East flooded the market and intensified the independent U.S. petroleum producers' insistence that the United States place import quotas on foreign oil. The multinational petroleum experts worried that Venezuela's success in securing a fifty-fifty split in oil revenues could prompt the new Middle Eastern producers to demand the same.

With luck and a degree of caution, Venezuela again—as in the days of Gómez—managed to survive the potential hazards inherent in its new importance to the United States. Before the dictatorship collapsed in 1958, key sectors of Venezuelan society lacked the experience or strength to counter the economic expansionism of the United States. Yet, just as Gómez's quiescence allowed Venezuela to escape the worst of the hegemonic expansiveness, the transitional dictatorships (mostly) from 1936 to 1958 effectively prevented the emergence of any dangerous challenges to the United States during the height of the cold war hysteria. Venezuela thus avoided being either President Theodore Roosevelt's Dominican Republic or Secretary of State John Foster Dulles's Guatemala.

Oil, Trade, and State Capitalism

Petroleum exploitation secured for the United States the economic goal that it had long held for Venezuela. The development of the oil industry in a context of free trade, free repatriation of profits, and minimal restrictions on U.S. imports produced a trade balance that favored the United States. Venezuelan presidents could not afford to overlook the fact that more than 60 percent of government revenues derived from oil and that over 40 percent of that oil went to the U.S. market. A strong Venezuelan and domestic commercial lobby demanded that U.S. exporters receive open door access to the increasingly lucrative Venezuelan consumer market. By 1962, 52 percent of Venezuela's total imports came from the United States, and Venezuela was America's best Latin American customer.

Venezuela did enjoy a modest surge of industrialization during the 1950s. Most of the new industry, however, derived from U.S. subsidiaries that established assembly plants in the country and from new state-owned industries. The two binational trade treaties signed during this time, in 1939 and in 1952, increased the advantage of U.S. investors over the nascent Venezuelan industrialists. Moreover, Venezuelan risk-adverse investors continued to prefer land speculation and commerce over manufacturing. State-owned corporations and subsidized mixed private-public industries provided the only effective competition to U.S. industrial expansion in Venezuela.

The Venezuelans who benefited from the industrial and commercial activity comprised a newly affluent class of advisers, legal consultants, shareholders, partners, and agents of U.S. companies. An outstanding example was Eugenio Mendoza, who rose from ownership of a modest hardware store in the 1930s to become one of the wealthiest and most diversified entrepreneurs in Venezuela. Mendoza became the principal supplier of U.S. construction materials to the Ministry of Public Works between 1936 and 1941. In 1943 Mendoza opened his own cement factory. As the minister of development under Medina, he supervised the distribution of import licenses for scarce U.S. products during the war; unsurprisingly, his own firms absorbed up to two-thirds of some shipments.[1] Mendoza won credit as a nationalist when he presided over the framing of the fifty-fifty petroleum legislation in 1943. After the war, in partnership with private capital from the United States and with credit from the U.S. Export-Import Bank, Mendoza diversified into other construction materials, animal foods, paper, and ultimately banking and financial organizations. Following the robber baron model to a T, the Venezuelan also generously established charitable foundations to redistribute some of his wealth. By maintaining close contact with the U.S. Embassy and business leaders in Venezuela, Mendoza prospered through all of the political changes between the 1930s and 1960s.[2]

Franklin Roosevelt's commitment to rescinding the high tariffs of the 1920s and opening foreign markets to U.S. goods paved the way for the new economic partnership. Historian David Painter has suggested that Roosevelt sought to replace U.S. military hegemony with a more subtle dominance that used private enterprise "to create a congenial atmosphere for the U.S."[3] The economic Good Neighbor policy further promised that U.S. economic recovery would create a greater "share" of the wealth for Latin America.[4]

Discussions of a new trade treaty with Venezuela began secretly in 1936. Roosevelt feared that independent American petroleum producers would subvert his strategic and political goals by demanding restrictions and higher tariffs on foreign oil. A favorable commercial treaty with Venezuela, the president believed, would not only benefit U.S. exports but would also heighten U.S. influence and help to secure access to strategic oil reserves in the event of war.

President López Contreras did not leap at the bait at once. In 1936, Venezuela was still active in the League of Nations and hoped to increase its commercial ties with Europe, thus avoiding a position unequivocally within the American sphere. López offered a series of feints and obstructions that dragged out the negotiations until 1938. By then, the inevitability of war dashed any hopes of relying on European markets and imports, and Caracas reluctantly accepted the U.S. treaty draft, although with some minor changes.

López initially opposed including petroleum in the trade treaty. The concessions for Venezuelan petroleum actually favored the multinational oil companies and the refiners on the Dutch islands of Aruba and Curaçao. In return, Venezuela's consumer market would be opened to imports from the United States and other countries, who would also demand most favored nation status. The black gold would be wasted on the purchase of foreign manufactured and agricultural products instead of being "sown," or invested, in Venezuela's own industrial development. Early in 1938, Foreign Minister Esteban Gil Borges offered to add petroleum to the list of preferred products if the oil companies would agree to refine 50 percent of the petroleum in Venezuela. The State Department responded that refining policies should be negotiated directly between Venezuela and the oil companies, not through the trade treaty.

López Contreras had silenced most of his political opposition after the 1936 demonstrations and thus could not call on popular support for a nationalistic position. U.S. minister Meredith Nicholson advised the State Department to moderate its position somewhat so as not to tempt López to publicize the negotiations and thus strengthen his hand.[5] Venezuelan commercial sectors threw in their interests with the oil companies, and the native industrialists lacked the numbers or influence to affect the negotiations. The Venezuelan government accepted most of the treaty's terms in 1939. The open door policy gave the United States an economic advantage and provided a "share" to some Venezuelans, but it delayed the development of a diversified Venezuelan economy over the long term.[6]

In July 1938, López Contreras's government tried to compensate for the projected loss in tariff revenues by raising taxes and asserting greater government control over the petroleum companies. The companies complained privately to the State Department but largely ignored López's new legislation. Although ineffective, the 1930s legislation began the cat-and-mouse game that the oil companies and the Venezuelan government would play for nearly forty years until the oil industry was nationalized in 1976. The government announced terms, won points for nationalism with the public, but frequently failed to implement the measures fully. The oil companies attacked each new measure but gradually complied in part, depending on the international oil climate and the perspicacity of the oil executives. By the postwar period the companies had become skilled at using public relations and Venezuelan allies to express their point of view. They sponsored television news programs (*El Observador Creole*), scholarships, safe driving campaigns, and the cultural activities of the Centro Venezolano Americano as well as the Consejo de Bienestar Rural (Rural Welfare Council), a kind of home demonstration project to teach rural Venezuelans proper nutrition.

Venezuela's 1943 petroleum legislation extended the foreign oil concessions in exchange for 50 percent of the profits. For the first time, President Isaías Medina Angarita actively sought the support of the Venezuelan public through the press, radio, and open meetings that drew as many as fifty thousand people. Washington policymakers, fearful of a groundswell of nationalism, asked Medina to avoid encouraging popular discussion of U.S. economic interests.[7] Medina won his gamble that he could control the populace. Only the nascent AD party attacked the 1943 legislation as too mild.

The oil companies resisted Venezuela's unprecedented demands, but Franklin Roosevelt's government refused to support the oilmen in the wartime situation. Prior to the passage of the Venezuelan legislation, U.S. petroleum adviser Max Thornburg signaled that "our primary interest is that Venezuelan oil remains available for the war."[8] The top priority was to maintain U.S. *control* of the Venezuelan oil industry, and Venezuela's insistence on a greater share of the profits did not affect that. U.S. observers further appreciated that President Medina's peaceful settlement with the companies "strengthened the hand of Venezuelan conservatives against the nationalists in the Acción Democrática party, whose chief concern was control over Venezuela's resources."[9]

The populist *trienio* that ruled from 1945 to 1948 pressed the oil companies further but essentially stayed within bounds the companies could tolerate. For example, Labor Minister Raúl Leoni intervened to secure higher wages for oil workers in the collective contract signed in February 1948 but squelched the unions' demands for more influence in the industry and greater worker security. The AD governments did lay the groundwork for a nationally controlled industry by exercising the privilege of accepting royalties in petroleum, pressing for more refining in Venezuela, and announcing that no new concessions would be awarded.

The Pérez Jiménez dictatorship favored the foreign companies with its suppression of the populist political parties and labor unions and its lax enforcement of the petroleum legislation, even granting new foreign concessions in 1956. Pérez Jiménez, however, displeased laissez-faire advocates in both Venezuela and the United States with his economic activism. He encouraged some diversification of the Venezuelan economy through state investment and state control. He allowed foreign companies like Bethlehem Steel and U.S. Steel a share in the impressive iron and steel industry in the Guayana region, but he also initiated direct government ownership of some industries and services. Posing a potential challenge to U.S. access to Venezuelan resources, in 1955 Pérez threatened to cut off the export of iron ore if the U.S. Congress imposed quotas on Venezuelan petroleum. He invested heavily in highway infrastructure, in dragging the sandbar at Lake Maracaibo, and in a modern military organization. The infrastructure and the military modernization at the same time secured the oil fields from internal subversion and raised the cost to any foreign power that might threaten them.

Venezuela's petroleum fields became even more precious in the face of the Korean Conflict, the Suez Crisis, and the 1951 Iranian expropriation of the Anglo-Iranian Oil Company. The windfall of increased revenues, along with the sale of new concessions, financed Pérez Jiménez's grandiose schemes, as well as new waves of corruption, waste, speculation, and conspicuous monument building. Even so, the independent oil producers in the United States kept Venezuela off-balance by pressing for import controls or quotas on foreign oil.

The petroleum revenues spurred both a rush of imports and some industrial expansion in Venezuela. In fact, Venezuela enjoyed the highest rate of industrialization in Latin America in the 1950s, although the total industrialization was still quite modest compared with the more developed Latin American countries such as Brazil and Mexico. Direct U.S. investment in manufacturing and commerce in Venezuela, primarily in the form of assembly plants like those opened by General Motors and Chrysler, grew at a faster rate than investment in petroleum. Many of the new industries continued to import heavily. Ironically in a country that boasted many native fruits, the Yukery firm bought fruit pulps from the United States to combine with Venezuelan water and sugar to make "Venezuelan" fruit juices.

Some older Venezuelan industries, and other aspiring ones, could not compete with the imported goods or the more modern industrial establishments. Venezuelan soap manufacturers complained that low duties on imported soap powders and detergents allowed those products to undercut Venezuelan products. Nor could the Venezuelan manufacturers switch quickly enough to production of the detergents that the newly imported washing machines required. By the time Procter and Gamble established its first detergent packaging plant in Venezuela in 1952, few Venezuelan soap manufacturers remained. In 1955, Rockefeller associate William Coles headed a group of Venezuelan and U.S. investors that purchased Las Llaves, one of the largest surviving Venezuelan soap companies.

U.S. retail firms further changed Venezuela's economic landscape. The growing American community demanded the familiar products that they had known at home or in the oil camp commissaries. Their preferences and their relatively high salaries fueled a revolution in retailing and consumer tastes among the growing Venezuelan middle classes. Sears, Roebuck and Company had six outlets in Venezuela by 1953. Nelson Rockefeller's Compañía Anónima Distribuidora de Alimentos (CADA) opened the first modern supermarket and shopping center in Maracaibo in 1949, soon followed by stores in Valencia and Caracas. CADA provided one outlet for some of the food products (fish, grains, chickens, eggs, milk, and other dairy products) in which Rockefeller's Venezuelan Basic Economy Corporation had invested in association with the state-owned Venezuelan Development Corporation. Sears and the CADA supermarkets claimed to have lower prices and to sell many Venezuelan products, but their main attraction probably was the variety of U.S. products available. These giant firms drove many Venezuelan merchants out of business.

Other U.S. investors benefited from "invisible" exports to Venezuela. U.S. shipping companies brought in the tons of U.S. imports and enjoyed the preference accorded them by U.S. merchants and their associates. Neither the Gran Colombian Merchant Fleet nor its Venezuelan successor, the Compañía Anónima Venezolana de Navegación, could compete, especially when the Caribbean shipping consortium penalized businesses that used the Venezuelan lines. Since most Venezuelan imports came from the United States, American exporters and the importing firms in Venezuela usually could favor U.S. shipping lines.

Construction, engineering, and architectural firms based in the United States also held a privileged position. The Orinoco Mining Company, a subsidiary of U.S. Steel, consistently gave all its contracts for dredging in the Orinoco River to foreign companies. U.S. Steel awarded the subcontract for the construction of a standard-gauge railroad and a highway to join the iron-rich Cerro Bolívar with the Orinoco River to Morrison-Knudson de Venezuela, an affiliate of the Boise, Idaho, firm of the same name. Don Hatch, an American architect resident in Caracas, designed the factory for U.S. Rubber de Venezuela CA, a subsidiary of U.S. Rubber.

Both Washington and Caracas offered incentives to U.S. investors. Pérez Jiménez allowed free convertibility of currency, unrestricted repatriation of profits, low tax rates, little regulation, and duty-free entry of the materials and equipment necessary for industrialization. After 1955, Venezuela withdrew from the International Labor Organization, continued to suppress unions, and invited waves of Italian, Spanish, and Portuguese immigrants to supplement Venezuelan workers, whom many employers considered to be poorly trained, overpaid, and too assertive.

The U.S. government in 1942 passed the Western Hemisphere Trading Corporation legislation, which allowed subsidiaries of U.S. corporations to receive a 14 percent savings on their federal income taxes if they did 95 percent of their business in the Western Hemisphere. Washington also helped North American farmers to unload their production profitably in the Western Hemisphere. In the 1950s, only Mexico and Cuba imported more agricultural products from the United States than Venezuela.

A new trade treaty with the United States, signed in 1952, further discouraged Venezuelan farmers and industrialists. The 1952 treaty awarded favorable tariff classifications to 179 U.S. products, up from 88 under the 1939 agreement. In return, Venezuelan crude oil was allowed to enter the United States duty free. The treaty effectively enabled U.S. businesses to reap the major portion of the benefits from Venezuela's 1943 taxation on the petroleum industry. The assistant secretary of state for Latin American affairs, John Moors Cabot, told members of the Export Managers Club and the Export Advertising Association in New York that the treaty "was designed to protect an important export market, and incidentally, to safeguard important U.S. investments."[10]

The trade treaty spawned enemies and friends on both sides of the Caribbean. In the United States, opposition came from the independent oil producers (who were somewhat mollified later, if briefly, when they were allowed to bid on new Venezuelan concessions in 1956), coal producers, the United Mine Workers, and other labor organizations that criticized the dictator's treatment of Venezuelan labor. The Venezuelan Chamber of Industrialists and Venezuelan economic nationalists could express only a muted, and ineffective, protest at the dictatorship's acquiescence to tying the Venezuelan market more tightly to U.S. agricultural and industrial exporters.

The treaty's advocates included the international oil companies and the Venezuelan American Chamber of Commerce (AmCham). The latter had been founded in Venezuela in 1950 by subsidiaries of U.S. firms and some Venezuelan companies that depended on U.S. trade. The oil companies were playing for high stakes. In 1954, 55 percent of the net earnings of the Standard Oil Company of New Jersey came from Creole, its Venezuelan subsidiary. When lobbyists pressed Congress to nullify the treaty and restrict foreign oil imports, the treaty's supporters marshalled a countercampaign in 1953–54. AmCham spokesman Joseph Foss wrote to the Congressional Committee on Foreign Economic Policy to point out the benefits that accrued from the purchase of Venezuelan oil:

In addition to this one-half billion dollars of American products purchased by Venezuela, the unrestricted remittances of profits and dividends and funds resulting from associated services such as banking, insurance, shipping, etc., amounted to some four hundred million dollars last year, *in other words a total of approximately one billion dollars of income to the United States from trade with Venezuela.*[11]

Voicing the usual cold war rhetoric, Foss further predicted that the restrictions would enable the Communists to make great headway in Latin America at the expense of the United States.

The lobbying campaign on the trade treaty and oil import policy highlighted the fragmentation of interest groups and the complex formation of trans-Caribbean alliances. Venezuelan commercial and importing firms depended on the political influence of Standard Oil and Gulf Oil in the United States. On the other hand, Venezuelan industrialists and farmers (and much organized labor in both countries) directly or indirectly fared better when the independent oil producers had the upper political hand, because Venezuela could then impose modest restrictions on U.S. imports in retaliation for the quotas on Venezuelan oil. In 1957, a glut of inexpensive Middle Eastern oil in the U.S. market forced President Eisenhower to bow to the pressure of the independent oil producers and impose voluntary quotas on imported oil; in 1959, the quotas became mandatory. The quotas did not fundamentally alter the economic relationship with Venezuela, but they did give a modest boost to Venezuelan nationalism and the framing of an import substitution policy.

The Spread of the American Entrepreneurial Culture

U.S. investment in nonpetroleum sectors of the Venezuelan economy accompanied a gradual transformation of financial and business practices. AmCham and other businesses urged Venezuelans to adopt sales, marketing, and accounting procedures like those used in the United States. For example, AmCham in 1956 sponsored Jolly D. Backer, the sales manager for Phillips Petroleum Company, to teach the Association of Venezuelan Sales Executives how to infuse salesmen with the ambition to make just one more sale.[12] Philip Gray, secretary of the National Association of Credit Men in the United States, advised Caracas credit managers to start a credit association in Venezuela. A local credit association, he explained, would perform an invaluable service to U.S. exporters who had no information on the creditworthiness of their Venezuelan customers.[13] The English-language *Caracas Journal* (after October 1955 the *Daily Journal*) fostered the new business values for a wider public than the AmCham *Review* reached. Founded in 1945 as "part of the Allied war effort," the paper boasted an executive committee that included prominent American businessmen residing in Venezuela.[14] Enjoying freedom from the Pérez Jiménez censorship, the paper had a daily circulation of ten thousand by 1955 and received the Venezuelan government's National Newspaper Prize.

The *Journal* endorsed all the intimidating theses espoused by the foreign oil companies with regard to Venezuelan control of the industry. In sum, Venezuelan nationalism or conservation would inevitably lead to poverty and disaster. When Iran nationalized foreign oil companies in 1951, the *Journal* ran a series of editorials condemning the action and praising Venezuela's sensible practice of allowing foreigners to run the industry. "In Iran, an inexperienced, foolish oligarchy is busying itself with the taking over of an oil concern which does not belong to it and which it cannot possibly run. This foolish oligarchy is taking this measure, apparently, in order to prove one thing: that it, and only it, has a right to rule the country."[15]

The *Journal* sometimes wrote admiringly of the repression of labor in Venezuela in the 1950s. Shortly after the 1948 *golpe*, the paper fretted that the inflated wages of petroleum workers limited the future growth of Venezuela's oil industry by raising the operating costs. When the dictatorship in 1951 imposed a new collective contract for petroleum workers without negotiating, the *Journal* expressed approval that conflict had been avoided.[16] A year later, with reference to a strike at Macy's in New York, the paper compared Venezuela's repressive labor policy favorably with that of the United States, where "such a fine firm like Macy's" had to suffer losses.[17] In 1955, the *Journal* counseled the

Venezuelan Ministry of Labor to reject a proposal for a five-day work week because it would be expensive for many businesses; and Venezuelans, the writer believed, were not "ready yet to take it so easy."[18]

Venezuelan consumers received no sympathy from these advocates of the free market. The paper praised the government's decision to abandon rent controls in 1952 and criticized the policy that set low fixed prices for gasoline, kerosene, and fuel oil sold domestically in Venezuela. Editor Jules Waldman, an avid music critic and agent for piano sales in Venezuela, even opposed government-subsidized free concerts by the Venezuelan Symphony. "It means that they will never appreciate the orchestra as much as when they have to pay something to hear it," he wrote.[19]

The paper occasionally reprised a whiff of social Darwinism. An article reported that a Venezuelan government official had expressed satisfaction because "Venezuela is getting to the point where the unfit are falling or are dropping by the wayside."[20] When smaller Venezuelan stores could not compete with Sears or Rockefeller's CADA supermarkets or the Venezuelan-owned BECO department store, the *Journal* wrote, "This denotes just another aspect of the 'survival of the fittest' maxim. . . . And it also denotes progress, right down the line."[21] The *Journal* frequently reminded its foreign readers of the opportunities for profit in Venezuela. "Why, anybody who came to Venezuela in 1950 and isn't a millionaire by 1970 ought to go to the Mayo Clinic and have his head examined, we're thinking."[22] The paper's writers evinced less concern about the prospects of those who were *born* in Venezuela in 1950.

Occasionally the paper veered from its social Darwinist dogma when a U.S. business needed help. For example, the journalists endorsed the protective measures that favored the products of Sudamtex, a Venezuelan subsidiary of a U.S. company, over less expensive Japanese textile imports.[23] In effect, the *Journal*'s economic philosophy was ambivalent, a 1950s version of Franklin Roosevelt's "give them a share—but not too much." Avowedly founded as "part of the Allied war effort," the *Journal* extended its mission into the cold war. As a Creole Oil spokesman wrote in the *Review* published by the American Chamber of Commerce:

"Still, the meaning of the Venezuelan trade figures is clear: the more prosperous the Free World becomes, the more it will be able to buy from us and thus contribute to our own prosperity."[24]

Unofficial Diplomats for the American Way of Life

The petroleum industry and U.S. investors most obviously affected Venezuela's business patterns, but U.S. citizens also encouraged broader cultural changes. U.S. ambassador Fletcher Warren said in 1951 that "the canons of free enterprise and individual liberty for which we stand are daily expressed by all of us in all walks of life. Those of you who live abroad are the unofficial diplomats of the American way of life."[25]

Like the oil companies that so many of them served, many U.S. citizens living in Venezuela benefited from good public and social relations with their Venezuelan associates. Away from the isolated segregation of the oil camps, Americans joined Venezuelans in social clubs, condominium associations, AmCham, the Centro Venezolano Americano, and charitable activities. They mentored and directed youth baseball teams, the YMCA, Boy Scouts, Girl Scouts, PTAs, and binational schools. A Venezuelan-American community of interests developed, especially in the business world but to some extent also among the social networks that included spouses and children. This community shared an affection for the "American way of life"—its consumer culture, its popular culture and language, its affluence, and its economic ideology.

English replaced French as the second language of preference for Venezuelans after World War II. The Centro Venezolano Americano (CVA), established in 1941 in Caracas to promote wartime good neighborliness, became the cultural core of the binational community. The CVA taught English classes—and the attitude that English was a necessary skill for those who wanted to be modern and get ahead. Familiarity with English became a mark of sophistication and culture, as many Venezuelan elite families increasingly turned to New York instead of Paris for education, travel, and shopping. The CVA acquired a certain cachet from one of its founders and directors, Margot Boulton, the daughter of a prominent Venezuelan family of English origin. U.S. films, the ubiquitous *Reader's Digest* (*Selecciones*, in Spanish), and business offices allowed Venezuelans ample opportunity to hone their new language skills. English speakers who wished to be good neighbors could also take Spanish classes at the CVA.

Critical to the spread of the English language and American customs was the growth and visibility of the U.S. community. Significant numbers of North Americans had lived in Venezuela since the beginning of oil exploitation in the 1920s, but many of them had lived in the oil camps. The opportunities created by the postwar oil boom lured more *estadounidenses* to Venezuela, especially to Maracaibo and Caracas. By the late 1950s an estimated thirty-five thousand persons boasted single U.S. citizenship, and that number again may have had double citizenship. It was the largest expatriate U.S. community in the world at the time.

If Venezuelans vacationed in New York, only a few U.S. citizens booked cruises or flights on Pan Am to visit sunny Venezuela. Prices were high, accommodations were minimal, and Venezuela could not compete with Cuba as a tourist destination. Most visitors were there on business, and Nelson Rockefeller, in association with Venezuelan investors, contributed to their comfort by financing and building several elegant hotels, including Caracas's Avila Hotel. In the 1950s, the larger and flashier Tamanaco Hotel replaced the Avila as Caracas's favorite luxury hotel. A 1954 letter to *El Heraldo* charged that the Indian cacique Tamanaco would have been outraged if he could have seen the English-language signs, books, menus, and foreign paintings that decorated his namesake establishment. The delegates to the Tenth Inter-American Conference who were to lodge there, the writer asserted, would conclude that Venezuela was not a country but a colony.[26] The letter writer overlooked the possibility that Tamanaco might not have been fond of hearing Spanish either!

In fact, the Tamanaco became a visible symbol of both what Venezuelans loved about the new hydrocarbon society and what they hated about it. Venezuelan essayist Mariano Picón Salas mocked the national and international businessmen who gathered there at lunch-time to drink martinis and make "deals" in English. At night, the bars and dance floors attracted the youth and bon vivants, who danced to Latin rhythms. The Tamanco became the national club, one that ex-cluded principally on the basis of wealth and proper dress. It did not replace the elegant, exclusive social clubs constructed in the 1930s and 1940s, but it fed the illusion of social equality for all those with the price of a martini or a glass of Johnny Walker Scotch.

U.S. citizens who left the oil camp enclaves for the cities attracted less attention than the flood of Italians, Portuguese, and Spaniards who came to Venezuela looking for work at the war's end. Especially among the popular classes, these immigrants added a "European" fla-vor to Caracas life. Many of them originated from the poorer working classes, however, and did not make as strong an imprint on the entre-preneurial or general culture as did the U.S. citizens with their afflu-ence, their businesses, and their entertainments.

Some U.S. citizens who came to Venezuela in the 1890s served as cul-tural brokers between the two communities and were held in high re-gard by both Venezuelans and Americans. For example, eighty-five-year-old Rudolf Dolge, acclaimed as the oldest American resident in 1949, had opened the National Association of Manufacturers (NAM) exhibit in Caracas in 1897 and subsequently served as a U.S. consul and an oil company employee. Over his long residence in Venezuela, Dolge collected books and manuscripts related to Venezuela and was a co-founder of the Venezuelan Society of Natural Sciences. After the war, Dolge donated his collection to his adopted country, and the Venezue-lan government honored him with the Order of Miranda in 1949.

A few other "pioneers" founded both dynasties and empires. The Phelps family formed part of what Venezuelan historian Domingo Alberto Rangel called the "money oligarchy." A strong interest in Venezuela's flora and fauna drew naturalist William H. Phelps to the country in the nineteenth century, but petroleum and the automobile spawned the family's commercial empire. William Phelps founded the first automobile dealership in 1925, and his Almacen Americano mar-keted U.S.-manufactured consumer durables in the 1920s and 1930s.

The family, in association with Procter and Gamble, diversified into the production of edible oils and also built William's early gamble on radio into a major communications network. In postwar Caracas, the Torre Phelps skyscraper in Plaza Venezuela emphasized the family's economic prominence. Ties to the United States remained important, however, and William's three sons attended Yale (Alberto), Harvard (William, Jr.), and Dartmouth (John). The U.S. Embassy in Caracas called on the family's local knowledge, and Alberto served as a special assistant to the U.S. ambassador in Venezuela during World War II. William Phelps, Jr., or Billy, and his Australian wife, Kathleen Deery, continued the family's interest in ornithology and natural history. Like the English Boulton family, the Phelpses became fully *venezolano* while also retaining their loyalty to and identification with their country of origin.

In later years, prominent American residents in Venezuela often began their Venezuelan careers as employees of the U.S. Embassy or Office of Inter-American Affairs, the petroleum companies, or other U.S. firms, especially those associated with Nelson Rockefeller. Rockefeller's wealth and prominence, his position as coordinator of inter-American affairs in the State Department in the 1940s, and his philanthropy and investments through the Venezuelan Basic Economy Corporation made him a key player in the postwar boom. He and his associates enjoyed a significant advantage in that competitive environment because of their ties with the Venezuelan government, the U.S. government, international banks and lenders, and oil companies. Significantly, and despite his Republican party and oil company affiliations, Rockefeller had a warm personal friendship with AD's Rómulo Betancourt. He took care, however, also to cultivate cordial relations with the post-1948 dictatorship and Pérez Jiménez.

Several of Rockefeller's associates formed an interlocking group of investors, entrepreneurs, leaders of the North American Association, the CVA, and AmCham, and directors of the *Daily Journal*. Dartmouth graduate (like Rockefeller) and native New Yorker Robert Bottome may have been the most prominent. He arrived in Venezuela in 1939 as a Rockefeller employee to supervise work on the Hotel Avila. During the war he became the coordinator of inter-American affairs in Venezuela. His marriage to Margot Boulton in 1942 secured his entry into Caracas's highest social and business circles. He opened an investment firm, became a founding member of the Caracas Stock Exchange in 1947, and invested in a cement factory. Bottome held leadership positions in the North American Association and AmCham, and owned a share of the *Daily Journal*.

William Coles, another Dartmouth graduate, had a similar trajectory. A lawyer, Coles arrived in Caracas in 1940 in association with Bottome and Rockefeller to promote the Hotel Avila and other hotels. Coles subsequently became vice president and manager of the Venezuelan Basic Economy Corporation and the founder of the Caracas law firm of Coles and Valera with partners Raúl Valera and Salvador Itraido. He was a member of the Caracas Country Club and served as president of AmCham (1970), the North American Association, and the CVA. His numerous investments in Venezuela included cattle farms, the *Caracas Journal*, Mavesa (margarine and oil products), Lav-O-Mat, and Las Llaves. Others who succeeded in the dynamic postwar economic boom were people who brought special skills or new services to Venezuela, sometimes branching out to open their own businesses. Gerald O'Conner came to Venezuela in 1931 as an engineer with Raymond Concrete Pile Company (RCPC) in charge of building roads, dry docks, housing, and sanitation works for the oil companies and the government. By 1951 he was president and general manager of RCPC of Venezuela and president of the North American Association. Similarly, Jack Reynolds came to Caracas to open an office for the U.S. Life Insurance Company. In 1949, he established and became president of Seguros Venezuela, a firm that benefited in part from the U.S. law that allowed U.S. citizens living abroad to purchase a tax-free straight life insurance policy that could be used to pay inheritance taxes.[27]

Some U.S. diplomats also followed the traditional trajectory from the embassy to the boardroom in oil-rich Venezuela. Walter J. Donnelly, ambassador from 1947 to 1950, settled in Venezuela again in 1952 as the representative of U.S. Steel in Latin America. Charles Urruela, second secretary of the political section of the U.S. Embassy from 1954 to 1957, became assistant to the general manager of Siderúgica Venezolana SA in 1957.

American women seldom achieved that kind of prominence. Their work with libraries, the American Church (ecumenically Protestant), the American School, the Caracas Little Theater, the Venezuelan American Association of University Women (VAAUW), benevolent foundations, and the *Caracas Journal* reinforced ties within the U.S. community, and often with the Venezuelan social and economic elite as well. The most visible were probably those who wrote for the *Caracas Journal*. Dorothy Kamen-Kaye, a Phi Beta Kappa graduate of Goucher College, arrived in Venezuela in 1938 with her husband, Maurice, a geologist employed by the Caracas Petroleum Company. With some colleagues she compiled a binational cookbook in 1943 entitled *Buen Provecho*. Through her column on Venezuelan folklore, geography, and customs in the *Caracas Journal*, Kamen-Kaye encouraged her compatriots to learn more about Venezuela and its people.[28] Similarly, Ruth Robertson arrived in Venezuela in the 1940s and spent thirteen years there working for the oil companies, *National Geographic*, and the Venezuelan government's international airline, Linea Aeropostal Venezolana. A professional journalist, photographer, pilot, and intrepid explorer, Robertson conveyed her affection for and knowledge of Venezuela to her readers. She was especially taken with the "lost world" of the Guayana highlands and Angel Falls, and her work—much of it published in the *Caracas Journal*—helped to promote the exotic spot as a tourist destination.[29]

A talented and energetic member of a wealthy, artistic, elite family who married an influential U.S. citizen, Margot Boulton de Bottome had more influence in binational circles than Kamen-Kaye and Robertson. Boulton, who also wrote a column for the *Caracas Journal*, received the newspaper's annual Good Neighbor Award in 1954. In addition to her work with the CVA, she founded and led Intercambio, a women's group that aspired to encourage common interests and friendship between Venezuelan and American women.

Popular Culture, Amusements, and Consumption

People like the Bottomes and the Coleses, and Dale Carnegie courses, influenced the values and preferences of the Caracas elites and business executives. U.S. films, periodicals, music, advertisements, consumer products, and the English-language newspaper gave Americans a taste of home while providing Venezuelans with glimpses of the American way of life. U.S. films served a cultural and a financial mission for their sponsors. Sixty-five percent of the films shown in Venezuela in the 1950s came from the United States, and U.S. film distributers found the country to be a lucrative market. Venezuelan cities had greater access to U.S.-made films than did the small rural theaters that used only sixteen-millimeter film, most of which came from Argentina and Mexico. In 1951, three of the top six films shown in Venezuela were U.S. products: *The Great Caruso*, *King Solomon's Mines*, and *Love Affair*. Two others were Mexican, and only one was Venezuelan, a situation that caused Venezuelan filmmakers to complain that their government had to do more if it really wanted to encourage Venezuela's fledgling movie industry.

Television, which arrived in Venezuela in 1952, was dominated by wrestling, comedy and variety shows, and Cuban artists. U.S. shows did not initially take over the new medium, since a 1954 law more concerned about immorally long kisses than nationalism forbade foreign dramas made for television to be shown in Venezuela. U.S. advertisers did seize the opportunity to air commercials extolling the U.S. products that were flooding the new supermarkets and the Sears, Roebuck store.

In the 1950s, six of the most popular magazines in Venezuela were edited in the United States: *Temas*, *Selecciones* (*Reader's Digest*), *Life*, *Visión*, *Time*, and *Newsweek*. The Venezuelan Press Association and the Venezuelan Chamber of Magazine Editors protested that these journals, which frequently had no Venezuelan content at all or carried unflattering articles, undercut the national media. Magazine distributers also introduced Venezuelans to another American custom: door-to-door salespersons. Five U.S. women reported to the *Daily Journal* in 1955 that, in spite of their limited Spanish, most Venezuelans they solicited purchased at least one magazine from them.

Margot Boulton de Bottome witnessed and recorded the changing habits of middle-class and elite women in Caracas. In past years these women had dispatched their servants to shop in the noisy, smelly public markets. With the opening of the American-style CADA supermarkets, Margot encountered many of her acquaintances shopping for themselves. After all, what would their poor servant women know of Libby fruit cocktail, Kraft cheese spreads, Swanson chicken broth, Kounty Kist peas, Pillsbury piecrust mix, Reddi-Whip, frozen whipped potatoes, or imported "American lettuce," celery, apples, pears, and grapes? The supermarket ads in the *Daily Journal* touted the highly processed canned and frozen foods that became so popular with U.S. housewives in the 1950s and so profitable for the food-processing conglomerates. The ads also encouraged Venezuelans to celebrate U.S. holidays with U.S. customs and food. For Thanksgiving 1954, CADA promised that shoppers could find turkeys, Ocean Spray cranberry sauce, Bordon's mincemeat, Broiled 'n Butter mushrooms, and Libby pumpkin pie filling, among other delicacies.

Of course, processed food and labor-saving appliances helped Caracas women cope with the radical changes that the postwar boom had brought to their lives. Former maids sought out better-paying, and more dignified, jobs in factories, shops, and other businesses. Middle- and upper-class women spent more time in charitable activities, women's groups, and the new office and government jobs that had opened to them. In Venezuela, the number of women employed in office work rose from 8,742 in 1950 to 24,068 in 1961. During the same time, the number of women employed in services, sports, and diversions rose from 30,889 to 45,057. The frequent requirement that a job applicant be a *señorita de buena presencia* (a good-looking young woman) drew complaints that foreign employers in particular wanted to use women as *carnada* (bait) to attract more clients.

Some Venezuelan traditionalists were also aghast at the *carnada* aspect of flaunting the human body in skimpy bathing costumes in international beauty contests. Once Susana Duijim won the Miss World contest in 1955, however, there was no turning back. Beauty contest mania seized the country, and national honor required that a Venezuelan place among the finalists in the major international contests. Like their counterparts in the United States, the Venezuelan "Misses" represented not only national honor and feminine pulchritude but also automobiles, favored brands of whiskey, and washing machines.

Other popular U.S. entertainments did not transplant well to Venezuela. Various anglophone groups—including the American Church and the Cub Scouts—put on minstrel shows in the 1950s. Venezuelans often assumed blackface disguises during Carnival and tolerated laws that excluded black immigrants, but racial issues were too complex in that diverse society to invite such satire. Priding themselves on their color-blind *café con leche* society, Venezuelans expressed outrage when three Caracas hotels, including the Avila, turned away the African-American singer Robert Todd Duncan in May 1945 because of his race. Many reasoned that the insult reflected a misguided effort to cater to prejudiced foreign guests, and a law prohibiting discrimination in public services was passed within a week. Since Acción Democrática included many people of mixed race, political pressure grew in the following years to avoid any appearance of racism.[30]

Venezuelan baseball gave further evidence of the Caribbean melting pot and of spreading professionalism and commercialism. Reputedly introduced into Venezuela in the 1890s by students who had studied in the United States, baseball had grown in popularity. By the 1940s, Venezuela, Panama, Cuba, Puerto Rico, Mexico, and the Dominican Republic had well-organized amateur baseball leagues and held their own World Series. U.S. players, especially the giants of the U.S. Negro League, often competed with and against the Caribbean players, foreshadowing the inevitable day of integrated teams in the United States. The famous Leroy "Satchel" Paige claimed to have been chased by Indians with poison darts when he played in Maracaibo in the late 1930s.[31] An all-star team from the Negro League that included Jackie Robinson, Roy Campanella, Quincy Trouppe, Buck Leonard, and Gene Benson severely embarrassed the Venezuelan team in 1947.[32]

In December 1945 Venezuelans decided to separate amateur from professional baseball in the country and to associate with professional organized baseball in the United States. As a Venezuelan journalist wrote, from that time "relations between teams and players became more like employer-employee relations. . . . [T]he club owners began to act and think more like business executives."[33] Even that fact could not dampen Venezuelans' pleasure and pride in Chico Carrasquel's successful career with the Chicago White Sox in the 1950s. In recognition of his popularity in both societies the *Caracas Journal* named Carrasquel Good Neighbor of the Year in 1952.

Visions of the Venezuelan Neighbor

Venezuelans could not escape learning about the United States and its culture. Even had they wished to do so, they could not have launched an equivalent cultural barrage on U.S. citizens. By and large, it was left to U.S. visitors, tourists, businesspeople, and writers to interpret Venezuela to the larger English-speaking audience.

Between the death of Gómez and the end of the Pérez Jiménez regime, a few new books in English proposed to educate the U.S. public about Venezuela. Most of the authors were popular writers or journalists rather than academics and scholars. One of the few scholarly volumes to appear, Edwin Lieuwen's *Petroleum in Venezuela: A History* (1954), appealed to people with more of a practical interest in black gold than in Gómez's prisons or exotic jungles. A few books, such as Henry Allen's *Venezuela* (1941) and Erna Fergusson's *Venezuela* (1939), introduced South Americans to their hemispheric allies in the global conflict. Two, Lavin's *A Halo for Gómez* (1954) and Rourke's *Gómez: Tyrant of the Andes* (1936), told the picturesque story of the late dictator, albeit with obviously differing theses. William D. Marsland and Amy L. Marsland's *Venezuela through Its History* (1954) attempted a full-scale history, with popular overtones, to explain this nation whose "'past'—the way of life its people followed for centuries before any European saw its jungled strand—still exists."[34] A few science, adventure, and exploration books (e.g., L. R. Dennison, *Devil Mountain* [1942]; William Beebe, *High Jungle* [1949]; Earle T. Hanson, *Journey to Manaos* [1938]; and Norman MacDonald, *The Orchid Hunters* [1939]) trickled out in the *Green Mansions* tradition, but the attraction of the exotic understandably gave way to more prosaic themes during World War II and the 1950s.

The new focus emerged in Alfred Jankus and Neil Malloy's *Venezuela, Land of Opportunity* (1956). Jankus was an international management consultant who worked for a Coca Cola bottler in Venezuela and sat on the boards of directors of other Venezuelan corporations. Malloy, an engineer with Consolidated Edison Company of New York, came to Venezuela in 1949 as a consulting electrical engineer for a Caracas public utility company. Their book, aimed at investors, businesspeople, and the occasional tourist, described the economic and business climate with a casual nod to history, customs, and the challenges of living in Venezuela. The authors lauded the opportunities in what the book jacket bubbled was "the most exciting and promising country in the Western hemisphere, if not the whole world."

Many of the works by U.S. writers in the 1940s and 1950s shared a similar political viewpoint. Reminiscent of the "democratic caesar" debates, they referred to the "political immaturity"[35] of the Venezuelan population. Allen found that "no political mind existed" and that "obviously" the illiterate Juan Bimba "isn't ready to contribute anything to the democracy."[36] Lavin lavishly praised the dictatorship of Juan Vicente Gómez, which had brought so much order and progress to Venezuela, although with an occasional excess of force; and Allen thought that López Contreras encouraged a "passion for social service and public welfare."[37] Although Jankus and Malloy rather pointedly ignored Venezuela's political regime in 1956, they praised the progress Venezuela had seen under Pérez Jiménez and tersely advised tourists and business travelers not to discuss politics. The Marslands provided an exception when they lamented the existence of the dictatorship even to govern such an "immature" population.[38]

The books of the 1940s and 1950s, however, provided a new justification for dictatorship when they pointed out that democratic freedom might allow Communists to exploit the unsophisticated population. Jankus and Malloy, Allen, and Lavin all considered Venezuela an attractive target for the Communists, and they all characterized Rómulo Betancourt as a dangerous radical who used chicanery to manipulate his naive compatriots. Jankus and Malloy subtly suggested that the 1947 election had been meaningless and the voters uninformed: "To many the elections meant getting a day off from work, going to the polls, dunking the small finger into indelible ink (so they would not be tempted to vote more than once), and placing a colored piece of cardboard in a box, which indicated the party they preferred, or at least they color they liked best."[39] The authors implied that the 1948 *golpe* had ended three years of corrupt and demagogic government. In contrast, they conveyed the results of the fraudulent 1952 election in deadpan prose with no suggestion of impropriety.[40]

While recoiling from the horrors of communism, these works also drove nails into the coffins of the New Deal, progressivism, and labor advocacy. Allen evoked conservative criticism of Franklin Roosevelt's policies when he referred to slow-moving stevedores in Willemstad, Curaçao, as having "WPA speed."[41] Acknowledging that Venezuelan suffrage under General López Contreras was limited, Allen still judged López's government "immeasurably better than that government which Pendergast gave to Kansas City or the Long brothers gave to Louisiana."[42] Like the *Caracas Journal*, these writers expressed suspicion of the higher standard of living that the AD government had brought to the workers. After the 1948 *golpe*, Jankus and Malloy reported that labor leaders "quickly took a well-earned vacation," allowing management to enjoy a "new era."[43] Allen worried that the "spiritual lives" of the Venezuelans might be ruined by "too great or too prolonged government spending." The oil companies' provision of houses, clean water, and sanitary facilities for their workers was laudable, but Allen thought that such generosity encouraged the workers "to look on the oil industry as a sort of Santa Claus with a bottomless sack."[44] Workers probably wasted their benefits in "celebrating," he concluded, but the cooperation between labor, management, and government made Venezuela a "haven compared to Mexico, where the laborer stands in confused and unrequited idleness amidst the industrial bankruptcy his radical leaders have brought upon him."[45] In sum, most of the authors of the 1940s and 1950s identified what they considered progressive in Venezuela with their own political values: anticommunism, hostility to labor, probusiness, and a conviction that working people and the illiterate should leave the business of governing to their betters. Just as the New Dealers had mildly encouraged their counterparts in Venezuela, the Cold warriors preferred their own doppelgangers as allies.

Venezuelan Reactions: The *Liquiliqui* and "Sowing the Petroleum"

How did Venezuelans react to the barrage of ideology, people, money, and popular culture from the United States? Obviously, some interpreted the changes as signs of progress, indicators that they had left behind that dusty, rural Venezuela of the *joropo* (a popular dance) and the *liquiliqui* (the loose-fitting traditional rural suit). Others expressed concern about the disappearance of authentically Venezuelan culture and values, the repression of workers and political opposition, and the wisdom of spending the petroleum wealth on imported consumer goods, from tomatoes to brandy to automobiles. After Gómez's death, Arturo Uslar Pietri, among others, advised Venezuelans to *sembrar el petróleo* (sow the petroleum) so that the nation would have a diversified and productive economy after the nonrenewable resource was used up.

Even Pérez Jiménez, whose New National Ideal praised materialistic progress and welcomed foreigners, had no intention of playing simple toll taker for the foreigners. The dictatorship served foreign interests, but it had no laissez-faire agenda. Like the AD government before him, Pérez Jiménez presided over an activist government that set the rules of the economic game and also participated actively in it. Unlike the AD government, however, Pérez had no penchant for investing in human capital, social infrastructure like schools, or the national bourgeoisie. The dictatorship's censorship usually did not extend to economic matters. Few Venezuelans objected in principle to a strong government hand in the economy, and some nationalists publicly called for protectionism against the U.S. subsidiaries and the flood of foreign imports. Alejandro Hernández of Pampero Industries, which specialized in food processing and canning, complained that even government agencies purchased foreign canned tomatoes while his products moldered in warehouses. He pleaded not only for legislation to protect national industries but for a campaign to encourage Venezuelans to purchase goods made in Venezuela. In 1952, the government did decree that all Venezuelan products had to be stamped "Hecho en Venezuela," but the dictatorship did little else to protect local industry. The business association, Fedecámaras (Federation of Chambers and Associations of Commerce and Production, founded in 1944), frequently featured Hernández's views in its publication, *Venezuela Económica*. Since the membership included associates of the oil companies and commercial firms as well as industrial ones, however, Fedecámaras could not take an uncompromising position in favor of industrial protectionism.

The major daily papers usually attacked the economic policy with impunity. A highly respected economist with nationalist credentials, Domingo Felipe Maza Zavala, had a regular column in *El Nacional*. Especially vituperative about the 1952 trade treaty, Maza charged that Venezuela was squandering its petroleum revenues on U.S. imports and enriching shareholders of U.S. companies based in Venezuela.[46] Ultimately finding Maza's criticisms too sharp, the government forced the editors of *El Nacional* to suspend his column but tolerated his articles in the lower-profile *Venezuela Económica*.

Exiled Venezuelans could be even more frank. A prolific writer, AD leader Rómulo Betancourt published the fervently nationalistic *Venezuela: Política y Petróleo* in 1956 in Mexico. He and his fellow Social Democrats advocated national agricultural development through agrarian reform and credit, irrigation, technology, and mechanization. Betancourt characterized Pérez Jiménez's economic policy as "submissive and colonialist" and his dictatorship as an "instrument" of the multinational oil companies. The nation should favor domestic entrepreneurs through import-substitution industrialization and should gain control of the petroleum industry in order to sow its benefits more widely, he said. Betancourt also insisted that economic development could proceed only in a climate of democracy and respect for civil liberties.

If some Venezuelans criticized the dictator's economic policies, others rejected the rampant materialism and cultural changes that they identified with the hydrocarbon society and the "American way of life." Many Venezuelans rejected the European influence as well, but essayist Mariano Picón Salas echoed César Zumeta when he wrote that the numerous Italian immigrants, the children of Botticelli, at least contributed to the survival of a Mediterranean identity in the face of the anglophone invasion. Picón also invoked the *arielismo* of José Enrique Rodó and the Enlightenment universalism of Bolívar when he called for a north-south concord based on true Jeffersonian principles rather than on the "greedy empiricism of businessmen." The spirits of Jefferson, Emerson, Henry George, Thorstein Veblen, and Simón Bolívar, among others, would bless such an alliance, Picón believed.[47] The true essence of the "good neighbor" was spiritual, he asserted, because good relations "can't be measured only in commercial trade or in exchange of material goods."[48]

Writers in the popular Venezuelan press sometimes lacked Picón's erudition, but they too expressed concern. Juana de Avila complained that in Caracas she could easily find hot dogs and "very hygienic sandwiches, wrapped in cellophane paper," but not the traditional "rich home-made *arepas* [corn meal muffins]" stuffed with mouth-watering butter and fresh local cheese. "This is not Caracas," she concluded, but an unknown world, filled with "humanity coming from the four corners of the earth, an ambience so cosmopolitan that in some restaurants we are almost embarrassed to speak Spanish."[49] One of the most frequent laments deplored the radical change in Christmas customs. In place of the traditional manger scenes, homemade *hallacas* (cornmeal dumplings with flavorful fillings), the celebration of the Three Wise Men, and folk games like "looking for the Christ child," Venezuelans had taken up Santa Claus, snow-decorated shop windows, and lighted

Christmas trees. One observer shuddered at watching the Three Wise Men speeding to their destination in 1951 in a convertible decorated with Pepsi Cola signs. "Our children look with curiosity at this other Christmas that comes to them in a ship's hold or in the belly of a Pan Am clipper."[50]

Novelist Enrique Bernardo Núñez, writing in *El Nacional*, was less troubled by external changes in the popular culture than by Venezuelans who scorned their country. Having heard of a pregnant Venezuelan who rushed to the United States so that her baby could be born there, Núñez pitied the child who had lost a national birthright. A Venezuelan might dance an authentic *joropo* and yet be indifferent to true nationalism, Núñez charged, for "customs alone do not make a national soul. Soul does not consist of eating criollo food, dressing like a *llanero* and dancing at traditional festivals."[51]

Thoughtful Venezuelans chronicled other behavior that violated their traditional moral standards. Although Venezuelans fought to adopt fair-skinned blond war orphans in 1950, they ignored the increasing numbers of abandoned children in Caracas. (One writer for the *Caracas Journal* proposed that the abandoned Venezuelan children be put to work serving visitors in luxury hotels like the Tamanaco.)[52] The burgeoning number of brothals, divorces, games of Russian roulette, and suicides in Caracas prompted Raúl Aguido-Freitez to write that Venezuela was "a society in a state of crisis, which easily absorbs foreign currents that stimulate evil, and in which only material values prevail."[53]

The newspaper *La Religión* outspokenly attacked the 1950s materialism that its writers identified with U.S. values and culture. Editorialists alleged that the "avalanche" of Protestants in the country brought poorly prepared pastors and those who, like the Jehovah's Witnesses, posed a danger to nationalism.[54] Moreover, "luxury in dress, in vehicles, in too many comforts in the home, in the dances of so-called high society" wasted money that could help the poor.[55] Easy wealth was causing Venezuelans to lose their "strong, manly customs" of hard work, and labor-saving appliances tempted housewives to hours of idleness painting their nails before the television set.[56]

The jeremiads of *La Religión* intensified after the publication of the 1 May 1957 pastoral of Monsignor Rafael Arias Blanco, archbishop of Caracas. The prelate took the dictatorship to task for its rampant materialism and callous inattention to social justice for the poor. In spite of the government's warnings, the editor of *La Religión*, Father Jesús Hernández Chapellin, stepped up the attacks and allowed the clandestine Junta Patriótica to publish some of its leaflets on the cathedral press. In January 1958 Pérez Jiménez arrested Father Hernández and other priests who had openly criticized the regime.[57]

By then, however, the dictator's days were numbered. He left the country on 23 January, making way for the ultimate return to power of Rómulo Betancourt and the civilian politicians. The dictatorship fell surprisingly easily, but the social and popular effects of the new hydrocarbon economy would remain.

From the 1930s to the 1960s, both Venezuela and the United States changed radically, and their interdependent relationship also altered. World War II and the nuclear bomb, the devastation of Europe, and the great fear of communism that drove the cold war propelled the United States to global power. Washington analysts believed that the maintenance of peace required a tranquil and homogeneous hemisphere and secure access to critical resources like petroleum. U.S. businessmen and investors fanned out across the globe, hoping to find opportunity and to fashion foreign economic structures more compatible with U.S. interests. U.S. journalists and media, advertisers and products, and purveyors and interpreters of popular culture also contributed to the crusade against communism and backwardness and for the "American way of life."

The *Vade-Mecum*'s hyperbole had become reality. Venezuela's petroleum finally drew the attention of the United States. More than at any other time in the nation's history, Venezuela stood unequivocally within the U.S. sphere of influence. The petroleum-producing country had less control over the pricing and marketing of its own product than did the transnational oil companies based in the United States. With European economies devastated by war and reshaped by the cold war, Venezuela found that its major petroleum customer and protector had also become its primary supplier of imports. Many Venezuelans welcomed the prosperity but deplored their excessive dependence on the United States. Nationalists wanted Venezuela to gain control of the petroleum industry, its nascent industrialization, and its own economic development. They hoped to construct an authentic national identity that would be modern while still retaining something of the ideals that they projected onto their historical hero, Simón Bolívar.

For the remainder of the twentieth century, Venezuela and the United States wrestled to accommodate their binational relationship to national interests and to the exigencies of a global economy and an increasingly global culture. Would there be room for both Coca Cola and Pampero rum? For Tío Conejo and Mickey Mouse?

8   From Hemispheric to Global Perspectives, 1958–1990s

> Today the Americas—North and South—recognize that they re-
> quire a global as well as a regional vision if they are to resolve their
> problems.
>
> —Henry A. Kissinger, 17 February 1976

Most of the shifting balance of U.S.-Venezuelan relations
after 1958 was played out in the global context of the cold war. Democratic Venezuela stood squarely with the United States and the West
but did not interpret all cold war issues in the same way that the United
States did. Secretary of State Henry A. Kissinger recognized that both
North and South America needed "a global as well as a regional vision," but he neglected to add that there were several global visions.[1]
As a developing nation, Venezuela did not share the priorities of the
United States, although its oil wealth occasionally limited its effective
alliance with other developing nations. A democratic ideology and the
hydrocarbon economy brought Venezuela and the United States closer
than ever, but the two nations viewed the world and each other from
different perspectives. As national issues intersected global ones, some
essentially binational diplomacy occurred in a broader context.

A democratic and Third World outlook revived Venezuela's commitment to the universalism first inspired by Simón Bolívar's generation.
The nature of petroleum exploitation and marketing, added to communication and transportation advances, further encouraged a global
strategy. Its relations with the United States continued to be primary
for Venezuela, but Caracas expanded and strengthened other international ties as well. The United Nations provided new opportunities for
weak nations to work together. The Organization of Petroleum Exporting Countries (OPEC) introduced new allies beyond the hemisphere
and reinvented the Mediterranean ties that César Zumeta and Mariano

199

Picón Salas had revered. This expansiveness did not represent a turning away from the Western Hemisphere. Venezuelans believed that many hemispheric issues were also global ones and that international coalitions might check U.S. hegemony more easily than the Washington-dominated Organization of American States.

Incidentally, the technical complexity of international issues placed a heavy burden on politicians and statesmen from developing nations. Venezuelans increasingly went to U.S. universities to study economics, ecology, administration, biotechnology, marine science, and engineering. Conversely, U.S. analysts studied and drew conclusions from Venezuela's geological, social, political, and economic landscapes. More than ever, a binational pool of technocrats informed the policies of both nations.

If oil and a new internationalism dominated Venezuela's outlook, Washington confidently exercised its global leadership until the 1970s, when the debacle of the war in Vietnam, the specter of an oil shortage that would alter the American way of life, the humiliation of the Iranian revolution, and a faltering economy made the world a hostile and unpredictable arena. The perceived arrogance of the OPEC cartel stoked fears that revolution, other races, and non-American systems posed new challenges to America. Even the Western Hemisphere seemed to be drifting out of control with Venezuela's nationalization of iron and oil in 1975 and 1976 and the rise of socialist governments in Grenada and Nicaragua in 1979.

Venezuela and the rest of the developing world, however, faltered on the shoals of the worst economic crisis they had seen since the 1930s—in Venezuela's case, since 1902. The late 1970s represented the high tide of what might have been a new configuration of global forces. The United States, under the twelve years of Ronald Reagan's and George Bush's leadership, recaptured the initiative with rhetoric, bluster, and a renewed willingness to deploy military force, covertly or overtly, in the hemisphere and elsewhere.

After 1989, the sudden collapse of the USSR and the communist world cleared the way for a different world order, but it was not clear how Latin America or the United States would fit into that new order.

In the face of thriving East Asian economies and the promise of the European Community, however, economic reality seemed to encourage an American economic community headed by the United States. Venezuela maintained a defensive, or cautious, approach of simultaneously seeking firmer economic ties both with the United States and with other global trading partners.

Petroleum and Globalism: New Strategies, Traditional Goals

The idiosyncrasies of the world petroleum market affected much of the interaction between Venezuela and the United States between 1958 and the 1990s. Simply stated, oil shortages strengthened Venezuela's autonomy and bargaining position, and oil gluts had the opposite effect. Venezuela's goals remained unchanged from the days of Gómez: to limit the power of the multinational petroleum companies and maximize the national return from the industry. A weak nation would have difficulty confronting either Standard Oil or the United States government. Venezuela's major contribution to the desired new international economic order for developing nations lay in the founding of the Organization of Petroleum Exporting Countries in Baghdad in September 1960.

From the time of the democratic *trienio*, Juan Pablo Pérez Alfonzo had puzzled over how Venezuela could control its petroleum industry. During his exile in the United States, Pérez found the model he sought in the Texas Railroad Commission, which had tried in the 1930s to regulate oil production.[2] Pérez Alfonzo realized that Venezuela alone could not bring the multinational companies to heel. Either the U.S. government or some other oil-producing nations had to join the effort. Outraged by the waste in the hydrocarbon societies of Venezuela and the United States, Pérez Alfonzo also became an advocate of conservation of the nonrenewable natural resource.

After Rómulo Betancourt became the president of Venezuela in 1959 and named Pérez Alfonzo to be his minister of mines and hydrocarbons, the minister worked to convert his ideas into policy. The struggling democratic government reeled under the impact of Washington's March 1959 quotas on imported oil, emphasizing Venezuela's vulnerability to foreign actions. The legislated quotas remained in force for fourteen years, with some tinkering, and replaced the 1957 system of "voluntary" quotas. The 1959 legislation reflected the political ascendency in the United States of the independent oil producers and some of their Texas advocates, including Speaker of the House Sam Rayburn and Senate Majority Leader Lyndon Johnson. The U.S. oilmen also used the 1958 recession to argue that national security demanded the protection of the domestic oil industry. The quota bill exempted Mexican and Canadian oil on the grounds that it arrived "overland," and hit Venezuela especially hard because 40 percent of Venezuela's exports went to the United States. Venezuelans felt doubly betrayed after their loyalty during World War II and their moderation toward the oil companies compared with Mexico's 1938 nationalization. Pérez Alfonzo lobbied U.S. government officials to assign petroleum quotas as they did sugar quotas; that is, the quotas should go to governments, not to the multinational companies. He received no response from the Eisenhower administration.[3]

Rebuffed in Washington, Pérez Alfonzo attended the Arab Oil Congress in Cairo in April 1959 and spoke with Saudi oil adviser Abdullah Tariki, whose views he knew to be similar to his own. Tariki and Pérez Alfonzo called a secret meeting with the representatives of Iran, Iraq, and Kuwait and hammered out a gentleman's agreement that advocated the formation of national oil companies, consultation among producing nations, defense of the price structure, development of domestic refining, and 60 percent of industry profits for the producing nations. In 1960 the multinational oil companies, hurt by the U.S. import quotas and by competition from the Soviet Union, which had reentered the global oil market, sharply cut their posted oil prices without consulting the host nations. Angered by that unilateral action, the signatories of the gentleman's agreement met in Baghdad in September 1960 to form the Organization of Petroleum Exporting Companies. The organization initially had little influence, but for Venezuela it simultaneously represented the Bolivarian call for a confederation of the weak against the strong and the beginning of national control over the petroleum industry.

Venezuela's democratic government further used its taxation policy and a wily strategy of divide and conquer to weaken the alliance between the multinational oil companies and the merchants and industrialists of Fedecámaras. In 1966 President Raúl Leoni's AD government decreed a modest increase in the low personal and corporate income taxes. The oil companies and the Venezuelan private sector joined forces to demand that the government roll back the changes. Leoni privately settled with the oil companies in September 1966, leaving the Venezuelan private sector looking selfish and foolish. Venezuelan entrepreneurs promptly lost their enthusiasm for defending the oil companies against the threats of regulation or even nationalization.

The shape of U.S.-Venezuelan oil relations in the 1970s also responded to factors beyond the control of the two nations: global market changes and Middle Eastern politics. By the late 1960s higher oil prices driven by unprecedented world demand and by the end of the surplus in the United States momentarily aided Venezuela's cause. One analyst summed up Venezuela's gains as attributable to "a remarkable mixture of acumen, skill, and outright luck."[4] The 1967 Six-Day War closed the Suez Canal, and in September 1969 Libya's Mu ammar al-Gadhafi threatened to shut down production if the posted price were not increased. The fact that the winter of 1969–70 was the coldest in thirty years in the United States helped OPEC win credibility and higher prices by 1971. In May 1973 President Richard Nixon signaled U.S. vulnerability—and the triumph of the multinationals over the independent producers—when he abolished the quota on imported oil.

Encouraged by the Middle Eastern producers, Venezuela announced in late 1970 that it would raise its share of profits to 60 percent and that in the future it would raise prices unilaterally, without consulting the companies.[5] The relationship between the petroleum producers and the multinationals had come full circle. The time seemed propitious for nationalization, and Caracas informed the companies in 1971 that their concessions would automatically revert to the state when they began to expire in 1983. The companies hastened the day of nationalization when they refused to finance new exploration and allowed machinery to depreciate.

Venezuela's Middle Eastern alliance bolstered the nation's influence worldwide but drove a wedge between Caracas and Washington. In 1973, in the wake of the Arab-Israeli War, the Arab nations implemented an OPEC oil embargo to punish Israel's allies. Although an OPEC member, Venezuela respected the importance of the U.S. market—and perhaps implicitly the priority of the Western Hemisphere over the Mediterranean—and defied the embargo by continuing to ship oil to the United States.

The petroleum-driven events fed a belief that a new world economic order had dawned. Venezuelan president Carlos Andrés Pérez (1974–80) flaunted his populism, nationalism, and Third World identity. In contrast, the debacle in Vietnam and the resignation of President Richard Nixon in 1974 made the United States seem on the verge of losing its position as hegemon. U.S. President Gerald Ford and Secretary of State Henry Kissinger employed bombastic public diplomacy to reassert U.S. dominance. Relations between Venezuela and the United States fell to a new low.

In early 1974 a State Department spokesman pointed out the enormous leap in earnings that petroleum producers had recently experienced, concluding that "never in history has such transfer of resources occurred without a war."[6] Such statements not only aroused the envy of non–petroleum producers among the developing nations but also suggested that the great powers would fight to retain their access to petroleum. Secretary Kissinger hinted that the United States was prepared to use force to seize petroleum fields if U.S. national security was at stake. Then, Washington launched an economic salvo in 1974 when the U.S. Congress excluded OPEC members, including Venezuela, from the tariff preferences granted to developing nations. Caracas railed against the injustice of punishing a nation that had shipped oil to the United States throughout the Arab boycott. Venezuelans, heavily dependent on U.S. food imports, charged that it was inhumane to use food as a weapon.

Rhetorical battles raged between Venezuelan and U.S. spokesmen. In September 1974 President Gerald Ford went before the United Nations and lamented the mood of economic confrontation and threatened that the United States would not permit the "wealthy" petroleum producers to gouge consumers with their high prices. In a letter distributed to major newspapers in the United States, President Carlos Andrés Pérez responded that the developed nations had exploited weaker nations for generations. They had paid artificially low prices for primary products from developing nations and then inflated the market value of the industrial products they exported. "Great countries have created the economic confrontation by denying equal participation to developing nations who need to balance their terms of trade."[7] Venezuela had not, and would not, use petroleum as a political weapon, Pérez stated. OPEC members wanted only to secure a fair balance between the value of raw materials and industrial goods in order to finance their own development. President Pérez's apologia circulated widely, but the principal focus of Caracas's campaign was the United States. Venezuelan leaders knew they had to frame their case skillfully for the U.S. Congress and public.

This particular campaign in public diplomacy was an uphill battle for Venezuela and its customary allies, the multinational oil companies. U.S. citizens hated the culprits who had made them lower their thermostats and wait in long lines at gas stations. Senator Henry "Scoop" Jackson, in hearings before the Senate Interior Committee (Permanent Subcommittee on Investigations), reflected that resentment when he referred to the "obscene profits" that the multinationals had made during the oil embargo. To defuse the public bitterness, Venezuela had to separate itself from the multinationals in the popular mind. Standard Oil might be a monster, but Venezuela had to portray itself as a hapless, but principled, victim.

Venezuela also took its case to an international audience. In October 1974 Foreign Minister Efraín Schacht Aristeguieta associated Venezuela with other poor and powerless developing nations. He threw down the gauntlet by asserting in the United Nations that "the welfare of one-third of the world is being achieved at the expense of the other two-thirds: one industrialized country alone, with only six percent of the world's population, uses, for itself, more than half of the mineral resources of the world."[8] The new international economic order could be achieved, Schacht promised, through collective action in the United Nations. The weak nations each had one vote; acting together they could end the hegemony of the few powerful and rich countries. As evidence of a real south-south alliance, the minister reported that Venezuela contributed up to 12 percent of its GDP in development aid to poorer nations, compared with an average of 1 percent of the GDP provided by developed nations. Schacht touched on another popular David and Goliath theme when he called for chemical and nuclear disarmament so that smaller states could not be victimized by the wars of the powerful. General disarmament would further enhance the value of small states by nullifying the argument that a state's greatness depended on its capacity for destruction, the minister argued.

Venezuelan writers and associations joined in the lobbying. Domingo Alberto Rangel, a popular analyst and pundit, began *La Invasión de Mr. Ford* with a quotation from Fidel Castro, who had characterized the petroleum crisis as a "crisis of a policy of irrational exploitation and waste of world energy resources" that simultaneously produced "astronomical earnings" for the multinational companies and took advantage of underdeveloped producing countries.[9]

Temperatures cooled a bit after Secretary of State Kissinger initiated a "new dialogue." Neither the United States nor the multinational companies raised obstacles to Venezuela's nationalization of the iron industry in 1975 and oil in 1976. Petroleum issues subsequently faded as sources of disagreement between the two nations. Conflicts over U.S. quotas, or, conversely, of U.S. access to Venezuela's petroleum, could always resurface, but Venezuela's nationalization of the petroleum industry altered the game. Instead of pitting the nation against the multinational companies—or the U.S. government—Venezuelan elites contended with each other to design the best national petroleum policy. New challenges abounded: the sometimes fragile OPEC cartel had to be maintained; non-OPEC nations offered unpredictable competition; the multinational companies retained control of oil transport, of technology, and of marketing. The new context for "sowing the petroleum" was global.

The international petroleum market turned against Venezuela and the south-south strategy when the petroleum shortage became another glut in 1985. The developed nations had slowed their consumption rates, and new fields in Alaska, Mexico, and the North Sea came into production. In 1977 the OPEC nations had controlled two-thirds of the free world's crude oil; by 1982 their share had shrunk to slightly less than half.[10] High prices returned briefly during the second oil shock that accompanied the Iranian revolution in December 1978 and continued with the Iran-Iraq War. In October 1981 OPEC prices went up for the last time for a decade. An expanded world supply ended panic buying and encouraged prices to ease back down. In late 1985 OPEC announced that the situation required a fight for market share, not profits. Petroleum producers, like other nations, were buffeted by a cycle of inflation, tighter money policy, and rising interest rates. Resources and capital flowed again in the traditional path from the poor producing nations to the rich consuming nations.

The international petroleum economy touched off Venezuela's worst economic downturn since the days of Cipriano Castro. Domestic political debate again focused on domestic issues of equity and development. Economic weakness, widespread corruption, and political divisions checked Venezuela's efforts to play a more aggressive international role. The 1970s rhetoric and policies had both fed the Bolivarian dreams of resuming a leadership role and aspired to use the developing nations' support to challenge U.S. hegemony. The 1980s required a change of tactics.

If the 1980s downturn transformed Venezuela from assertive creditor to cautious debtor, the nation could not afford to return entirely to a defensive or isolationist policy. Democratic Venezuela's participation in global forums continued to place a high priority on democratic values and human rights, international economic justice, the juridical equality of states, decolonization, and disarmament. On all issues, Caracas kept a wary eye fixed on Washington, trying to accommodate Venezuelan interests to U.S. priorities. After all, Washington retained the power to express displeasure by throwing Venezuela's economy into a tailspin with import restrictions.

Venezuela and the United States on the Global Stage

Venezuela's international interests and perspectives sometimes corresponded with those of the United States and sometimes conflicted. For example, Washington and Caracas usually defended human rights, but they did not always agree on how to deal with Castro's Cuba. Venezuela's OPEC alliance with the Arab nations made it difficult to consistently endorse Washington's uncompromising support of Israel. If Venezuelan statesmen were wary of relations with Israel, however, they admired and tried to emulate some aspects of that nation's foreign policy. Venezuelan analysts recommended that Venezuela should, like other small and weak countries, use multilateral bodies and alliances to compensate for its weakness. The Organization of American States provided a hemispheric forum, but the international membership of the United Nations was a more promising venue. The United States was omnipotent in the OAS but less able to ride roughshod over the UN.

Like many developing nations, Venezuela used the bully pulpit of the United Nations to make points at home as well as abroad. Many Venezuelan speeches in the UN, complete with attacks on the great hegemonic powers, were carried live on national television. Mediterranean ties with OPEC nations and cooperation with African leaders played well in Venezuela's *café con leche* population. The highly visible (and mostly sincere) commitment to the new international economic order preempted some dissatisfaction at home by diverting attention away from Venezuela's own wealthy families and companies. Venezuela's sometimes rhetorical embracing of developing nations and attacks on the United States projected an image of autonomy and confidence. The Venezuelan media's coverage of their nation's international role fomented a stronger global outlook among informed Venezuelans. The nation's internationalism, and the strategy of multilateral alliances, contrasted with many U.S. citizens' continuing belief in the exceptionalism and unquestioning right to world leadership of the United States.

Domestic conditions and Washington's priorities both tempered Venezuela's global activism. The vulnerable democratic Venezuelan government in the 1960s frequently echoed Washington's cold war perspective in the United Nations (and even more so in the OAS). Between 1959 and 1970, the communist guerrillas supported by Fidel Castro posed a greater threat than either the U.S. government or multinational firms. Venezuela did not even restore diplomatic relations (broken in 1952) with the Soviet Union until 1970. Although eager for allies among the developing nations, Caracas remained aloof from the Non-Aligned Movement because of its aggressive political agenda and Castro's high visibility in the group. Instead, the Venezuelans concentrated on UN bodies that focused on economic issues, like the United Nations Conference on Trade and Development (UNCTAD) and the "Group of 77" developing nations.

Higher oil revenues, the apparent popularity of the democratic government, the end of the guerrilla threat, and the lessening of U.S.-USSR tensions allowed Venezuela to strike out more independently in the 1970s. Germany's Willy Brandt and his Social Democrats (often through the Socialist International) and the Christian Democratic International encouraged AD and COPEI, respectively, in some debates. Venezuelan statesmen Simón Alberto Consalvi, Ramón Escovar Salom, Manuel Pérez Guerrero, Kaldone Nweihed, Juan Pablo Pérez Alfonzo, and Arístides Calvani, among others, earned credibility in the United Nations through their experience in specialized issues. If these men won acclaim for their talents and expertise, Venezuela's other diplomatic appointments sometimes served their country less well. Limited university education in international affairs meant that, aside from petroleum policy, Venezuela lacked a deep pool of experts. For example, scholar Jorge Rondón Uzcátegui advocated that Venezuela expand relations with African nations but had to acknowledge that few Venezuelans had studied or knew much about Africa.[11]

The UN Law of the Sea Conference, one session of which was held in Caracas in 1974, illustrated the complexity of Venezuelan international politics. Venezuela joined the developing nations to insist on international control of deep seabed minerals, the "common heritage of mankind," in spite of U.S. resistance to such a policy. On the other hand, since Venezuelan oil had to traverse the narrow Caribbean passageways, Venezuela voted with the United States and other maritime powers to limit the expanse of territorial sea that a nation could claim and potentially close to maritime traffic. Caracas supported the establishment of a moderate twelve-mile territorial sea (a claim that Pérez Jiménez had asserted for Venezuela unilaterally in 1956) but sided with the developing nations to establish a nation's full economic rights over its continental shelf and an extended economic zone (EEZ) of two hundred miles. The EEZ, unlike the territorial sea, allowed free, unrestricted passage of international shipping. Venezuela's Third World sympathies gave way to national interests in other cases. The Windward Islands lost access to a broader economic zone, for example, when Venezuela insisted that Aves Island merited its own economic zone. The island, far to the north of the Venezuelan coast, arguably was uninhabited in spite of the tenuous presence of a naval station.

In the end, both the United States and Venezuela refused to ratify the Law of the Sea when the final draft emerged in 1982. The United States objected to the plan that would distribute wealth from the deep seabeds and require developed nations to share technology with poor nations. (After securing changes in these clauses, Washington ratified the treaty in 1994.) Venezuela would not accept binding and obligatory arbitration of disputed maritime boundaries. Obligatory arbitration had been attractive in the 1890s dispute with Great Britain, but Venezuela's armed forces in the 1970s opposed forced arbitration of Venezuela's boundary disputes with Guyana and Colombia.

Venezuela's internationalism had fewer contradictions when the UN debate turned to halting the arms race, especially the proliferation of nuclear arms. Simón Alberto Consalvi, the Venezuelan ambassador to the UN, argued that small nations had both economic and strategic stakes in disarmament. "Limited" nuclear war meant that the nuclear powers expected limited destruction in their own territories, but small neighboring nations might well be devastated by tactical nuclear weapons. In 1976–77, Consalvi sat on a UN study commission that highlighted the relationship between the money spent on arms and the poverty of the developing world. The developed nations, the report concluded, made money by exporting arms. In spite of its high-minded stand, Venezuela became the only developing nation to purchase sophisticated F-16 fighter-bombers from the United States in the early 1980s. During that decade, Venezuela had the highest per capita military expenditures in Latin America, although the sum represented a relatively small portion of its GDP. The presence of Cuba and the necessity to defend the oil fields, Venezuelan leaders argued, necessitated the military expenditures.

Conflicting interests required Venezuela to temporize in condemning violence and intervention. Venezuela held a seat on the UN Security Council in 1986 when the United States bombed Libya, an OPEC member. Caracas compromised by abstaining on the UN resolution that condemned the U.S. bombing but refusing to support an OPEC oil embargo against the United States. President Jaime Lusinchi accompanied the pragmatic actions in the United Nations with a public statement that criticized the use of violence to resolve international conflicts.

Drawing again on Bolívar, Venezuela sided in the UN with those who endorsed national self-determination and decolonization. Caracas voted for the independence of Namibia, for a homeland for Palestine (with obvious implications for the U.S. support of Israel in the UN), and, usually, for Cuban-sponsored calls for the full independence of Puerto Rico. At the height of the Venezuelan economic crisis in August 1987, however, the U.S. ambassador to Venezuela, Otto Reich (an advocate of Jeanne Kirkpatrick's argument that rhetorical stands do have consequences), conducted an energetic campaign in Venezuela against the Puerto Rican independence resolution. Reich arranged a satellite hookup that allowed the U.S. ambassador to the United Nations, Vernon Walters, to speak directly with Venezuelan opinion leaders. Cowed for the moment, President Jaime Lusinchi ordered Venezuela to abstain on the vote.

Consistent with its history of acting to secure control over its own petroleum resources, Venezuela supported a new international economic order in the UN. Manuel Pérez Guerrero, chair of the UNCTAD in the

1970s, was an outstanding internationalist whose long experience and conciliatory skills gained the respect of representatives from both rich and poor nations. Even while working to secure a transfer of resources from wealthy to poorer nations, however, Venezuelan spokesmen continued to insist that progress should not be measured by material factors alone. Speaking before the UN General Assembly in October 1975, Foreign Minister Ramón Escovar Salom denounced "unrestrained consumerism" and an exclusive focus on material assets as "the most notorious aberrations of that world order."[12]

In 1988 Foreign Minister Consalvi acknowledged that the developing nations had failed to alter the world's economic order. The economic crisis of the 1980s, he observed, was global, but the developed nations had the power to deal unilaterally or bilaterally with the issues. Consalvi might also have censured the erratic nature of cooperation among the developing nations whose interests, like those of wealthier countries, varied from issue to issue. Venezuela voted sometimes as a relatively wealthy petroleum producer and sometimes as a developing nation with a $3,881 per capita gross domestic product (1982).

Finally, Venezuela's democratic governments forcefully defended human rights and condemned racism in the United Nations. President Carlos Andrés Pérez reminded visiting African diplomats of the "strong presence of African tradition in our people, in our folklore."[13] At minimal risk of inciting U.S. retaliation Caracas could express a Third World solidarity and sometimes defy cold war policies. For example, Caracas condemned apartheid in South Africa and refused to support the racist minority in Zimbabwe. Like Cuba and many developing nations, Venezuela espoused a broad humanitarian definition of human rights, including the fulfillment of basic human needs like food, shelter, education, and health care.

By the 1980s some Venezuelans believed that the Cuban government did not deserve to be singled out by Washington's unwavering hostility, and Caracas often abstained or voted against U.S. resolutions in the UN to censure Cuba. The UN votes against censure, like the one in March 1987, often provoked controversy at home, for some Venezuelans deplored Cuba's lack of liberty and could not forgive Castro's support of Venezuelan guerrillas in the 1960s.

In sum, Venezuela played a game of Tío Conejo and Tío Tigre with the United States in the United Nations. Caracas sometimes joined the other rabbits to tease the tiger and sometimes expediently bowed before the tiger's roar.

Hemispheric Legacies: Monroe and Bolívar

Within the hemisphere, Venezuela shared with other Latin American nations a cultural affinity, a Third World perspective, and the legacy of Bolívar's Pan-Americanism. At the same time, the nation's relative wealth and the dependence of its hydrocarbon economy on the United States weakened its Latin American solidarity. Moreover, Washington still drew on the tradition of James Monroe and John Quincy Adams to claim the Western Hemisphere, especially the Caribbean, as a special zone of U.S. influence. Policies that advanced Venezuelan (and Latin American) goals of autonomy or a new international economic order directly reduced the U.S. hegemony. Washington gave lip service to continental unity but generally preferred bilateral relations to effective multilateral action. Thus, the inter-American system—including the Organization of American States, the Rio Treaty, and the Inter-American Bank—customarily reflected Latin American priorities poorly. As Carlos Andrés Pérez put it, Latin America did not take "an active part" in designing the OAS or in "defining the objectives of the inter-American system."[14]

After 1958, three issues remained paramount for Venezuela in the hemisphere: support for democracy, negotiation of regional economic pacts and debt relief, and encouragement of effective multilateral action. Although the United States avowed commitment to the same goals, Washington's definitions and priorities often diverged from those of Venezuela.

President John F. Kennedy's Latin American policy, epitomized by the Alliance for Progress, called for a commitment to democracy, social reform, and economic development in the hemisphere. Rómulo Betancourt's (1959–64) unwavering democratic values made him an outstanding model for the new era. Betancourt's years in exile and his

State Department mentors had taught him the acceptable limits to Latin American nationalism. Since his principal domestic enemies were communist guerrillas, Betancourt easily secured the military and diplomatic support that Washington had been unwilling to grant in 1948. Presidential visits were exchanged. President Kennedy visited Caracas in December 1961 to emphasize his support of Betancourt's democratic reformism, and Betancourt made an official trip to the United States in early 1963. The two presidents appeared to enjoy a warm personal relationship based on mutual trust.[15]

Betancourt found, however, that his own commitment to hemispheric democracy surpassed that of Kennedy and subsequent U.S. presidents. Washington appreciated Betancourt's anticommunism but balked at his demand that the American nations break relations with all dictatorships, including those of the Somoza family in Nicaragua and Rafael Trujillo in the Dominican Republic. In 1961 President Kennedy mused on what sort of government would arise in the Dominican Republic following Trujillo's assassination: a democratic regime, a dictatorship like Trujillo's, or a communist government like Fidel Castro's. He concluded, "We ought to aim at the first, but we really can't renounce the second until we are sure that we can avoid the third."[16] The United States still feared that the "immaturity" of Latin American populations made them susceptible to demagogic appeals. Betancourt countered that popular Latin American hostility toward the United States, seen in the 1958 attacks on Vice President Richard Nixon, derived from the valid resentment at Washington's courting of dictators, and not from immaturity.

After Rafael Trujillo underwrote a bomb attack that nearly killed Betancourt in 1960, Eisenhower's government reluctantly agreed to OAS sanctions against the Dominican Republic, but neither Eisenhower nor Kennedy would adopt a general policy of isolating dictators. When new democratic governments succumbed to military takeovers (El Salvador in 1961, Peru and Argentina in 1962, Ecuador and Honduras in 1963, Brazil and Bolivia in 1964), the United States routinely extended diplomatic recognition to the de facto regimes. Betancourt could not convince Washington that a continental isolation of dictators had the same priority as the World War II hemispheric solidarity against fascists.

Betancourt did, however, win one symbolic victory in his campaign against dictators. Former Venezuelan dictator Marcos Pérez Jiménez had taken up residence in Miami after he was ousted from power in January 1958, and in 1959 Betancourt's government requested his extradition, arguing that his self-enrichment in office and his abuses of human rights were common crimes for which he should be held legally responsible. The five years of U.S. court hearings on the Pérez Jiménez case demonstrated that both Betancourt and Pérez Jiménez had learned to cultivate allies within the United States. The case became a political referendum on U.S. policy in Latin America, similar to James Welch's 1930s dispute with the Venezuelan government. Betancourt engaged the prestigious law firm Covington and Burling to represent the Venezuelan government, influenced by a friendship with the senior partner, Dean Acheson. Many Democrats advocated Pérez's extradition, citing him as an example of a failed U.S. policy of supporting Latin American dictators. Pérez Jiménez found his allies among many Republicans and the John Birch Society, who appreciated the predictability of strongman rule in Latin America and argued that the United States should not turn its back on a former friend. Other Latin American exiles watched the court hearings anxiously and urged respect for the tradition of political asylum, as did the American Civil Liberties Union. Many Venezuelans applauded U.S. attorney general Robert Kennedy's comparison of Pérez's corruption with that of the criminal mobs he pursued in the United States. The democratic thesis won, if narrowly, and in 1963 the United States extradited Pérez Jiménez to stand trial in Venezuela for embezzlement. By the time the Venezuelan Supreme Court found him guilty of minor financial crimes and released him to go into exile in Spain in 1968, the dictator had been all but forgotten in the United States.

Betancourt had to overcome U.S. reluctance to extradite Pérez Jiménez, but he found Kennedy eager to punish another Latin American dictator: Fidel Castro of Cuba. Rómulo Betancourt's personal antipathy toward Castro intensified when the Cuban refused to hold elections and then executed some of Fulgencio Batista's henchmen in 1959. Furthermore, as noted previously, Castro had inspired the Venezuelan guerrillas who threatened Betancourt's government and the scheduled 1963 elections. Betancourt broke relations with Cuba in November 1961, voted to expel Cuba from the OAS in January 1962, and successfully petitioned to have OAS sanctions imposed on the nation after the discovery of a cache of arms on a Venezuelan beach, allegedly dropped by Cubans for the use of Venezuelan guerrillas. Betancourt secured U.S. military assistance for a counterinsurgency program that both defeated the guerrillas and gave the Venezuelan armed forces an honorable and well-compensated patriotic mission.

Venezuelan presidents after Betancourt tempered his strident antidictatorial policy. They actively encouraged democracy, but their commitment to nonintervention effectively accepted ideological pluralism in the hemisphere. An increasing Third World identification, the waning of the guerrilla threat in Venezuela, and Castro's renunciation of exporting revolution allowed a sometimes shaky rapprochement with Cuba. Venezuela restored diplomatic relations in 1974, subsequently agreed to supply Cuba with oil, and advocated its reintegration into the OAS. On international issues like decolonization, the Venezuelan government found Castro a more natural ally than the United States. Cordial relations with Cuba also reinforced at home and abroad Caracas's claim to Third World solidarity and to a degree of independence from the United States. The Venezuelan-Cuban relationship still had its flash points, however, especially regarding Venezuela's handling of the terrorists who blew up a Cubana airplane in 1976 and of the Cubans who sought refuge in Venezuela's Havana embassy in 1980.

Taking pride in their own democratic institutions, Venezuelans often urged other American governments to adopt similar values. Their success was about as mixed as that of U.S. initiatives to "export democracy," especially when their initiatives were not strongly seconded in Washington. Caracas angered some authoritarian partners of the Andean Pact in the 1970s with its expressed disapproval of military dictatorship. Pinochet's Chile withdrew from the pact in 1976, for example, complaining that Venezuela was trying to impose a political patina on an economic pact. After the collapse of the communist bloc, many Venezuelans urged Castro to implement democratic reforms in Cuba. Teodoro Petkoff, several times Venezuelan presidential candidate for the Movimiento al Socialismo, spoke at a plenary meeting of the Caribbean Studies Association in Havana in May 1991. If Castro would agree to hold elections, Petkoff proposed, the United States would have no excuse to continue the damaging economic blockade. The best of Cuba's exemplary social reforms might then survive to inspire the Latin American Left. A Cuban spokesman rebuffed Petkoff's tutelage, predicting that the United States would be unlikely to soften no matter what Cuba did. Washington wanted only to see a Cuba *fracasada* (failed), not a Cuba *reformada* (reformed), he retorted. Certainly, President Ronald Reagan gave no indication that he might ameliorate U.S. policy toward Cuba.

Unlike the United States, Venezuela could unequivocally support reformist governments in the Americas. From experience, that nation had seen that a policy of tolerance and flexibility could divide and weaken the Marxist Left. Venezuelan guerrillas had been defeated by military force, but also by the willingness of Presidents Raúl Leoni (1964–69) and Rafael Caldera (1969–74) to offer amnesty and to allow Marxist parties to operate freely. Moreover, if Venezuelan politicians refrained from attacking leftist governments abroad, Venezuelan Marxists had less reason to cause trouble at home. The Socialist International, of which Acción Democrática was a member, further encouraged assistance to and warm relations with a variety of leftist governments. Thus, Venezuelan presidents supported and welcomed as Third World allies leaders such as Juan Bosch of the Dominican Republic, Michael Manley of Jamaica, Salvador Allende of Chile, Maurice Bishop of Grenada, Omar Torrijos of Panama, and Daniel Ortega of Nicaragua. Caracas condemned U.S. pressure and threats against these reformist governments as strongly as it dared, considering its own vulnerability to Washington's displeasure. President Raúl Leoni was reported to be so furious at the U.S. invasion of the Dominican Republic in 1965 that he contemplated breaking relations with Washington. President Luís Herrera Campins (COPEI, 1979–84) displayed more ambivalence since he hoped that the U.S. military presence in Central America would help his friend and fellow Christian Democrat José Napoleon Duarte in El Salvador. Disappointed, however, at what he characterized as Washington's lukewarm support for Duarte and its betrayal of hemispheric allies in the Falklands War, Herrera cooled regarding U.S. use of force in the region. The president worried about the ramifications of the murder of Grenadan leader Maurice Bishop but offered scant support of the U.S. invasion in 1983.

Venezuela's Third World perspective had contradictions in the economic realm as well as the political one. Venezuelan governments called for an international redistribution of wealth and regional economic integration, but they also fully endorsed free enterprise, free trade, and capitalism. The lust for imported goods, the presence of U.S. manufacturing subsidiaries, and the 1952 Reciprocal Trade Treaty with the United States limited the development of a significant, diverse, and autonomous industrialization. At the same time, the funds channeled to transportation, communication, services, and the huge petrochemical and steel industries gave Venezuela one of the largest public sectors in Latin America. Presidents Betancourt and Leoni used the trade treaty's "escape clause" to regulate some imports through quotas and licenses. (Washington used the escape clause to apply quotas on Venezuelan petroleum.) Only after President Rafael Caldera canceled the treaty in 1972 could Venezuela try to apply a systematic protectionist program. Even then, the hardy commercial and petroleum sectors resisted the encouragement of domestic consumer industries. The peculiarities of Venezuela's economy thus limited the avowed goal of participation in the regional economic integration schemes endorsed by the Alliance for Progress.[17]

Venezuelan industrialists and the Third World identity did press the nation to take some steps toward regional economic ties. The oil and iron nationalization and the emphasis on a new international economic order independent of the great powers accompanied participation in the Andean Pact (1973), the Latin American Economic System (SELA, 1975), and regional lending agencies like the Caribbean Development Bank. Carlos Andrés Pérez urged other Latin American leaders that "either we must achieve the integration of Latin America, or the transnational companies will do it for us."[18] The rhetoric did not disguise the difficulties of integrating with other Latin American economies. The debt crisis in the 1980s and the desperate need for foreign capital shifted economic strategy to an emphasis on producing competitive exports rather than protecting the manufacture of domestic consumer goods. The export strategy required greater harmony both with the U.S. market and with regional Latin American free trade networks. The 1980s and 1990s emphasis on a hemispheric market whose centerpiece was the United States—rather than one that excluded the United States—accommodated Venezuela's international petroleum economy better than the earlier anti-American strategy employed by other developing nations.

Thus, Venezuela began to privatize and dismantle much of its public sector and to revitalize regional trade blocs. SELA, with Caracas as its headquarters, became more active, as did the Andean Pact, which was more politically compatible after the Andean nations returned to elected governments in the mid-1980s. Venezuela joined with Colombia and Mexico to form the Group of Three, with professed goals of economic and geopolitical cooperation within the Caribbean basin. The group signed free trade agreements with most of the Caribbean nations, allowing the "Big Three" indirectly to benefit from the U.S.-sponsored Caribbean Basin Initiative (announced in 1982).

The desperate economic situation and the prevelance of free trade ideology drew Latin American's attention to the North American Free Trade Agreement (NAFTA) between the United States, Canada, and Mexico. In the early 1990s, the stalled Uruguay Round of GATT (General Agreements on Tariffs and Trade) talks; the challenge of the European Economic Community, Japan, and the Asian Tigers; and the evaporation of the cold war economic blocs had driven the United States to act boldly to reseize the global economic initiative. Washington hoped

to construct a free trade zone within the Americas, to guide new investment toward Latin America, and to encourage debt-for-nature swaps.
Venezuelans, like most Latin Americans, feared isolation as the economic blocs took shape. Certainly, no Latin American nation could
afford to be left out. Still, Laura Rojas, director of Venezuela's Foreign
Trade Institute, predicted that Venezuela would gain from the new
initiatives only if three conditions were met: if Venezuela, unilaterally
or jointly with other Latin American nations, took a strong negotiating position toward the United States; if Venezuela could gain access
to the U.S. market without entirely surrendering its own domestic
market to U.S. goods and services; and if Washington continued to give
priority to the Enterprise for the Americas Initiative.[19] Rojas, like other
Venezuelans, could recall that the goal of James Blaine's "America for
Americans" had been to encourage U.S. exports in a time of recession,
not to build up other American economies. Moreover, Washington had
shown little long-term consistency in its Latin American economic initiatives like the Alliance for Progress.

The foreign debt crisis of the 1980s reawakened Latin American interest in increasing foreign trade, but it also prompted radical proposals.
Some nations advocated forming a debtors' cartel to consider collective
means of managing, reducing, or renouncing the crippling foreign
debts. Venezuela, however, generally resisted coordinated negotiations
with the U.S. banks, preferring a bilateral approach. Venezuelan experts
were convinced that they had such strong economic cards to play that
they could only be damaged by cooperating with weaker Latin American nations. In June 1984 Caracas did sign the Cartagena Consensus,
which stated that creditor and debtor nations, multilateral lending
agencies, and commercial banks all shared responsibility for the economic crisis. The consensus stopped with such pieties, however, and
carried no obligation for its signers to employ collective tactics against
the banks. Caracas proudly continued to negotiate separately with the
U.S. bankers' committee, earning perhaps the most stringent terms in
Latin America because of Venezuela's assumed ability to pay. The *Wall
Street Journal* in 1988 called Venezuela "one of Latin America's most

compliant debtors." The eagerness of Presidents Lusinchi's (1984–89) and Carlos Andrés Pérez's (1989–93) governments to win the approval of U.S. bankers and investors led to the imposition of austerity measures. The popular distress that followed culminated in public rioting in February 1989, two attempted military coups in 1992, and the resignation of Carlos Andrés Pérez in 1993 during his second presidency.

Venezuela's economic ties to the United States limited its full-fledged commitment to effective Latin American solidarity in the postwar period. U.S. creditors held 85 percent of Venezuela's foreign debt. Nonetheless, Caracas consistently supported initiatives to enhance Latin American action within the hemisphere. The difficulty of maintaining sometimes contradictory loyalties—to the United States and to other Latin American nations—could be seen in Venezuela's reactions to the Central American crisis of the 1980s.

President Ronald Reagan's efforts to restore a cold war hegemony in the hemisphere intensified regional conflicts in the Caribbean and placed a strain on Venezuela's ambivalent diplomacy. Venezuela's fervent advocacy of disarmament in the United Nations reflected the certainty that any great power conflict in the Caribbean could threaten the entire region in a number of ways. "Any conflict that disturbs relations in the hemisphere," declared Carlos Andrés Pérez, "will have very negative repercussions in our country."[20] Any Caracas position toward U.S. military actions in the region was certain to outrage some Venezuelans, perhaps enough to endanger the democratic government. Thus, all Venezuelan governments, regardless of their sympathy or antipathy for the Frente Sandinista de Liberación Nacional (FSLN), the Frente Farabundo Martí de Liberación Nacional (FMLN), Maurice Bishop's New Jewel movement, or Panama's Manuel Noriega, tried to lower tensions in order to avoid U.S. action.

The Central American situation became troublesome after the Sandinista (FSLN) party came to power in Nicaragua in 1979. Implementing radical and rapid reforms within Nicaragua, the Sandinistas also endorsed the armed struggle of the FMLN in El Salvador. After 1981, Washington worked to defeat the FMLN and to overthrow the

Sandinistas by arming and supporting the Nicaraguan counterrevolutionary guerrillas, or contras. The neighboring countries of Honduras and Costa Rica feared the extension of conflict into their territory and felt the burden of the thousands of refugees who fled the war zones. Conciliation proved especially difficult because the U.S. government would accept nothing short of defeat and annihilation of the Sandinistas and the FMLN.

Venezuelan efforts to put off U.S. military action did not necessarily imply approval of the Sandinistas. Most Venezuelans had welcomed the overthrow of the tyrant Anastasio Somoza, but, as noted earlier, President Luís Herrera Campins (Christian Democrat, 1979–84) disliked the Sandinistas because of their support of the Salvadoran guerrillas. After 1982, however, Herrera was ready to join a multilateral effort to resolve the Central American conflict.

In January 1982 Venezuela joined with Mexico, Colombia, and Panama to form the Contadora Group, which tried to construct a diplomatic firewall between the United States and Nicaragua. Venezuela's economic distress and Washington's obvious distaste for Contadora led Caracas to play a relatively quiet role within the group. The Contadora Group directed its efforts both at Central American leaders and at the U.S. Congress and public opinion, gradually gaining credibility as a disinterested intermediary. Perhaps overshadowed by the 1987 initiatives of President Oscar Arias of Costa Rica and the Esquipulas II Accords, the Contadora Group nonetheless became the yeast for increased diplomatic activism in Latin America.

The multilateral initiative broadened when it spawned the Contadora Support Group (the original four plus Argentina, Brazil, Peru, and Uruguay), also known as the Rio Group. In December 1987, the group held an unprecedented summit conference of Latin American presidents, encouraging more personal friendships and confidence among them. Some diplomats foresaw the birth of a Pan-Americanism that excluded the United States. The Latin Americans voiced their chagrin at the way U.S. leaders treated them. Venezuelan foreign minister Simón Alberto Consalvi recounted a meeting of the Group of 8 with Secretary of State George Shultz in February 1986. Characterizing the "discussion" as a "multilateral monologue," Consalvi said that Shultz implied that Latin American leaders were not competent to solve Central America's problems. Consalvi concluded that "without Washington there was no way to progress in the search for peace in the region, and with Washington it didn't seem probable."[21]

If Consalvi accepted the clumsiness of the United States with a certain diplomatic fatalism, some of his compatriots offered a "trapped tiger" explanation for U.S. actions. Domingo Alberto Rangel judged that Ronald Reagan's reactionary government displayed its inherent weakness by seeking easy victories in Central America to assuage the memory of U.S. failures in Vietnam and Iran. Breaking its own laws in the Iran-Contra debacle, Rangel mused, further revealed the United States as a desperate power in decline.[22] Alfredo Toro Hardy, an international lawyer and adviser to several Venezuelan foreign policy agencies, characterized U.S. policy as incoherent, a situation from which Venezuela could benefit. Drawing on his associations with Harvard, Stanford, Princeton, and the Universities of Pennsylvania and Paris, Toro urged Venezuelans to achieve their foreign policy aims by lobbying key groups within the United States. They would get nowhere by imagining that they were confronting a unitary foreign policy apparatus in Washington.[23]

Venezuelan statesmen also demonstrated that they understood the value of public diplomacy. In September 1985 U.S. assistant secretary of state for inter-American affairs Elliott Abrams leaked a "secret" document that said that Washington preferred no Contadora treaty in Central America to a bad treaty. When Venezuelan journalists asked Foreign Minister Consalvi for his reaction to the news, he tersely replied that it was bad manners to discuss other people's secrets. A few days later, however, the Venezuelan Foreign Ministry leaked a Venezuelan secret document expressing a preference for "a bad treaty to a good war." Consalvi's public response thus made his point without directly challenging Abrams.

For Venezuela, Latin American cooperation expressed both a useful defensive strategy and a treasured cultural value. Carlos Andrés Pérez compared the fight for economic independence with Simón Bolívar's continent-wide fight for political independence, pointing out that both battles required Latin American cooperation. Yet, Bolívar in the end had had the simpler task.

Carlos Andrés Pérez and Henry Kissinger could agree on one thing: hemispheric issues had become global ones. Beyond that truism, different national conditions implied different strategies. The United Nations, the Group of 77, OPEC, and other organizations opened and changed the terms of debate. Binational discussions might occur in conference rooms in Geneva, Tel Aviv, and Paris as well as in Caracas and Washington. Petroleum issues absolutely critical to Venezuela were no longer negotiated only between Venezuela and the United States. Nor were many other issues of importance. The dialogue had become a choir of many voices—or sometimes multilateral monologues. Venezuela joined poorer nations to call for an international redistribution of wealth and power. Washington and other developed nations demonstrated again that the quality of an argument matters less than the economic and military forces that support it. The OAS became part of the emerging Third World bloc but still suffered from the curse of James G. Blaine. Venezuelan, and Latin American, efforts to re-create Pan-Americanism could not eject the United States from the hemisphere. Only time would tell whether the postwar changes implied a real, or a prematurely announced, death of U.S. hegemony in the hemisphere.

Notes

Introduction

1. Michael H. Hunt, *Ideology and U.S. Foreign Policy* (New Haven: Yale University Press, 1987), 14; see also, for example, Akira Iriye, "Culture and International History," in *Exploring the History of American Foreign Relations*, ed. Michael J. Hogan and Thomas G. Patterson (New York: Cambridge University Press, 1991), 214–25.
2. Arturo Uslar Pietri, "Tío Tigre y Juan Bobo," in *Letras y hombres de Venezuela*, 4th ed. (1948; Madrid: Editorial Mediterráneo, 1978), 245–51.
3. Tony Perrottet, ed., *Insight Guides: Venezuela* (Boston: Houghton Mifflin, 1993), 67.
4. Ibid., 73.
5. See, for example, Gaddis Smith, *The Last Years of the Monroe Doctrine, 1945–1993* (New York: Hill & Wang, 1994).
6. Charles Krauthammer, "Goodby, Monroe Doctrine," *Washington Post*, 2 August 1994.
7. Walter Russell Mead, "Mr. Monroe's Neighborhood," *New York Times Book Review*, 21 August 1994, 6–7.

1. The Origins, 1790–1830

I am grateful to Ann Farnsworth-Alvear for her contributions to an earlier version of this chapter.

1. Most of this chapter concentrates on Venezuela with its six provinces: Caracas, Mérida de Maracaibo, Barinas, Guayana, Cumaná, and Margarita. Within Venezuela, the political and economic elite of Caracas has always dominated events. Venezuela was, of course, part of the Viceroyalty of New Granada and subsequently part of the nation-confederation of Gran Colombia between 1822 and 1830. In most cases, even when technically discussing New Granada or Gran Colombia, I focus on the Venezuelan leaders.

2. Manuel Lucena Salmoral, "The Commerce of La Guaira with the United States during the Venezuelan Revolutionary Juncture, 1807–1812," in Jacques Barbier and Allan Kuethe, eds., *The North American Role in the Spanish Imperial Economy, 1760–1819* (Manchester: Manchester University Press, 1984), 158–76; Lester D. Langley, *Struggle for the American Mediterranean* (Athens: University of Georgia Press, 1976), 37; *Gazeta de Caracas*, 10 May 1811.

3. Mercedes M. Alvarez, *Comercio y comerciantes y sus proyecciones en la independencia venezolana* (Caracas: n.p., 1963), 25.

4. *Las proclamas de Filadelfia de 1774 y 1775 en la Caracas de 1777* (Caracas: Centro Venezolano Americano, 1973).

5. James Biggs, *The History of Don Francisco de Miranda's Attempt to Effect a Revolution in South America* . . . (Boston: Edward Oliver, 1810), 6.

6. Ibid., 4.

7. Ibid., 5.

8. Ibid., 25, 27.

9. Elías Pino Iturrieta, *La mentalidad venezolana de la emancipación* (Caracas: Facultad de Humanidades y Educación, Universidad Central de Venezuela, 1971), 43.

10. Francisco de Miranda, *Fragments from an XVIIIth Century Diary*, trans. Jordan H. Stabler (Caracas: Tipógrafo "La Nacion," 1931), 60.

11. *Richmond Enquirer*, 4 July 1806.

12. *Richmond Enquirer*, 28 February 1806.

13. Arthur Whitaker, *The United States and the Independence of Latin America 1800–1830* (Baltimore: Johns Hopkins University Press, 1941), 37.

14. Jefferson to Humboldt, quoted in Whitaker, *The United States and the Independence of Latin America*, 188.

15. William Gribbin, "A Matter of Faith, North America's Religion and South America's Independence," *The Americas* 31 (April 1975):472.

16. Ibid.

17. Manuel Pérez Vila, "La accidentada misión diplomática de Juan Vicente Bolívar Palacios," *Boletín Histórico* 47 (May 1978):270–71.

18. "Informaciones transmitidas por Robert K. Lowry, . . ." in *Anales Diplomáticos de Venezuela*, 7 vols. (Caracas: Ministerio de Relaciones Exteriores, 1976), 6:7.

19. Juan Germán Roscio, "Instrucciones para el señor Manuel Torres, . . ." in *Anales Diplomáticos*, 6:112.

20. Cristóbal Mendoza, *Las primeras misiones diplomáticas de Venezuela*, 2 vols. (Caracas: Academia Nacional de la Historia, 1962), 2:32.

21. Ibid., 1:175.
22. Orea to Sanz, 10 September 1811, in *Anales Diplomáticos*, 6:32–33.
23. Orea to Secretary of State Monroe, *Anales Diplomáticos*, 6:51.
24. Orea to Government of Venezuela, 14 May 1812, *Anales Diplomáticos*, 6:54.
25. *Providence Gazette*, 5 September 1812, quoted in Bruce Solnick, "American Opinion concerning the South American Wars of Independence: 1808–1830" (Ph.D. diss., New York University, 1975), 59.
26. "El Plan de Briceño . . . ," in Santos Rodulfo Cortés, ed., *Antología documental de Venezuela 1492–1900*, 3rd ed. (Caracas: n.p., 1960), 295–96.
27. Alfred Hasbrouk, *Foreign Legionaries in the Liberation of Spanish South America* (New York: Columbia University Press, 1928), 350.
28. "Biographical Sketch of Doctor Alexander Macaulay (Collected from Authentick Sources)," in *The Portico* (Baltimore), vol. 4 (1817), 128.
29. Ibid., 474.
30. Jane Lucas de Grummond, *Renato Beluche: Smuggler, Privateer, and Patriot, 1780–1860* (Baton Rouge: Louisiana State University Press, 1983), 256.
31. Ibid., 224.
32. Charles C. Griffin, "Privateering from Baltimore during the Spanish American Wars of Independence," *Maryland Historical Magazine* 35 (1940):13.
33. *Anales Diplomáticos*, 7:207–59.
34. David Bushnell, "The Florida Republic: An Overview," in David Bushnell, comp., *La República de las Floridas: Texts and Documents* (Mexico City: Pan American Institute of Geography and History, 1986), 9, 10.
35. "Draft Constitution of the República de las Floridas," in Bushnell, comp., *La República de las Floridas*, 62–64.
36. "Exposición y protesta presentada por Vicente Pazos al Secretario de Estado . . . ," in *Anales Diplomáticos*, 6:69.
37. Ibid.
38. Bolívar to Lino de Clemente, *Anales Diplomáticos*, 6:103.
39. José Rafael Fortique, "El Corso Venezolano y las Misiones de Irvine y Perry en Angostura," *Boletín de la Academia Nacional de la Historia* 51, no. 202 (1968):216.
40. Ibid.
41. Quoted in ibid., 217.
42. Ibid.
43. Ibid., 218.
44. Quoted in ibid., 222.
45. Quoted in ibid., 223, 225, 227.

46. Harold A. Bierck, Jr., *Vida pública de Don Pedro Gual*, trans. Leopoldo Landaeta (Caracas: Ministerio de Educación Nacional, 1947), 393–97.

47. Vicente Lecuna, comp., and Harold A. Bierck, Jr., ed., *Selected Writings of Bolívar*, 2 vols., trans. Lewis Bertrand (New York: Banco de Venezuela, 1951), 2:508.

48. Ibid., 513.

49. Quoted in John J. Johnson, *A Hemisphere Apart: The Foundations of United States Policy toward Latin America* (Baltimore: Johns Hopkins University Press, 1990), 77.

50. John V. Lombardi, *The Decline and Abolition of Negro Slavery in Venezuela 1820–1854* (Westport, Conn.: Greenwood, 1971), 47.

51. Lecuna and Bierck, *Selected Writings of Bolívar*, 2:513.

52. Quoted in C. Parra Pérez, *La monarquía en la Gran Colombia* (Madrid: Ediciones Cultura Hispánica, 1957), 377.

53. Ibid., 520.

54. Ibid.

55. Ibid., 523–24.

2. Gunboats and Caudillos, 1830–1866

1. Miguel Izard, *Series estadísticas para la historia de Venezuela* (Mérida: Universidad de los Andes, 1970), 63.

2. Quoted by Pedro José Rojas in *Pensamiento político venezolano del siglo XIX*, 15 vols. (Caracas: Congress, 1983), 7:233.

3. Jane Lucas de Grummond, *Las comadres de Caracas: historia de John G. A. Williamson, primer diplomático norteamericano en Venezuela* (Barquisimeto: Editorial Nueva Segovia, 1955), 73.

4. Fermín Toro, "Europa y América," in *Pensamiento político*, 1:58–59.

5. Juan Vicente González, "Washington y Bolívar," in *Pensamiento político*, 2:447.

6. Toro, "Europa y América," 61.

7. Antonio Leocadio Guzmán, "Discurso . . . ," in *Pensamiento político*, 6:149.

8. Simón Camacho, *Cosas de los Estados Unidos* (New York: n.p., 1864). The book, published under the pseudonym "Nazareno" in 1864, reflects Camacho's travels and observations in the 1850s.

9. De Grummond, *Las comadres*, 41.

10. Shields to Department of State [hereafter DS], 20 October 1849, Diplomatic Despatches from U.S. Ministers to Venezuela, 1835–1906 (National Archives Microfilm Publication M79) [hereafter cited as Despatches; all references are to the microfilm publication].

11. DS to Williamson, 1 April 1835, Diplomatic Instructions of the Department of State to U.S. Legation in Venezuela, 1835–1906 (National Archives Microfilm Publication M77) [hereafter cited as Instructions; all references are to the microfilm publication].

12. Benjamin Frankel, "Venezuela and the United States, 1810–1888" (Ph.D. diss., University of California, Berkeley, 1964), 210.

13. Culver to DS, 2 February 1865, Despatches.

14. De Grummond, *Las comadres*, 95.

15. Williamson to DS, 8 October 1836, Despatches.

16. Shields to DS, 7 January 1848, Despatches.

17. Forsyth to Williamson, 1 April 1835, Instructions.

18. Hall to DS, 28 October 1844, Despatches.

19. De Grummond, *Las comadres*, 114.

20. Quoted in Elías Pino Iturrieta, *Las ideas de los primeros venezolanos* (Caracas: Fondo Editorial Tropykos, 1987), 62.

21. Shields to DS, 29 January 1848, Despatches.

22. Shields to DS, 7 February 1848, Despatches.

23. Buchanan to Shields, 22 March 1848, Instructions.

24. Shields to DS, 10 July 1849, Despatches; Clayton to Shields 25 October 1849, Instructions.

25. Turpin to DS, 7 September 1859, Despatches. In 1854, the chief officer of the United States mission became the minister resident instead of the chargé.

26. Blow to DS, 11 February 1862, Despatches.

27. Steele to DS, 9 May 1853, Despatches.

28. Culver to DS, 4 August 1864, Despatches.

29. Shields to DS, 7 January 1848, Despatches.

30. Steele to DS, 24 August 1852, Despatches.

31. José Gil Fortoul, *Historia constitucional de Venezuela*, 5th ed., 3 vols. (Caracas: Librería Píñango, 1967); 2:285–86.

32. Blow to DS, 22 November 1861, Despatches.

33. Seward to Culver, 9 March 1863, Despatches.

34. Culver to DS, 21 November 1862, Despatches.

35. Enclosure, Culver to DS, 30 January 1863, Despatches.

36. Culver to DS, 30 January 1863, Despatches.
37. Shields to DS, 20 August 1845, Despatches.
38. Culver to DS, 3 December 1864, Despatches.
39. Seward to Culver, 9 January 1865, Instructions.
40. Ellis to DS, 16 June 1845, Despatches.

3. Rogues and Heroes, 1866–1896

1. Reprinted in *La Opinión Nacional*, 8 February 1890, from *Washington Post* interview.
2. Walter LaFeber, *The American Search for Opportunity, 1865–1913*, vol. 2 of *The Cambridge History of American Foreign Relations*, ed. Warren Cohen (New York: Cambridge University Press, 1993).
3. Wilson to DS, 17 June 1887, Despatches.
4. Pile to DS, 19 July 1872, Despatches.
5. Jesús Múñoz Tébar, *Personalismo y legalismo* (New York, 1890; Caracas: Fundación Sánchez, 1977), 62–64.
6. Quoted in Pile to DS, 5 October 1871, Despatches.
7. Scruggs to DS, 28 June 1892, Despatches.
8. Wilson to DS, 31 January 1867, Despatches.
9. Stilwell to DS, 26 December 1867, Despatches.
10. Pile to DS, 27 January 1873, Despatches.
11. Pile to DS, 6 August 1873, Despatches.
12. Carter to DS, 25 January 1882, Despatches.
13. A. Barrett, in *New York Herald*, enclosed with Scruggs to DS, 15 February 1890, Despatches.
14. Scruggs to DS, 8 August 1889, Despatches.
15. Baker to DS, 3 October 1883, Despatches.
16. Ministerio de Relaciones Exteriores (Venezuela), *Libro Amarillo 1882*, 1:528–29.
17. Pile to DS, 8 April 1872, Despatches.
18. Russell to DS, 26 September 1876, Despatches.
19. Plumacher to DS, 30 April 1881, 3 January 1887, Despatches from U.S. consuls to Maracaibo, 1824–1906 (National Archives Microfilm T62) [hereafter Maracaibo Despatches; all references are to the microfilm edition unless otherwise indicated].
20. Plumacher to DS, 3 February 1888, Maracaibo Despatches.

21. Plumacher to DS, 26 March 1880, Maracaibo Despatches.

22. Scruggs to DS, 7 July 1891, Despatches.

23. Blaine to Scruggs, 28 October 1891, Instructions; Scruggs to DS, 21 November 1891, Despatches.

24. LaFeber, *American Search for Opportunity*, 129 and passim.

25. Arturo Uslar Pietri, "Tío Tigre y Juan Bobo," 247–48.

26. Guzmán Blanco to U. S. Grant, quoted in Armando Rojas, *Historia de las relaciones diplomáticas entre Venezuela y los Estados Unidos* (Caracas: Presidencia de la República, 1979), 217.

27. Partridge to DS, 8 August 1869, Despatches.

28. Fish to Partridge, 20 November 1869, Instructions.

29. Russell to DS, 31 May 1875, Despatches.

30. Russell to DS, 30 June 1876, Despatches.

31. Partridge to DS, 16 January 1870, Despatches.

32. Baker to DS, 22 April 1883, Despatches.

33. Russell to DS, 23 October 1876, Despatches.

34. *Libro Amarillo 1882*, 1:503.

35. *Libro Amarillo 1886*, 207–8, 321–26.

36. Partridge to DS, 12 July 1893, Despatches.

37. Miguel Izard, *Series estadísticas para la historia de Venezuela*, 63.

38. William E. Curtis, *Venezuela: A Land Where It's Always Summer* (New York: Harper & Brothers, 1896), 29.

39. Richard Harding Davis, *Three Gringos in Venezuela and Central America* (New York: Harper & Brothers, 1896), 225.

40. U.S. historian Frederick Jackson Turner delivered his famous address on the closing of the American frontier in 1893. British novelist and naturalist W. H. Hudson published *Green Mansions: A Romance of the Tropical Forest* in 1904, based on Venezuela. In 1912, Sir Arthur Conan Doyle set his Jurassic fantasy, *The Lost World*, in Venezuela's Guayana territory.

41. Davis, *Three Gringos*, 269.

42. Baker to DS, 18 January 1881, Despatches.

43. Baker to DS, 4 February 1884, Despatches.

44. Baker to DS, 16 February 1881, Despatches.

45. Múñoz Tébar, *Personalismo*, 200–201. Múñoz Tébar (1847–1909), as the first minister of public works (1874), was responsible for many of Guzmán's works of infrastructure, including the Caracas–La Guaira railroad and numerous roads. A bit of a visionary, he completed plans for canals and for removing the sandbar in Lake Maracaibo and was in charge of numerous

public works in Caracas, including the Municipal Theater and the General Cemetery of the South. As president of Zulia State (Maracaibo region) from 1894 to 1896, he promoted the construction of an aqueduct, a colonization project, a stenography school, and an 1895 state exposition. Even more remarkable for that corrupt age, he was reknowned for being an honest and effective administrator of public funds, repeating the aphorism "Public funds should be administered in a glass box."

46. Ramón Páez, *Ambas Américas: contrastes* (New York, 1872), 13–14.
47. *Libro Amarillo 1886*, 196.
48. *La Opinión Nacional*, 28 January 1890.
49. *La Opinión Nacional*, 21 January 1890.
50. *La Opinión Nacional*, 2 August 1890, 14 November 1890, 14 February 1891.
51. *La Opinión Nacional*, 28 January 1890.
52. Translated by Ernest Plumacher, U.S. consul in Maracaibo, and enclosed with his dispatch of 7 April 1880, in Maracaibo Despatches.
53. *La Opinión Nacional*, 25 April 1890.
54. *La Opinión Nacional*, 10 December 1890, 16 January 1891.
55. John A. S. Grenville and George Berkeley Young, *Politics, Strategy and Diplomacy: Studies in Foreign Policy, 1873–1917* (New Haven: Yale University Press, 1966), 32.
56. Enclosure, Thomas to DS, 19 December 1895, Despatches.

4. Venezuela Dodges the Big Stick, 1897–1912

1. Hernández had lost an arm in one of his earlier military encounters, thus the nickname El Mocho, "the maimed."
2. Manuel Vicente Magallanes, *Los partidos políticos en la evolución histórica venezolana*, 5th ed. (Caracas: Ediciones Centauro, 1983), 148.
3. Shields to DS, 19 April 1898, Despatches.
4. Loomis to DS, 9 September 1897, Despatches.
5. Enclosure with Loomis to DS, 25 April 1898, Despatches.
6. Loomis to DS, 2 May 1898, Despatches.
7. DS to Loomis, 3 June 1898, Instructions.
8. Loomis to DS, 6 June 1898, Despatches.
9. Enclosure with Loomis to DS, 6 August 1898, Despatches.
10. Loomis to DS, 9 September 1898, Despatches.
11. Loomis to DS, 20 June 1899, Despatches.

12. Loomis to DS, 7 November 1899, Despatches.

13. Venezuela's total population in 1891 was 2,323,827, and the Federal District numbered 113,204 persons. Táchira's population made it the fifth most populous state in the nation, ranking just ahead of Zulia (capital, Maracaibo), whose population was 150,776 in 1891, and 69,233 in 1873.

14. Nikita Harwich Vallenilla, "El modelo económico del Liberalismo Amarillo. Historia de un fracaso, 1888–1908," in *Política y economia en Venezuela, 1810–1976* (Caracas: Fundación John Boulton, 1976), 206.

15. Domingo Alberto Rangel, *Los andinos en el poder*, 3rd ed. (Valencia: Vadell Hermanos, 1975), 66.

16. Bowen to DS, 6 August 1904, Despatches.

17. Theodore Roosevelt, *The Letters of Theodore Roosevelt*, 8 vols. sel. and ed. Elting E. Morison et al. (Cambridge: Harvard University Press, 1951–52), 4:1156.

18. Ibid., 6:957.

19. James Weldon Johnson, *Along This Way: The Autobiography of James Weldon Johnson* (1933; New York: Viking Press, 1968), 229, 257.

20. Hutchinson to DS, 14 May 1905, Despatches. Hutchinson confused the name of Castro's revolution, the Causa Liberal Restauradora, with that of M. A. Matos's revolt, the Revolución Libertadora.

21. For a full account of the asphalt saga, see Nikita Harwich Vallenilla, *Asfalto y revolución: la New York & Bermúdez Company* (Caracas: Monte Avila Editores and FUNRES, 1991).

22. William Sullivan, "The Rise of Despotism in Venezuela: Cipriano Castro, 1899–1908" (Ph.D. diss., University of New Mexico, 1974), 374.

23. Bowen to DS, 25 June 1904, Despatches.

24. Bowen to DS, 22 January, 4 March 1905, Despatches.

25. Roosevelt, *Letters*, 4:917.

26. Ibid., 5:135.

27. Ibid., 5:761.

28. Ibid., 6:1148.

29. Ibid., 4:1164.

30. Ibid., 4:1249.

31. Ibid., 4:1164.

32. Maurice Belrose, *La sociedad venezolana en su novela, 1890–1935* (Maracaibo: Universidad del Zulia, 1979), 19.

33. Hiram Bingham, *The Journal of an Expedition across Venezuela and Colombia, 1906–1907* (New Haven: Yale Publishing Association, 1909), 50. In fact, the

Venezuelan minister of foreign relations who gave permission for Bingham and his group to follow Bolívar's route to gather scientific, historical, and geographical information commented that the expedition looked suspiciously military, but that it was purely scientific.

34. Johnson, *Along This Way*, 231.
35. Loomis to DS, 4 March 1901, Despatches.
36. Martí and Zumeta were both associated with the New York newspaper *La América* between 1884 and 1889.
37. César Zumeta, "Nota Editorial," in *Pensamiento político venezolano del siglo XIX*, 14:48.
38. Zumeta, "La Revolución," in *Pensamiento político*, 14:69.
39. Zumeta, "La ley del cabestro," in *Pensamiento político*, 14:55.
40. Zumeta, "Hoy," in *Pensamiento político*, 14:65–66.
41. Zumeta, "Sobre Cipriano Castro," in *Pensamiento político*, 14:94.
42. Zumeta, "El continente enfermo," in *Pensamiento político*, 14:121.
43. Ibid., 121.
44. Zumeta, "Cartas de Nueva York," in *Pensamiento político*, 14:187.
45. Whitehouse to DS, 7 June 1910, Department of State, General Records, Record Group 59, 831.00/299, National Archives, Washington, D.C. (National Archives Microfilm Publication M366, Internal Affairs) [hereafter cited as RG 59].
46. *Libro Amarillo 1910–11*, xxv.
47. Ramón González Escorihuela, *Las ideas antimperialistas y socialistas en el Táchira: Horizontes, 1903–1920* (San Cristóbal: n.p., 1988), 103–4).
48. *Libro Amarillo, 1911–12*, 313.

5. Oil and the Democratic Caesar, 1912–1935

1. Germans had been coffee factors and bankers in the Andes for years, inspiring both respect and occasional resentment for their economic astuteness.
2. DS to Wilson, 25 October 1917, RG 59, 831.00/811.
3. McGoodwin to Secretary of State [hereafter SS], 3 November 1917, RG 59, 831.11/810.
4. Wilson to SS, 16 February 1918, RG 59, 831.00/834 1/2.
5. McGoodwin to DS, 29 October 1918, RG 59, 831.00/860.

6. Adee to Legation in Bogotá, 8 May 1919, RG 59, 831.00/899.

7. Wiley to SS, 15 October 1920, RG 59, 831.00/954.

8. William Sherwell, "The Political Situation in Venezuela," sent by L. S. Rowe, Director General of the Pan-American Union, to Sumner Welles, Chief, Division of Latin American Affairs, DS, 10 May 1921, RG 59, 831.00/991 1/2.

9. Ibid.

10. Stabler to Kellogg, 22 September 1927, RG 59, 831.00/1337 1/2.

11. Kellogg to Cook, 11 November 1927, RG 59, 831.00/1339.

12. "Official Statement of and Commentary upon the Monroe Doctrine by the Secretary of State," 28 February 1929, in *The Papers relating to the Foreign Relations of the United States* [hereafter *FRUS*] *1929*, 1:718.

13. "Legendary" because many Venezuelans trace the birth of popular social democracy to this revolt and its leaders.

14. Engert to DS, 7 and 22 March 1928, RG 59, 831.00/1350 and 1355.

15. Engert to DS, 25 December 1929, RG 59, 831.00/1449.

16. H. Eric Trammell to DS, 19 November 1931, RG 59, 831.00/1466.

17. McGoodwin to DS, 11 October 1915, RG 59, 831.00/736.

18. McGoodwin to DS, 10 April 1916, RG 59, 831.00/766.

19. Diógenes Escalante to Gómez, 12 August 1921, *Boletín del Archivo Histórico de Miraflores* 52–58 (January 1968–February 1969):257.

20. Rafael Requena to Gómez, 20 September 1923, *Boletín del Archivo Histórico de Miraflores* 61–63 (July–December 1969):262–63.

21. Pedro M. Arcaya to Gómez, 8 November 1923, in ibid., 272.

22. Carlos Grisanti to Ministerio de Relaciones Exteriores [hereafter MRE], 28 February 1928, in Archive of Ministerio de Relaciones Exteriores (Caracas) [hereafter AMRE].

23. Jones to Minister of Foreign Relations Rafael Cayama, 25 June 1929, AMRE.

24. Mark Gilderhus, *Pan American Visions: Woodrow Wilson in the Western Hemisphere, 1913–1921* (Tucson: University of Arizona Press, 1986), 6.

25. Hughes to McGoodwin, 8 October 1921, RG 59, 831.00/111.

26. For Gómez's relations with the oil companies, see B. S. McBeth, *Juan Vicente Gómez and the Oil Companies in Venezuela, 1908–1935* (Cambridge: Cambridge University Press, 1983); and Stephen Rabe, *The Road to OPEC: United States Relations with Venezuela, 1919–1976* (Austin: University of Texas Press, 1982).

27. Stabler to DS, 22 September 1927, RG 59, 831.00/1337 1/2.

28. Pérez Soto to Gómez, 5 July 1926, *Boletín del Archivo Histórico de Miraflores* 70 (January–February 1972):327.

29. Pérez Soto to Gómez, 29 July 1926, in ibid., 336–37.

30. One of Gómez's positivist advisers wrote a book in which he argued that Venezuelan society needed a strong hand until the population could become advanced enough to implement a true democracy. To many, Gómez fulfilled the role of the democratic caesar who should rule during the transition period. See Laureano Vallenilla Lanz, *Césarismo democrática: estudios sobre las bases sociológicas de la constitución efectiva de Venezuela* (Caracas: Empresa El Cojo, 1919).

31. Letter and report forwarded by Ambassador Arcaya to MRE, 8 May 1933, AMRE.

32. Chargé Warden M. Wilson to DS, 25 November 1931, RG 59, 831.00/1498.

33. Daniel Yergin, *The Prize: The Epic Quest for Oil, Money, & Power* (New York: Simon & Schuster, 1991), 520.

34. Arcaya to MRE, 8 July 1930, AMRE.

35. Herbert Spencer Dickey, *My Jungle Book* (Boston: Little, Brown, 1932), 101.

36. Ibid., 110.

37. Cook to DS, 17 July 1925, RG 59, 831.00/1274 1/2.

38. Quoted in Vernon Charles Connelly, "Juan Vicente Gómez and the Venezuelan Worker, 1919–1929" (Ph.D. diss., University of Maryland, 1975), 139.

39. Quoted in ibid., 148–49.

40. Ibid., 150.

41. *Occidente*, 13 May 1930.

42. *Occidente*, 2 June 1928.

43. Wilson to DS, 20 July 1933, RG 59, 831.00/4061.

44. *Occidente*, 3 June 1931.

45. *Occidente*, 31 March 1928.

46. *Occidente*, 23 June 1928.

6. Good Neighbors and the Dismantling of Democracy, 1936–1958

1. Venezuelan Legation in Washington to MRE, 23 April 1937, AMRE; Memorandum of Governor of the Federal District to MRE, 13 December 1937, AMRE; *New York Times*, 10 June 1939.

2. Consul James P. Moffitt to DS, 19 November 1943, RG 59, 831.00/1898.

3. Corrigan to DS, 9 January 1941, RG 59, 831.00/1739. In 1939, Washington raised the rank of the U.S. emissary to Venezuela from minister plenipotentiary to ambassador.

4. Pedro Manuel Arcaya, *Memorías* (1962; Caracas: n.p., 1983), 77.

5. Hull to Chargé in Venezuela, 19 January 1941; Chargé to Hull, 6 February 1941, *FRUS 1941*, 6:607–9; MRE, 29 September 1943, *Libro Amarillo 1943*, 89–90.

6. Corrigan to SS, 2 October 1945, *FRUS 1945*, 9:1439–41.

7. Corrigan to DS, 26 October 1945, RG 59, 821.00/10-2645; Corrigan to DS, 6 November 1945, RG 59, 831.00/11-645.

8. Corrigan to SS, 28 October 1945, *FRUS 1945*, 9:1415.

9. Corrigan to SS, 27 October 1945, *FRUS 1945*, 9:1414.

10. Corrigan to DS, 1 April 1946; Flack to Corrigan, 28 March 1946, *FRUS 1946*, 11:1315–17.

11. Irwin F. Gellman, *Good Neighbor Diplomacy: United States Policies in Latin America, 1933–1945* (Baltimore: Johns Hopkins University Press, 1979), 225–28; Bryce Wood, *The Dismantling of the Good Neighbor Policy* (Austin: University of Texas Press, 1985).

12. See *FRUS 1946*, 11:1298–1302, for correspondence on López's plotting.

13. Maleady to SS, 7 January 1947; Byrnes to Venezuelan Ambassador, 10 January 1947, *FRUS 1947*, 8:1055.

14. Butler to SS, 19 June 1947; Marshall to Butler, 1 August 1947, *FRUS 1947*, 8:638–42, 648.

15. See *FRUS 1947*, 8:131–40, for correspondence on the arms sale.

16. Mills to Daniels, 22 November 1948, *FRUS 1948*, 9:126.

17. Donnelly to SS, 4 December 1948, *FRUS 1948*, 9:135–36.

18. Secretary of the Army Royall to Secretary of Defense Forrestal, 9 December 1948, *FRUS 1948*, 9:147.

19. Memorandum by Director Policy Planning Staff (Kennan) to Acting Secretary of State, 10 December 1948, *FRUS 1948*, 9:141–43.

20. John Kieffer, "Geopolítica: Conferencias pronunciadas por el Teniente Coronel John Elmer Kieffer," *Revista de las Fuerzas Armadas*, supplement 48 (1955).

21. *Hispanic American Report* 8 (March 1955):2.

22. Charles Urruela to Maurice Bernbaum, 21 June 1955, RG 59, 731.00/6-2155.

23. Warren to DS, 28 November 1952, RG 59, 731.00/11-2852.

24. "Preliminary analysis of recent political developments in Venezuela," Wolf to DS, 10 December 1952, RG 59, 731.00/12-1052.

25. Warren to DS, 15 April 1953, RG 59, 731.00/4-1553.

26. Dulles to Caracas Embassy, 28 May 1954, RG 59, 731.000/5-2654.

27. Bernbaum (Caracas) to Dulles, 31 May 1954, RG 59, 731.00/5-3154.

28. Quoted in Holland to SS, 20 December 1954, RG 59, 731.00/12-2054.

29. Rubottom to Murphy, 19 May 1958, RG 59, 731.00/5-1958, XR090.31.

30. Stewart, Memorandum of conversation (with Betancourt, Fishburn, Davis, and Bartch), 21 December 1956, RG 59, 731.00/12-2156.

31. Anthony Swezey, First Secretary U.S. Embassy, Bern, to DS, 30 July 1957, RG 59, 731.00/7-3057.

32. Yervant Maxudian, petroleum consultant, to Howard Pyle (White House), 28 August 1957, filed with W. P. Snow, Deputy Assistant Secretary for Inter-American Affairs, to Maxudian, 29 August 1957, RG 59, 8-2957.

33. Saunders to Rubottom, 24 September 1957, RG 59, 731.00/9-2457.

34. Rubottom, Memorandum of conversation (with Proudfit, Metzgar, Bernbaum, and Bartch), 13 December 1957, RG 59, 731.00/12-1357.

35. Rubottom, Memorandum of conversation (with Caldera, Bernbaum, and Hank Hoyt), 29 January 1958, RG 59, 731.00/1-2958.

36. Rubottom, Memorandum of conversation (with Betancourt and Bernbaum), 31 January 1958, RG 59, 731.00/1-3158.

37. Porter to Eisenhower, 3 February 1958, filed with William B. Macomber, Jr., Assistant Secretary of State, to Porter, 13 February 1958, RG 59, 731.00/2-358.

7. The Hydrocarbon Economy and the American Way of Life, 1936–1958

1. Joseph Flack to DS, 30 April 1943, RG 59, 831.00/1843.

2. The general outline of Mendoza's career comes from Domingo Alberto Rangel, *La oligarquia del dinero*, 3rd ed. (Caracas: Editorial Fuentes, 1972), 195–210.

3. David Painter, *Oil and the American Century: The Political Economy of U.S. Foreign Oil Policy, 1941–1954* (Baltimore: Johns Hopkins University Press, 1986), 129.

4. See David Green, *The Containment of Latin America: A History of the Myths and Realities of the Good Neighbor Policy* (Chicago: Quadrangle Press, 1971).

5. Nicholson to Secretary of State, 28 March 1938, *FRUS 1938*, 5:969.

6. For a fuller discussion of the trade issue, see Clemy Machado de Acedo and Marisela Padrón Quero, *La diplomacia de López Contreras y el tratado de reciprocidad comercial con Estados Unidos* (Caracas: Ministerio de Relaciones Exteriores, 1987).

7. Corrigan to SS, 23 January 1943, *FRUS 1943*, 6:812.

8. Memo by the Petroleum Adviser (Max Thornburg) to Bonsal, Duggan, and Welles, 23 September 1942, *FRUS 1942*, 6:751.

9. Painter, *Oil and the American Century*, 22.

10. *Caracas Journal*, 19 March 1953.

11. American Chamber of Commerce in Venezuela [hereafter AmCham], *Review* 1 (April 1954):3; emphasis in original.

12. AmCham, *Review* 3 (March–April, 1956):23.

13. AmCham, *Review* 4 (May–June, 1957):40.

14. *Caracas Journal*, 28 September 1955. In that year, the Executive Committee of the *Caracas Journal* consisted of Jules Waldman, George Speirs, Elbert Boylan, Robert Bottome, Morse Travers, and Earl Elrick.

15. *Caracas Journal*, 9 July 1951.

16. *Caracas Journal*, 16 April 1951.

17. *Caracas Journal*, 17 April 1952.

18. *Caracas Journal*, 7 September 1955.

19. *Caracas Journal*, 2 May 1952.

20. *Daily Journal*, 10 April 1956.

21. *Caracas Journal*, 25 May 1955.

22. *Caracas Journal*, 23 July 1951.

23. *Daily Journal*, 3 May 1957.

24. AmCham, *Review* 4 (July 1957):16.

25. *Caracas Journal*, 19 November 1951.

26. *El Heraldo*, 4 March 1954.

27. *Caracas Journal*, 25 September 1954.

28. Some of Kamen-Kaye's articles were collected and published as *Caracas Everyday* (Caracas: Caracas Journal, 1947), later reprinted as *Venezuelan Folkways* (Detroit: Blaine Ethridge Books, 1976).

29. Robertson published an account of her experiences titled *Churún Merú— The Tallest Angel: Of Jungles and Other Journeys* (Ardmore, Pa.: Whitmore Publishing, 1975).

30. Winthrop R. Wright, *Café con Leche: Race, Class and National Image in Venezuela* (Austin: University of Texas Press, 1990), 97–100.

31. Richard Donovan, "The Fabulous Satchel Paige," in *The Baseball Reader*, ed. Charles Einstein (New York: Lippencott & Crowell, 1980), 68–101. The original essay was written in 1953.

32. Donn Rogosin, *Invisible Men: Life in Baseball's Negro Leagues* (New York: Atheneum, 1983), 164–66, 175.

33. Eleazar Díaz Rangel, *El beisbol en Venezuela* (Caracas: El Diario de Caracas, 1979), 63–64.

34. William D. Marsland and Amy L. Marsland, *Venezuela through Its History* (New York: Thomas Crowell, 1954), 1.

35. Ibid., 259.

36. Henry J. Allen, *Venezuela, a Democracy* (New York: Doubleday, Doran, 1941), 51.

37. Ibid., xi.

38. Marsland and Marsland, *Venezuela through Its History*, 259.

39. Alfred Jankus and Neil Malloy, *Venezuela, Land of Opportunity* (New York: Pageant Press, 1956), 20.

40. Ibid., 22.

41. Allen, *Venezuela*, 4.

42. Ibid., 52.

43. Jankus and Malloy, *Land of Opportunity*, 21.

44. Allen, *Venezuela*, 236–37.

45. Ibid., 243.

46. *El Nacional*, 20 April 1953.

47. Mariano Picón Salas, "Américas desavenidas," in *Obras Selectas*, 2nd ed. (Madrid: Ediciones Edime, 1962), 1058–61.

48. Picón Salas, "La espinge en America," in *Obras Selectas*, 1214–15.

49. *El Nacional*, 21 June 1950. Avila was the pen name of Pomponette Planchart de García.

50. *El Nacional*, 23 December 1955.

51. *El Nacional*, 29 December 1955.

52. *Caracas Journal*, 19 March 1953.

53. *El Heraldo*, 24 July 1953.

54. *La Religión*, 21 September 1957.

55. *La Religión*, 24 July 1957.

56. *La Religión*, 28 April 1957.

57. Glen Kolb, *Democracy and Dictatorship in Venezuela, 1945–1958* (Hamden, Conn.: Connecticut College and Archon Books, 1974), 166–72.

8. From Hemispheric to Global Perspectives, 1958–1990s

1. Speech given by Henry A. Kissinger to the U.S.-Venezuelan Symposium II at Macuto, Venezuela, 17 February 1976, published as Henry A. Kissinger, *The Americas in a Changing World* (Washington, D.C.: Department of State, Bureau of Public Affairs 1976), 4.
2. Yergin, *The Prize*, 511.
3. Ibid., 513.
4. Franklin Tugwell, *The Politics of Oil in Venezuela* (Stanford: Stanford University Press, 1975), 5.
5. Yergin, *The Prize*, 580.
6. Quoted in "Descarto la acción militar el secretario de defensa de EE.UU.," in *El Presidente Pérez, la nación venezolana, y la guerra del petróleo declarada por Mr. Ford* (Caracas: Ediciones Centauro, 1974), 128.
7. Pérez, "Repuesta pública del Presidente de Venezuela al de Estados Unidos," in ibid., 92.
8. "El Canciller Schacht en las Naciones Unidas," in ibid., 188.
9. Quoted in Domingo Alberto Rangel, *La invasión de Mr. Ford* (Valencia: Vadell Hermanos, 1975), 5.
10. Yergin, *The Prize*, 718.
11. Jorge Rondón Uzcátegui, "Las relaciones de Venezuela y Africa," *Política Internacional* 5 (January–March 1987):16–19.
12. Ramón Escovar Salom, *Nuevas alternativas para la solidaridad internacional* (Caracas: Ministerio de Relaciones Exteriores, 1976), 24.
13. Carlos Andrés Pérez, "Presencia de la tradición africana en nuestro pueblo," in *La política internacional de Carlos Andrés Pérez*, 2 vols. (Caracas: Ediciones Centauro, 1980), 2:241.
14. Pérez, "Un continente americano sin vasallajes, opresión o rezagos colonialistas," in ibid., 2:134.
15. Robert Alexander, *Rómulo Betancourt and the Transformation of Venezuela* (New Brunswick, N.J.: Transaction Books, 1982), 554.
16. Quoted in Stephen E. Ambrose, *Rise to Globalism: American Foreign Policy 1938–1970* (Baltimore: Penguin Books, 1971), 323.
17. M. Ignacio Purroy, *Estado e industrialización en Venezuela* (Valencia: Vadell Hermanos, 1982), 228.
18. Pérez, "La Integración de Latinoamerica la hacemos nosotros o la harán por nosotros las compañías transnacionales," in *La política de Pérez*, 1:169–70.

19. Laura Rojas, "Aspectos económicos de la política exterior de Venezuela, in *Reforma y política exterior en Venezuela*, ed. Carlos A. Romero (Caracas: Instituto Venezolano de Estudios Sociales y Políticos and Editorial Nueva Sociedad, 1992), 169–70.

20. Pérez, "El Canal de Panamá, preocupación esencial de mi gobierno," in *La política de Pérez*, 2:426.

21. Simón Alberto Consalvi, *Una política exterior democrática en tiempos de crisis* (Caracas: Editorial Pomaire, 1988), 143.

22. Domingo Alberto Rangel, *La caída de los Estados Unidos y sus consecuencias internacionales* (Caracas: Consejo de Profesores Universitarios Jubilados U.C.V., 1989).

23. Alfredo Toro Hardy, *El desafío venezolano: como influir las decisiones políticas estadounidenses* (Caracas: Instituto de Altos Estudios de América Latina, Universidad Simón Bolívar, 1988).

Bibliographical Essay

The monographs and scholarly works on Venezuela are uneven in quality and coverage. One can find quite a lot in both Spanish and English on the Bolivarian period of the early nineteenth century, a smattering of works on the 1890s crises and their aftermath, and quite a bit on the post-1958 democratic period, especially with relation to petroleum. Other periods and topics have received much less coverage. Thus, I have relied more on primary published and unpublished works than on secondary surveys. The most useful have included U.S. diplomatic and consular reports (principally Record Group 59 of the U.S. National Archives records), *The Papers relating to the Foreign Relations of the United States* (*FRUS*), some archival material from the Venezuelan Foreign Ministry (Cancillería), and the Venezuelan Foreign Ministry's *Memoria y Cuenta* (known as the *Libro Amarillo*, issued since 1868). For anyone with the patience, the post-1945 period can also be examined in newspapers and magazines such as the *Daily Journal* (and its precursor, the *Caracas Journal*), *Venezuela Económica*, *El Nacional* (Caracas), and *El Universal* (Caracas); in oil company publications like *El Farol*; and in newsmagazines and political party publications. Two relatively recent journals contain articles by and about Venezuelan foreign policy experts: *Perfiles Internacionales* and *Política Internacional*.

This essay is limited to works dealing directly with United States–Venezuelan relations or with Venezuelan topics that illuminate those relations. Lamentably for the general reader, many of the best works are available only in Spanish-language editions or as unpublished doctoral dissertations. For more general bibliographies on inter-American relations, U.S. relations with Latin America, and the history of U.S. foreign policy, see appropriate guides to these topics. For example, David Trask, Michael Meyer, and Roger Trask, *A Bibliography of United States–Latin American Relations since 1810* (Lincoln, 1968); and Michael Meyer, *Supplement to "A Bibliography of United States–Latin American Relations since 1810"* (Lincoln, 1979), may be used in conjunction with the annual *Handbook of Latin American Studies* for more recent citations.

The most comprehensive bibliographical guide to Venezuelan materials is John Lombardi, Germán Carrera Damas, Roberta Adams, et al., *Venezuelan History: A Comprehensive Working Bibliography* (Boston, 1977). It should be supplemented with the excellent D. A. G. Waddell, *Venezuela* (Oxford, 1990), for more recent titles and annotated entries. Venezuela's Biblioteca Nacional publishes periodic guides to more recent works (see *Bibliografía Venezolana* and *Anuario Bibliográfico Venezolana*) as well as a guide to government publications, *Catálogo de publicaciones oficiales, 1840–1977* (Mérida, 1978). William Sullivan and B. S. McBeth compiled *Petroleum in Venezuela: A Bibliography* (Boston, 1985), which concentrates on Venezuela's most critical topic. William Sullivan also published another useful guide, *Dissertations and Theses on Venezuelan Topics, 1900–1985* (Metuchen, N.J., 1988).

Francisco J. Parra sketches a digest of Venezuelan foreign policy positions and their origins in the five volumes of *Doctrinas de la cancillería venezolano* (New York, 1953). The Ministerio de Relaciones Exteriores de Venezuela includes some documents and a chronicle of important foreign relations in the *Anales diplomáticos de Venezuela* (Caracas, 1975); volumes 6 and 7 treat relations with the United States. Manuel Pérez Vila et al., *Diccionario de historia de Venezuela* (Caracas, 1990), is an invaluable three-volume reference source for scholarly sketches of important people, regimes, and events. More accessible for English speakers, but less useful, is Donna Keyse Rudolph and G. A. Rudolph's slight *Historical Dictionary of Venezuela* (Metuchen, N.J., 1971).3

For statistics, Miguel Izard's *Series estadísticas para la historia de Venezuela* (Mérida, 1970) gives longer runs of data than does the annual and more inclusive *Anuario Estadístico*, published since 1877. The Banco Central de Venezuela's *La economía venezolana en los últimos treinta y cinco años* (Caracas, 1978) can be updated with the Inter-American Development Bank's annual, *Social and Economic Progress in Latin America*.

Venezuelan Published Document Collections

A number of document sets assist historians of Venezuela. The Academia Nacional de la Historia has an especially strong series for the colonial period, but see also its list of titles under the Fuentes para la historia republicana de Venezuela. Two major collections provide access to essays and political tracts by most major Venezuelan figures from independence to the late twentieth century: *Pensamiento político venezolano del siglo XX: Documentos para su estudio* (Caracas, 1985–) and *Pensamiento político venezolano del siglo XIX* (Caracas, 1983). For the independence period and Bolivarian thought, see Harold Bierck, Jr., ed., *Selected Writings of Bolívar* (2 vols., New York, 1951). Pedro Grases has published several independence era collections; see especially *Preindependencia y emanci-*

pación (protagonistas y testimonios) (Barcelona, 1981) and *Traducciones de interés político-cultural en la época de la independencia de Venezuela* (Caracas, 1961).

A collection intended for Venezuelan students is Santos Rodulfo Cortés's *Antología documental de Venezuela, 1492–1900* (Caracas, 1971). Naudy Suárez Figueroa continues the work for the first half of the twentieth century in *Programas políticos venezolanos de la primera mitad del siglo XX* (Caracas, 1977). The *Boletín del Archivo Histórico de Miraflores* reproduces documents from that presidential archive, especially the 1899–1935 period. The *Boletín* of the Academia Nacional de la Historia focuses on the colonial and independence periods but also prints some nineteenth-century documents. Most recent presidents (and some foreign ministers) have published their key foreign policy statements. The two volumes devoted to Carlos Andrés Pérez are especially interesting for their scope; see *La política internacional de Carlos Andrés Pérez* (Caracas, 1980). Two collections of interviews with prominent Venezuelans provide further grist for historians of the late twentieth century; see the volumes by journalist Alfredo Peña (*Conversaciones con . . .* Luís Herrera Campíns, Uslar Pietri, Carlos Andrés Pérez, and other prominent figures) and Agustín Blanco Múñoz's *Testimonios violentos* (interviews with guerrillas, politicians, Seguridad Nacional head Pedro Estrada, and Marcos Pérez Jiménez).

General Histories of Venezuela

There are few good general histories of Venezuela. Of them, John Lombardi's *Venezuela: The Search for Order, the Dream of Progress* (New York, 1982) is the best in English. Guillermo Morón's *A History of Venezuela* (London, 1964) gives slight attention to the twentieth century, as is also true of his five-volume *Historia de Venezuela* (Caracas, 1956). J. L. Salcedo-Bastardo frequently revises and updates his *Historia fundamental de Venezuela*, now in its eighth edition (Caracas, 1979). Manuel Vicente Magallanes, in *Los partidos políticos en la evolución histórica venezolana*, 5th ed. (Caracas, 1983), traces the programs, rise, and fall of major and minor political parties from the early nineteenth century.

The works of Venezuela's positivist historians still stand up for basic narrative of the nineteenth century. The fifteen volumes of Francisco González Guinán, *Historia contemporánea de Venezuela* (Caracas, 1909, 1954), have much of the flavor of a chronicle; while José Gil Fortoul's *Historia constitucional de Venezuela*, 5th ed., (3 vols. Caracas, 1967) advances more interpretative material. Malcolm Deas published two essays in the *Cambridge History of Latin America* that deal with Venezuela: "Venezuela, Colombia and Ecuador: The First Half-Century of Independence" (vol. 3, 1985) and "Colombia, Ecuador and Venezuela, 1880–1930" (vol. 5, 1986). Judith Ewell concludes the series with "Venezuela since 1930" (vol. 8, 1991). See also the bibliographical essays that accompany these essays.

For the twentieth century, the multivolume work of Juan Bautista Fuen-mayor, *Historia de la Venezuela política contemporánea 1899–1960* (Caracas, 1978–), somewhat echoes González Guinán's chronicle approach, but with the Marxist fervor of one who participated in much of the drama. Judith Ewell's *Venezuela: A Century of Change* (Stanford, 1984) is an overview of Venezuelan history since the 1890s. Especially for the post-1958 period, see the work of political scientists John Martz and David Myers, eds., *Venezuela: The Democratic Experience* (New York, 1977, 1986); John Peeler, *Latin American Democracies: Colombia, Costa Rica, Venezuela* (Chapel Hill, 1985); Richard Hillman, *Democracy for the Privileged* (Boulder, Colo., 1994); and David Blank, *Venezuela, Politics in a Petroleum Republic* (New York, 1984). The multiauthor collections of Ramón J. Velásquez et al., *Venezuela moderna: medio siglo de historia 1926–1976*, 2nd ed. (Caracas, 1979); and Mariano Picón Salas et al., *Venezuela independiente: evolución política y social 1810–1960* (Caracas, 1975), have some good essays.

For economic history, both Federico Brito Figueroa's *Historia económico y social de Venezuela* (2 vols., Caracas, 1966) and Domingo Alberto Rangel's, *Capital y desarrollo* (3 vols., Caracas, 1969) employ a Marxian or dependency approach. Loring Allen's *Venezuelan Economic Development: A Politico-Economic Analysis* (Greenwich, Conn., 1977) is more balanced, as is Sergio Aranda, *La economía venezolana* (Mexico, 1977).

Travel, Description, and Popular Accounts

Venezuela does not have as rich a travel literature as Mexico and Cuba, but there are some useful accounts, especially those written by continental Europeans and British travelers in the nineteenth century. Alexander von Humboldt's *Personal Narrative of Travels to the Equinoctial Regions of the New Continent during the Years 1799–1804* (London, 1822) is the classic source for geography, society, and resources of the late colonial period. Italian Giovanni Agustín Codazzi's three-volume work, *Resumen de la geografía de Venezuela* (Caracas, 1841), remained the standard on geography until the mid-twentieth century. J. Hawkshaw, *Reminiscences of South America from 2½ Year's Residence in Venezuela* (London, 1838); F. DePons, *Travels in South America during the Years 1801, 1802, 1803, and 1804* (London, 1807); and E. B. Eastwick, *Venezuela: Or Sketches of Life in a South American Republic* (London, 1868), recount the authors' views of society and politics. See also the collection edited by Elías Pino Iturrieta and Pedro Enrique Calzadilla, *La mirada del otro: viajeros extranjeros en la venezuela del siglo XIX* (Caracas, 1992).

Most U.S. travelers who recorded early impressions of the new republic (of Venezuela or Gran Colombia) were diplomats, adventurers, or commercial agents, and many of these accounts were not published until much later. A collection of the accounts of Americans who joined Francisco Miranda's 1806 expedition is found in Edgardo Mondolfi, *Testigos norteamericanos de la expedición de Miranda: John Sherman, Moses Smith, Henry Ingersoll* (Caracas, 1992). William Duane's account—*A Visit to Colombia in the Years 1822 and 1823* (Philadelphia, 1826)—is excellent, as is Jane Lucas de Grummond's edition of the diary of the first U.S. minister to Venezuela, *Las comadres de Caracas: Historia de John G. A. Williamson* (Barquisimeto, 1955); and Alfred Tischendorf's edition of *The Diary and Journal of Richard Clough Anderson, Jr., 1814–1826* (Durham, 1964). Richard Harding Davis, *Three Gringos in Venezuela and Central America* (New York, 1896), gives a late nineteenth-century novelist's view.

A few Venezuelans reciprocated by chronicling their impressions of the United States. Among these works are Francisco de Miranda, *The New Democracy in America: Travels of Francisco de Miranda in the United States, 1783–84* (Norman, Okla., 1963); Nazareno (pseudonym of Consul Simón Camacho), *Cosas de los Estados Unidos* (New York, 1864); Jesús Múñoz Tébar, *Personalismo y legalismo* (New York, 1890); and Ramón Páez, *Ambas Americas* (New York, 1872). Páez, the son of President José Antonio Páez, spent a number of years in the United States and also interpreted his country—and father—for a U.S. audience in *Wild Scenes in South America; or, Life in the Llanos of Venezuela* (New York, 1862).

The work of William E. Curtis, secretary to the U.S. mission that traveled to South America prior to the 1889 Pan-American Conference, represents a transition from the informal early nineteenth-century memoirs to the descriptive guides that reflected the boosterism of James Blaine's new Pan-Americanism. Blaine's *Venezuela: A Land Where It's Always Summer* (New York, 1896) and *The Capitals of Spanish America* (New York, 1888) point up the opportunities to be found in Venezuela for the alert commercial traveler or tourist. In the same era, the work of William Scruggs, former U.S. minister and lobbyist for the Venezuelan government in the 1890s, sought to publicize the history and plight of the small nation threatened by British expansionism; see *Colombian and Venezuelan Republics, with Notes on Other Parts of Central and South America* (Boston, 1900).

For the twentieth century, the following works combine description, history, and an account of the nation's rich resources for a popular—or business—audience. British geologist and petroleum expert Leonard Dalton stresses the mineral resources and commercial possibilities of the country in *Venezuela* (London, 1912). Other works include Erna Fergusson, *Venezuela* (New York, 1939); Henry J. Allen, *Venezuela, a Democracy* (New York, 1941); William D. Marsland and Amy L. Marsland, *Venezuela through Its History* (New York, 1954); John Gunther's chapter on Venezuela in his *Inside Latin America* (New York, 1966); and Stan Steiner, *In Search of the Jaguar: Growth and Paradox in Venezuela* (New York, 1979). The book by Alfred Jankus and Neil Malloy, *Venezuela, Land of Opportunity* (New York, 1956), reflects the postwar enthusiasm to cash in on the nation's oil wealth. By the 1960s, tourist guides regularly carried minimal references to Venezuela but found little to tout compared with Mexican or Peruvian archaeological wonders or Caribbean luxury resort accommodations. The essays found in the 1990s Insight Guides resemble classically idiosyncratic travelers' accounts more than a tourist guide; see *Venezuela* (Boston, 1993). A few U.S. literary figures have made reference to Venezuela. Of special note is the autobiography of African-American writer James Weldon Johnson, *Along This Way: The Autobiography of James Weldon Johnson* (New York, 1933). Johnson spent two years as U.S. consul in Puerto Cabello in the first decade of the twentieth century.

U.S. scientists, naturalists, and anthropologists became fascinated with the less-traveled areas of Venezuela. Although their focus was on science or adventure, they often included their observations on Venezuelan history and society. The height of this interest fell between the 1920s and the 1950s, inspired by searches for exotic flora and fauna, "primitive" peoples (like the legendary "white Indians" of the far south), and geographic marvels like the source of the Orinoco River and the world's highest waterfall. Some of the best works are Hiram Bingham, *The Journal of an Expedition across Venezuela and Colombia, 1906–07* (New Haven, 1909); Arthur Friel, *The River of Seven Stars* (New York, 1924); Herbert Spencer Dickey, *My Jungle Book* (Boston, 1932); Earl Parker Hanson, *Journey to Manaos* (New York, 1938); Norman MacDonald, *The Orchid Hunters* (New York, 1939); L. R. Dennison, *Devil Mountain* (New York, 1942); Ruth Robertson, *Churún Merú—The Tallest Angel* (Ardmore, Pa., 1975); and Charles W. Beebe, *High Jungle* (New York, 1949).

Venezuelan–United States Relations in the Nineteenth Century

Only Sheldon Liss has made a gallant stab at analyzing the entire history of U.S.-Venezuelan relations; see his *Diplomacy and Dependency: Venezuela, the United States, and the Americas* (Salisbury, N.C., 1978). A few works deal comprehensively with the nineteenth century. Benjamin Frankel's Ph.D. dissertation, "Venezuela and the United States, 1810–1888" (Berkeley, 1964) gives much attention to claims issues and is also available in a published edition in Spanish as *Venezuela y los Estados Unidos, 1810–1888* (Caracas, 1977). Two broad Venezuelan works are Dilio Hernández, *Historia diplomática de Venezuela, 1830–1900* (Caracas, 1986); and Armando Rojas, *Historia de las relaciones diplomáticas entre Venezuela y los Estados Unidos, 1810–1899* (Caracas, 1979). Of these works, only Liss goes much beyond narrative to analysis.

As is true of much of Venezuelan historiography, the works that cover the Bolivarian period are most numerous and are frequently more scholarly than those that discuss some of the more polemical later topics. The general works often treat early commercial ties with the United States, the influence of U.S. independence and ideology, and the effort to secure the assistance of the United States in the independence struggle. See, for example, Cristóbal Mendoza, *Las primeras misiones diplomáticas de Venezuela* (Madrid, 1962); Mauro Páez-Pumar, *Las proclamas de Filadelfia de 1774 y 1775 en la Caracas de 1777* (Caracas, 1973); Mercedes Alvarez, *Comercio y comerciantes y sus proyecciones en la independencia venezolana* (Caracas, 1963); C. Parra Pérez, *Historia de la primera república de Venezuela* (2 vols., Caracas, 1959); Francisco José Urrutía, *Páginas de historia diplomática; los Estados Unidos de America y las repúblicas hispanoamericanas de 1810 a 1830* (Bogotá, 1917); and Elías Pino Iturrieta, *Las ideas de los primeros venezolanos* (Caracas, 1987).

U.S. historians have generally dealt with U.S. relations with all of Latin America during the independence epoch rather than focusing just on Gran Colombia or Venezuela, but these works contain much useful information on Bolívar and on Caribbean commerce. The following include information on relations with Venezuela: John J. Johnson, *A Hemisphere Apart: The Foundations of United States Policy toward Latin America* (Baltimore, 1990); Charles C. Griffin, *The United States and the Disruption of the Spanish Empire 1810–1822* (New York, 1937); Arthur P. Whitaker, *The United States and the Independence of Latin America 1800–1830* (Baltimore, 1941); and William R. Manning, ed., *Diplomatic Correspondence of the United States concerning the Independence of Latin American Nations*

(New York, 1925). David Bushnell collected documents relating to the strange Amelia Island affair in *La República de las Floridas: Texts and Documents* (Mexico, 1986). For commercial topics, see Jacques Barbier and Allan Kuethe, *The North American Role in the Spanish Imperial Economy, 1760–1819* (Manchester, 1984); Peggy Liss, *Atlantic Empires: The Network of Trade and Revolution, 1713–1826* (Baltimore, 1982); and William Olson, "Early North Americans in Venezuelan Commerce, 1810–1830" (Ph.D. diss., University of North Carolina, 1974). Jane Lucas de Grummond recounts the adventures of a successful Caribbean privateer in *Renato Beluche: Smuggler, Privateer, and Patriot, 1780–1860* (Baton Rouge, 1983). For the Gran Colombian period, see the useful E. T. Parks, *Colombia and the United States, 1765–1934* (Durham, 1935); the more recent *Colombia and the United States: Hegemony and Interdependence* (Athens, Ga., 1992), by Stephen Randall; and David Bushnell's *The Santander Regime in Gran Colombia* (Newark, Del., 1954). William Henry Harrison reveals his dislike of Bolívar but proclaims his innocence of conspiracy against him in *Remarks of Gen. Harrison, . . . on Certain Charges Made against Him by That [Gran Colombian] Government* (1830; Louisville, Ky., 1975).

Few notable events ruffled the diplomatic horizon between the two countries from the time of Venezuela's separation from Gran Colombia in 1830 until late in the century, and only a smattering of monographs on specialized topics are available. Foreign claims occupied the most attention until the concern about British expansionism in the 1890s became more important. Pedro Manuel Arcaya devotes considerable attention to claims by U.S. citizens in *Historia de las reclamaciones contra Venezuela* (Caracas, 1965). See also James R. Hibbs, "Caracas Award of 1868; Chapters in the Diplomatic History of Venezuela and the United States, 1865–69" (Ph.D. diss., University of Pennsylvania, 1941). For the Aves Island guano conflict, see William L. Harris, *Las reclamaciones de la Isla de Aves* (Caracas, 1968). Profiles of some Venezuelan foreign ministers and their actions supplement their writings, found in *Pensamiento político*, and give some insight into their actions. See, for example, F. Villanueva Berrizbeitia's sketches of sixteen Venezuelan foreign ministers in *Dieciséis cancilleres de Venezuela* (Caracas, 1960); Rafael Armando Rojas, *Los creadores de la diplomacia venezolana* (Caracas, 1965); Harold Bierck, Jr., *Vida pública de Don Pedro Gual* (Caracas, 1976); and William Lane Harris, *La diplomacia de José María Rojas, 1873–1883* (Caracas, 1984). More specialized topics include Richard H. Bradford's account of Venezuela's interest in the Cuban Ten Years' War in *The Virginius Affair* (Boulder, 1980); Alfred J. Hanna and Kathryn A. Hanna's history of the ill-fated Price grant in Guayana in *Confederate Exiles in Venezuela* (Tuscaloosa, 1960); Rafael A.

Rojas's narrative of late nineteenth-century diplomatic initiatives in *Las misiones diplomáticas de Guzmán Blanco* (Caracas, 1972); and Nikita Harwich Vallenilla's compelling history of the asphalt claims and conflicts in *Asfalto y revolución: la New York & Bermúdez Company* (Caracas, 1991). Not many of the corrupt or inept U.S. emissaries inspired biographies. Jane Lucas de Grummond drew on the subject's diary to write about the first U.S. minister to Venezuela in *Envoy to Caracas. The Story of John G. A. Williamson, Nineteenth Century Diplomat* (Baton Rouge, 1951); and William G. Wolff takes on the public life of the controversial William Scruggs in "The Diplomatic Career of William L. Scruggs: United States Minister to Colombia and Venezuela, and Legal Adviser to Venezuela, 1872–1912" (Ph.D. diss., Southern Illinois University, 1975).

Of the numerous works about British/European activities in Venezuela at the turn of the century, the tensions they generated, and the effects of the U.S. "rediscovery" of the Monroe Doctrine, see William L. Scruggs's own *British Aggressions in Venezuela, or the Monroe Doctrine on Trial* (Atlanta, 1895); Miriam Hood, *Diplomacia con cañones 1895–1905* (Caracas, 1978); Manuel Rodríguez Campos, *Venezuela 1902, la crisis fiscal y el bloqueo* (Caracas, 1977); Grover Cleveland, *The Venezuelan Boundary Controversy* (Princeton, 1913); Gordon Ireland, *Boundaries, Possessions and Conflicts in South America* (Cambridge, Mass., 1938); and the classic account by Dexter Perkins, *A History of the Monroe Doctrine*, rev. ed. (Boston, 1955). Walter LaFeber places the Venezuelan events in a provocative context in *The American Search for Opportunity, 1865–1913* (New York, 1993).

Castro, Gómez and the Táchira Dynasty, 1899–1958

Much of the twentieth-century bibliography on U.S.-Venezuelan relations naturally centers on the importance of petroleum. Most of the books specifically about petroleum are listed in a later section, but Stephen Rabe also provides an excellent general overview of binational relations in *The Road to OPEC: United States Relations with Venezuela, 1919–1976* (Austin, 1982). Three accounts in English of the chaotic Cipriano Castro period are William Sullivan's comprehensive "The Rise of Despotism in Venezuela: Cipriano Castro, 1899–1908" (Ph.D. diss., University of New Mexico, 1974); Embert J. Hendrickson, "New Venezuelan Controversy. The Relations of the United States and Venezuela, 1904 to 1914" (Ph.D. diss., University of Minnesota, 1964); and Charles Carreras, *United States Economic Penetration of Venezuela and Its Effects on Diplomacy: 1895–1906* (New York, 1987).

The long regime of Juan Vicente Gómez (1908–35) has not yet received the scholarly attention it merits. For contrasting popular views, see John Lavin, *A Halo for Gómez* (New York, 1954); and Thomas Rourke, *Gómez: Tyrant of the Andes* (New York, 1941). An excellent history of Gómez's dealings with the oil companies is found in B. S. McBeth, *Juan Vicente Gómez and the Oil Companies in Venezuela, 1908–1935* (Cambridge, 1983). Also useful is Edward Duff, "The Politics of Expediency: U.S.-Venezuelan Relations under Gómez" (Ph.D. diss., Pennsylvania State University, 1969). Ramón González Escorihuela examines traces of anti-imperialism in the Gómez era in *Las ideas antimperialistas y socialistas en el Táchira: Horizontes, 1903–1920* (San Cristóbal, 1988). Pedro Manuel Arcaya gives a highly colored version of the James Welch case in a booklet intended for the U.S. political audience: *The Venezuelan Courts and the Welch Case* (Washington, 1930).

Scholarly coverage is also uneven (with respect to nonpetroleum topics) for the period between the death of Gómez in 1935 and the overthrow of Pérez Jiménez in 1958. Clemy Machado de Acedo and Marisela Padrón Quero give a masterful account of the Venezuelan perspective on the negotiation of the 1939 trade treaty in *La diplomacia de López Contreras y el tratado de reciprocidad comercial con Estados Unidos* (Caracas, 1987). Glen Kolb provides a general history of the Pérez Jiménez regime in *Democracy and Dictatorship in Venezuela, 1945–1958* (Hamden, Conn., 1974). Winfield Burggraaff's *The Venezuelan Armed Forces in Politics, 1935–1959* (Columbia, Miss., 1972) analyzes the professionalization of military officers and their growing nationalism. Charles Ameringer traces the intersection of traditional political rivalries with the anticommunist cold war paranoia in *The Democratic Left in Exile: The Antidictatorial Struggle in the Caribbean, 1945–1959* (Coral Gables, Fla., 1974), and shows that Rómulo Betancourt's Acción Democrática colleagues found common cause in exile with democratic reformers from Costa Rica, the Dominican Republic, Nicaragua, and Puerto Rico. Redolent of the spirit of the 1950s, John A. Clements Associates allege the communist or subversive associations of Betancourt, Rutgers scholar Robert Alexander, Eleanor Roosevelt, and others in *Report on Venezuela* (New York, 1959). By contrast, Manuel Caballero, in *Latin America and the Comintern, 1919–1943* (Cambridge, 1986), argues that the Communists were singularly uninterested in Venezuela.

Venezuelan scholars have written some excellent studies of the origins of Venezuelan twentieth-century internationalism. See, for example, Fermín Toro Jiménez, *La política de Venezuela en la conferencia inter-Americana de consolidación de la paz: Buenos Aires, 1936* (Caracas, 1977); and Freddy Vivas Gallardo, *Venezuela en la sociedad de las naciones, 1920–1939* (Caracas, 1981). Vivas Gallardo suggests that the experience in the League of Nations allowed Venezuelan statesmen to experiment with rebuilding European and hemispheric ties without U.S. interference.

The United States, Venezuela, and the World after 1958

Venezuela's role as a petroleum democracy with an active foreign policy inspired a new spurt of scholarship after 1958. Overviews are provided by Rabe (already cited), and by Franklin Tugwell in *The Politics of Oil in Venezuela* (Stanford, 1975). Tugwell focuses on the Venezuelan government's luck and skill in its bargaining with the United States and the multinational oil companies. Collections of essays on Venezuelan foreign policy and its relationship to U.S. interests are more plentiful than monographs. Excellent studies may be found in Instituto de Estudios Políticos, UCV, *La agenda de la política exterior de Venezuela* (Caracas, 1983); Robert Bond, ed., *Contemporary Venezuela and Its Role in International Affairs* (New York, 1977); Elizabeth Ferris and Jennie Lincoln, eds., *Latin American Foreign Policies: Global and Regional Dimensions* (Boulder, Colo., 1981); and Carlos Romero, ed., *Reforma y política exterior en Venezuela* (Caracas, 1992).

Venezuelan scholars recognize the central role of the United States in their foreign policy agenda, whether or not they perceive a decline in the U.S. global hegemony. See, for example, Domingo Alberto Rangel, *La caída de los Estados Unidos y sus consecuencias internacionales* (Caracas, 1989); and Alfredo Toro Hardy's two excellent studies: *Venezuela, democracia y política exterior* (Caracas, 1986) and *El desafío venezolano: como influir las decisiones políticas estadounidenses* (Caracas, 1988). José Francisco Sucre Figarella discusses the crisis-filled contemporary world in *Venezuela en un mundo en crisis* (Caracas, 1988); and José Herrera Oropeza, in *Venezuela en el tercer mundo* (Caracas, 1969), notes with approval Venezuela's Third World stance. Venezuelan Carlos Rangel's *Third World Ideology and Western Reality: Manufacturing Political Myth* (New Brunswick, N.J., 1986) is more critical of Third World politics. For an indicator of Venezuela's shifting positions in the United Nations, see the collection of speeches by presidents and foreign ministers published by the Ministerio de Relaciones Exteriores: *Venezuela en las Naciones Unidas, 1945–1985* (Caracas, 1986).

While not as enamored of geopolitics and national security doctrines as their brethren in the Southern Cone, some Venezuelans have adopted that perspective. Rubén Carpio Castillo sums up most of the critical themes in *Geopolítica de Venezuela* (Caracas, 1981) and in his earlier *Mexico, Cuba y Venezuela. Triángulo geopolítico del Caribe* (Caracas, 1961), in which he makes a case for Venezuela's Caribbean identity and interests. The essays contained in Aníbal Romero, ed., *Seguridad, defensa y democracia en Venezuela* (Caracas, 1980), recapitulate much of the discussion over Venezuela's national security law, passed in 1976.

The Cuban Revolution of 1959, decolonization in the English Caribbean, geopolitical theories, the Venezuelan boundary dispute with Guyana, and, more recently, the Central American crises compelled greater Venezuelan attention to Caribbean affairs. Most Caribbean issues directly or indirectly affected Venezuelan relations with the United States. Eloy Lanza argues that Venezuela is only a stalking horse for Washington in the region in *El sub-imperialismo venezolano* (Caracas, 1980). Antonio Montilla Saldivia reiterates the more classic argument about U.S. imperialism in *Estados Unidos, América Latina y el Caribe: continuidad histórica de una política de dominación* (Caracas, 1988). More balanced and scholarly analyses appear in Andrés Serbín, *El Caribe: ¿ zona de paz?* (Santiago, 1989); in Demetrio Boersner, *Venezuela y el Caribe: presencia cambiante* (Caracas, 1978); and in two essay collections edited by Serbín: *Geopolítica de las relaciones de Venezuela con el Caribe* (Caracas, 1983) and *Venezuela y las relaciones internacionales en la cuenca del Caribe* (Caracas, 1987). The Serbín collections showcase the work of the Venezuelan scholars who formed the Venezuelan Caribbean Studies Association in the 1970s to provide a counterweight to some less responsible advocates of Caribbean activism.

Since so much of Venezuela's post-1958 foreign policy has been intertwined with its identity as a democratic nation, studies of political parties and politics can be useful. Classic works on the formative years of the Acción Democrática include Robert Alexander's *Rómulo Betancourt and the Transformation of Venezuela* (New Brunswick, N.J., 1982), and *The Venezuelan Democratic Revolution* (New Brunswick, N.J.,1964); and John Martz, *Acción Democrática. Evolution of a Modern Political Party in Venezuela* (Princeton, 1966). Judith Ewell's *Indictment of a Dictator: The Extradition and Trial of Marcos Pérez Jiménez* (College Station, Tex., 1981) focuses on the AD's efforts to secure Pérez's extradition from the United States. Other studies widen the political perspective; see David Blank, *Politics in Venezuela* (Boston, 1973); and Daniel Levine, *Conflict and Political Change in Venezuela* (Princeton, 1973). Other major political parties have received less attention, but see Donald Herman, *Christian Democracy in Venezuela* (Chapel

Hill, 1980); and Steve Ellner, *Venezuela's Movimiento al Socialismo: From Guerrilla Defeat to Innovative Politics* (Durham, 1988). One of the best accounts of the political effects of the 1970s oil boom is Terry Karl's "The Political Economy of Petrodollars: Oil and Democracy in Venezuela" (Ph.D. diss., Stanford, 1982).

Petroleum Relations

The most significant relations between the United States and Venezuela in the twentieth century have concerned petroleum and the petroleum companies. Daniel Yergin gives a dense but readable general account of the growth of the international oil business in *The Prize: The Epic Quest for Oil, Money & Power* (New York, 1991). Yergin's focus is primarily on the United States, but he places the history of petroleum in an international context that includes Venezuela, the Middle East, and OPEC.

The classic account of the intersection of petroleum, politics, and foreign companies in Venezuela is Rómulo Betancourt, *Venezuela: Oil and Politics*, trans. Everett Bauman (Boston, 1979; original Spanish edition published in Mexico, 1956); see also the English translation of some of Betancourt's speeches and articles in *Venezuela's Oil* (London, 1978). Edwin Lieuwen's *Petroleum in Venezuela: A History* (Berkeley, 1954) treats the same time period more dispassionately. For the origins of foreign exploitation in Venezuela, see R. Arnold et al., *The First Big Oil Hunt: Venezuela, 1911–1916* (New York, 1960). As noted previously, B. S. McBeth, *Juan Vicente Gómez and the Oil Companies in Venezuela, 1908–1935* (Cambridge, 1983); and Stephen Rabe, *The Road to OPEC* (Austin, 1982), provide excellent accounts of petroleum diplomacy, as does Franklin Tugwell's *The Politics of Oil in Venezuela* (Stanford, 1975). Wayne C. Taylor's useful *The Creole Petroleum Corporation in Venezuela* (Washington, 1955) sketches in the history of the Standard Oil subsidiary and its prominent role in Venezuela. James Petras et al., cover the process of the 1976 nationalization in Venezuela in *The Nationalization of Venezuelan Oil* (New York, 1977); and Laura Randall continues the story into the mid-1980s in *The Political Economy of Venezuelan Oil* (New York, 1987). David S. Painter, in *Oil and the American Century: The Political Economy of U.S. Foreign Oil Policy, 1941–1954* (Baltimore, 1986), analyzes the critical transition period from the FDR era to the cold war, with much attention to U.S. petroleum machinations. Aníbal Martínez guides the general reader to the history of the Venezuelan petroleum industry in *Cronología del petróleo venezolano* (Caracas, 1970) and several other books.

Several books examine the history and strategies of Latin American state oil companies, including Venezuela's PDVSA. See George Philip, *Oil and Politics in Latin America: Nationalist Movements and State Companies* (Cambridge, 1982); and the collection edited by John Wirth, *Latin American Oil Companies and the Politics of Energy* (Lincoln, 1985).

Economic histories of Venezuela have dwelt on the opportunities brought by oil and the distortions of society caused by the petroleum industry. In addition to the general studies by F. Brito Figueroa, Domingo Alberto Rangel, Loring Allen, and Sergio Aranda that I have already mentioned, see the International Bank for Reconstruction and Development, *The Economic Development of Venezuela* (Baltimore, 1961), for coverage of the major issues of Venezuelan economic development. An analysis of the weak industrial structure can be found in Weine Karlsson, *Manufacturing in Venezuela: Studies on Development and Location* (Stockholm, 1975). Optimism and positive thinking prevailed at the time of nationalization; for example, see Jorge Salazar Carrillo, *Oil in the Economic Development of Venezuela* (New York, 1976); and Luís Vallenilla, *Oil: The Making of a New Economic Order: Venezuelan Oil and OPEC* (New York, 1975). Marxist economists and other Venezuelan analysts have long sounded warnings about the nation's neglect of agriculture and preference for luxury imports over efficient domestic industrialization; for example, see Domingo F. Maza Zavala, *Problemas de la economía exterior de Venezuela* (Caracas, 1962), and *Venezuela. Crecimiento sin desarrollo* (Caracas, 1974). Even the omniscient "father" of OPEC became quite critical of waste, corruption, and the misuse of Venezuela's petroleum moment; for example, see Juan Pablo Pérez Alfonzo: *Hundiéndonos en el excremento del diablo* (Caracas, 1976), *El pentágano petrolero* (Caracas, 1967), and *Petróleo y dependencia* (Caracas, 1971). After the crash and devaluation of 1983 presaged the nation's awareness of its crippling foreign debt, pessimism became even more prevalent. The following works have chapters on the Venezuelan debt: Miguel Wionczek, ed., *Politics and Economics of External Debt Crisis: The Latin American Experience* (Boulder, Colo., 1985); and Esperanza Durán, *Latin America and the World Recession* (Cambridge, 1985). Carlos Marichal gives an admirable background history of all Latin America in *A Century of Debt Crises in Latin America from Independence to the Great Depression, 1820–1930* (Princeton, 1989).

The weakness of the agricultural economy and the role of U.S. multinationals is covered in George Schuyler, *Hunger in a Land of Plenty* (Cambridge, Mass., 1980); and Eleanor Witte Wright, "The Political Economy of Venezuelan Food Policy 1958–1978" (Ph.D. diss., University of Maryland, 1982).

José Antonio Mayobre analyzes the history of foreign investments in the country in *Las inversiones extranjeras en Venezuela* (Caracas, 1970); and Nikita Harwich Vallenilla, in *Asfalto y revolución: la New York & Bermúdez Company* (Caracas, 1991), covers the history of one of the earliest major U.S. investments.

Culture and National Identity

The line between national identity and national stereotypes sometimes is thin and overly fungible. Venezuelan intellectuals and foreign writers often identify with European or United States culture and denigrate the value of what is uniquely *venezolano*. Laureano Vallenilla Lanz's *Cesarismo democrático* (Caracas, 1919) remains the classic account; Carlos Rangel's provocative *The Latin Americans: Their Love-Hate Relationship with the United States* (New Brunswick, N.J., 1987) is a more recent example. The essays and novels of intellectuals Arturo Uslar Pietri and Mariano Picón Salas treat many twentieth-century cultural issues and often comment on historical ones as well.

Venezuelan writers often skirt the topic of race, stymied by a discomfort with the Afro-Venezuelan past and the near nonexistence of a surviving indigenous culture. Winthrop R. Wright brings the topic to the fore and analyzes it in *Café con Leche: Race, Class, and National Image in Venezuela* (Austin, Tex., 1990). John Lombardi discusses the last years of slavery in *Decline and Abolition of Negro Slavery in Venezuela, 1820–1854* (Westport, Conn., 1971).

Contemporary Marxist Rodolfo Quintero, in *La cultura nacional y popular* (Caracas, 1976), discusses Venezuelan popular culture, but the classical nineteenth-century studies of Arístides Rojas may be more useful for background. Dorothy Kamen-Kaye sympathetically portrays Venezuelan traditions of the 1940s in *Venezuelan Folkways* (Detroit, 1947, 1976). Angel Rosenblatt's works on Venezuelan language contain many clues to national culture; see *Buenas y malas palabras en el Castellano de Venezuela* (Caracas, 1960) and *Lengua y cultura de Venezuela, tradición e innovación* (Caracas, 1957).

Twentieth-century Venezuelan novelists, although generally less known than writers from other Latin American countries, offer many insights into Venezuelan character and attitudes. The novels of Rómulo Gallegos (many of them translated, published between 1920 and the early 1950s), especially the classic *Doña Barbara*, depict the diversity of the Venezuelan ethnicity and landscape. Ramón Díaz Sánchez's often bitter novels treat themes of race and the early impact of the petroleum industry in Maracaibo. Miguel Otero Silva's fiction similarly portrays Venezuelan societal changes in the transition from a dusty rural past to the tensions of the postwar urban nation. Arturo Uslar Pietri's excellent historical novels simultaneously sketch out the national past and reveal Uslar's erudite and often pessimistic views. See also Maurice Belrose, *La sociedad venezolana en su novela, 1890–1935* (Maracaibo, 1979).

José Egidio Rodríguez relates national image to international policy in *Imagen y política internacional* (Caracas, 1987). The classic work by historian Germán Carrera Damas dissects Simón Bolívar's image in the minds of his countrymen and women; see *El culto á Bolívar* (Caracas, 1969).

Index

Abrams, Elliott, 223
Acción Democrática (AD): in exile, 154, 158, 159, 161, 162, 164–65; petroleum policy of, 173, 194, 201–3; and Socialist International, 209, 217; and *trienio* policies, 149–52, 184, 189, 192, 193
Acheson, Dean, 155, 215
Adams, John, 16
Adams, John Quincy, 16, 27, 28, 31, 32
Adams-Onís Treaty, 29
Afro-Venezuelans, 3, 50, 86, 155
Aguido-Freitez, Raúl, 196
Alexander, Robert, 161, 162
Allen, Henry, 190–92
Alliance for Progress, 213, 218, 220
AmCham. *See* Venezuelan American Chamber of Commerce (AmCham)
Amelia Island, 25, 26, 30
American Civil Liberties Union, 215
American Federation of Labor, 137
Americanization, 5, 118; and American way of life, 6, 167, 181, 197; and consumption, 132, 146, 175, 181, 188; and films, 141, 187; and holidays, 188, 195, 196; and magazines, 187; in oil zones of 1920s, 141; and radio, 129
Andean Pact, 219
Andrade, Ignacio, 94–96, 98, 110
Andrews, Avery D., 101
Andueza Palacio, Raimundo, 74, 75
Anglo-Iranian Oil Company, 174, 179
Angostura, Congress of, 32
Anti-Americanism, 5, 97, 109, 140, 141; under Gómez, 114, 120, 123; in 1958, 164; in nineteenth century, 35, 51, 93, 96

AP. *See* Associated Press
Arbenz, Jacobo, 160
Arcaya, Pedro Manuel, 112, 115, 127, 137; as ambassador to Washington, 124, 125, 129; views of, on democracy, 147–48; and Welch case, 139
Arias, Oscar, 222
Arias Blanco, Rafael, 197
Arms race, 210, 211
Asphalt, 63, 70, 73, 92, 100–102, 105, 109, 134
Associated Press, 118, 129, 138
Astucia, 2, 5, 76, 77, 79, 124
Aury, Louis, 25, 26
Aves Island, 8, 60, 61, 210
Avila, Juana de, 195
Ayacucho, battle of, 22, 31

Baker, Jehu, 68, 71, 78, 83, 84
Baltimore merchants, 23, 24
Baseball, in Venezuela, 5, 189, 190
Beauty contests, 188, 189
Beluche, Renato, 23, 40
Benton, Thomas, 32
Berle, Adolf, 149
Betancourt, Rómulo, 154, 192, 197; as democratic model, 8, 213, 214; in exile, 160, 161, 162, 163, 165; as president, 166, 201, 218; and *trienio*, 147, 149–52, 184; and *Venezuela: Política y Petróleo*, 194
Biaggini, Angel, 149
Bidlack Treaty, 46
Biggs, James, 14, 15
Bingham, Hiram, 108

Blaine, James G., 90, 109, 220, 224; and Pan-American Conference, 9, 68, 88; and tariff policy, 75

Blockade of 1902–3, 101–2, 104, 105

Blow, Henry T., 52, 53, 55

Bolet Peraza, Nicolás, 88

Bolívar, Juan Vicente, 18, 19

Bolívar, Simón, 25, 38, 87, 97, 99, 211; book on, 121; cult of, 65, 67, 92, 114, 198; death of, 35; liberalism of, 14, 40, 199; monarchical tendencies of, alleged, 6, 33–35; Pan-Americanism of, 7, 9, 30–33, 68, 128, 195, 213; statue of, in Washington, 68, 124; and wars for independence, 21, 22, 23, 27–30, 43, 223–24; compared with Washington, 1, 4, 80, 82–83

Bottome, Robert, 179, 184–86, 188

Boulton, Margot, 12, 185, 186, 188

Boulton family, 45

Bowen, Herbert, 91, 99, 101–3, 106, 110; as arbiter for Venezuela in 1903, 102; dismissed from foreign service, 106

Boyacá, battle of, 29

Brandt, Willy, 209

British Guiana, 3, 42, 87, 89

Bryan, William Jennings, 94

Buchanan, William I., 113

Buchanan Protocol, 113

Buckley, William F., 134

Bush, George, 200

Byrnes, James, 151–52

Cabot, John Moors, 177

Cacao. *See* Cocoa

CADA, 175, 180, 188

Caffrey, Jefferson, 119

Caldera, Rafael, 163–66, 217, 218

Calvani, Arístides, 209

Calvo, Carlos, 76

Calvo Doctrine, 76, 79, 100, 111

Camacho, Simón, 38, 41, 42, 57, 84, 87; and criticism of U.S. democracy, 41; publications of, 84

Carabobo, battle of, 22, 29

Caracas Journal, 168, 177, 179–81, 185, 186, 190, 192, 196; editorial policy of, 179; history of, 179. See also *Daily Journal*

Cardenas, Román, 126

Caribbean Basin Initiative, 219

Carner, Ambrose H., 73

Carnevali, Alberto, 161–62

Carrasquel, Chico, 190

Cartagena Consensus, 220

Castro, Cipriano, 92, 93, 117, 126, 162, 207; considered anti-American, 99; career of, 98, 99; enemies of, 101, 102; in exile, 106, 114; U.S. plans to remove, 103, 104, 105, 106; and Zumeta, 110–13

Castro, Fidel, 209, 215, 216

Catholic church, 197

Centro Venezolano Americano, 14, 173, 181

Christian Democratic International, 209

Civil War: Spanish, 144; U.S., 54, 56, 57, 69, 78, 80, 81; Venezuelan, 47, 75, 92

Claims, 44, 54, 58, 59, 76, 109; Commission of 1868, 60, 77, 78, 90

Clay, Henry, 32, 130

Clemente, Lino de, 25–27, 29

Cleveland, Grover, 75, 79, 89, 91

Clinton, Daniel Joseph (pseud. Thomas Rourke), 146, 190

Cocoa, 12, 13, 45, 63, 70, 72, 74, 75, 83, 131

Coffee, 12, 45, 63, 70, 71, 74, 75, 83, 98–100, 109, 119, 131

Cold war, 9, 161, 169; and *Daily Journal*, 180; and Reagan, 221; and Venezuelan democracy, 8, 199, 209, 212; and Venezuelan dictatorship, 145, 150, 154–56, 158, 178

Coles, William, 175, 185

Comité de Organización Política Electoral Independiente. *See* COPEI

Communism, 117, 159, 192, 197, 214; and Gómez, 123, 125; and guerrillas of 1960s, 8, 209, 217; and Pérez Jiménez, 155, 158, 160; and transition of 1958–59, 163–66

Compañía Anónima Distribuidora de Alimentos. *See* CADA

Consalvi, Simón, 209, 210, 212, 222, 223

Consejo de Bienestar Rural, 173

Constitutions, Venezuelan: of 1857, 55; of 1864, 52; of 1928, 125

Consuls, Venezuelan, 85

Contadora, 9, 222, 223

Cook, W. C., 121–22, 140

Coolidge, Calvin, 118

COPEI, 154, 159, 163, 165, 166, 209, 218

Corporación Venezolana de Fomento, 157

Corrigan, Frank, 147, 149–51, 173

Corruption, 53, 54, 65, 127, 174, 215

Counterinsurgency, Venezuelan, 216

Craig, John, 13

Creole Petroleum Company, 159, 164, 172, 177, 180

Crespo, Joaquín, 69, 73, 75, 88, 94, 95

Cuba, 32, 87, 104, 123; Venezuelan relations with, after 1959, 212, 216, 217

Cúcuta Constitution, 32

Culver, Erastus, 46, 53, 55–57

Curtis, William, 81, 82

Daily Journal, 179, 180, 184, 185, 188. See also *Caracas Journal*

Dallett and Company, 71

Danels, John Daniel, 24, 25

Davis, Richard Harding, 63, 82, 83

Dawson, Allan, 150, 151

Debt, Venezuelan, 9, 46, 220, 221

Decolonization, in Caribbean, 207, 211, 216

Delgado Chalbaud, Carlos, 149, 152, 154, 158

Democracy, 4, 41, 54, 209; and cold war, 160, 161, 163–65; and "democratic caesar," 4, 47, 92, 116, 117, 137, 143–45, 154, 160, 191; exporting of, 1, 6, 14, 216, 217; and Gómez as "democratic caesar," 107, 112, 113, 140; in international relations, 212–17, 221; opinions on Venezuelan capability for, 34, 36, 42, 67, 109, 123, 147, 159, 214; and *trienio*, 149–51, 153, 154; and Woodrow Wilson, 119–21

Democratic party, U.S., 138, 139, 215

Depons, Francisco, 13

Díaz, Porfirio, 8, 110, 113, 115, 117, 118, 123

Díaz Sánchez, Ramón, 141–43

Dickey, Spencer, 139–40

Dolge, Rudolf, 70, 183

Dominican Republic, 169, 189, 217; and relations with Betancourt, 151, 152, 214; and relations with Pérez Jiménez, 154, 160; U.S. intervention in, 104, 118

Dominici, Santos, 121, 128

Donnelly, Walter J., 150, 153, 185

Doyle, William T. S., 133, 137

Drago, Luis H., 76

Drago Doctrine, 76, 79

Driggs, Seth, 38, 59

Duijim, Susana, 188–89

Dulles, John Foster, 160, 169

Earthquake of 1812, 19, 20, 38

Eisenhower, Dwight D., 155, 158, 166, 178, 202, 214

Ellis, Vespasian, 56, 58, 59, 114

Embargo of 1807, 17, 20

Engert, C. Van H., 123

Escalante, Diógenes, 127, 128

Escovar Salóm, Ramón, 209, 212

Esquipulas II Accords, 222

Essequibo River, 90
Estrada, Pedro, 157, 160
Expositions, 70
Extended economic zone, 210
Extradition, 79, 80, 215
Exxon, 134

Fairs, 70
Falcón, Juan Crisostomo, 57
February Program of 1936, 146
Federal War (1859–63), 52, 55, 65
Federation of Chambers and Associations
   of Commerce and Production
   (Fedecámaras), 194
Fergusson, Erna, 190
Figueres, José, 160
Filibusters, 8, 22, 51, 60
First Republic of Venezuela, 17–21
Fish, Hamilton, 87
Flack, Joseph, 150, 170
Florida, Spanish, 18, 21, 25
Ford, Gerald, 204–6
Forsyth, John, 44, 47
Foss, Joseph, 177, 178
Franco, Francisco, 154
French Cable Company, 86, 96, 97, 101

Gallegos, Rómulo, 143, 152–54
General Asphalt, 100
Geopolitics, 10, 155, 156
Gil Borges, Esteban, 127, 172
Gil Fortoul, José, 54, 112
Girard, Stephen, 18
Golpe: of 1945, 149, 150; of 1948, 153, 192
Gómez, Juan Vicente, 8, 46, 93, 146, 147,
   163, 169, 190, 193; books about, 191, 192;
   dictatorship of, 107, 112–30 passim,
   132–44 passim; neutrality of, in World
   War I, 119; seizes power, 106, 107; as sur-
   rogate policeman, 92; U.S. views on, 117
González, Juan Vicente, 1, 40, 42

González Guinán, Francisco, 113, 115
Good Neighbor Award, of *Caracas Journal*,
   186, 190
Good Neighbor policy, 8, 124, 144, 195;
   dismantling of, 167; and economic
   policy, 171
Gran Colombia, 33, 34, 35, 42
Grant, Frances R., 162
Grant, Ulysses S., 68
Great Britain, 3, 36, 43, 45, 46, 91. *See also*
   British Guiana
Gresham, Walter, 89
Gual, Pedro, 25, 26, 30–32
Guano, 60, 61
Guanoco Lake, 73, 100, 113
Guayana, 186; British threat to, 46, 75, 89,
   99; and Confederate immigration, 81;
   goldfields in, 70, 74; steel industry in,
   157, 174
Guevara, Ernesto "Che," 165
Gulf Oil, 133, 134, 140, 178
Guzmán, Antonio Leocadio, 38, 41, 48, 49,
   66
Guzmán Blanco, Antonio, 57, 64, 69, 82,
   85, 90, 94, 99, 100, 110; and asphalt
   concessions, 72, 73; and claims disputes,
   76, 77, 78, 88; and foreign policy, 46, 57,
   67, 68, 74; and modernization, 66, 72;
   Pan-Americanism of, 57, 67, 68; U.S.
   views of, 66, 67

Haiti, 9, 12, 25, 114
Hall, A. A., 48
Hambledon, John N., 29
Hamilton, Alexander, 14
Hamilton, Horatio, 73
Hancox, J. W., 64, 77
Harding, Warren G., 118, 120, 124, 133
Harrison, Benjamin, 65
Harrison, William Henry, 6, 34, 35, 47
Hay, John, 104, 106

Hernández, Alejandro, 194
Hernández, José Manuel "El Mocho,"
    94–96, 98, 101, 104, 108, 122; political
    program of, 95; and presidential
    campaign of 1897, 94
Hernández Chapellin, Jesús, 197
Herrera Campins, Luís, 218, 222
Herter, Christian, 165
Hoover, Herbert, 118
Hoover, Herbert, Jr., 157
Hoover, J. Edgar, 149
Hughes, Charles E., 132
Human rights, 143, 208, 212; and Gómez,
    122, 125, 137; and Pérez Jiménez, 215,
    169; Venezuelan advocacy of, in 1980s,
    207
Humboldt, Alexander von, 85
Hunt, Michael, 1
Hutchinson, Norman, 100

Immigration, to Venezuela, 80, 81, 183
Import substitution, 178, 195
Independence wars, 3, 7
Independent Petroleum Association of
    America, 133, 138; and FDR, 171; and
    Gómez, 134; and Pérez Jiménez, 169,
    174, 177, 178
Industrialization, 170, 174, 175, 176
Inter-American Association for
    Democracy and Freedom, 162, 166
Inter-American Conferences: of 1889, 82,
    88; of 1933, 124; of 1954, 182
International Committee for Political
    Prisoners, 137
International Labor Organization (ILO),
    137, 176
International Telephone Company, 72, 73
Investment, in Venezuela, 71, 174, 176
Iran, 174, 179, 200, 202, 207, 223
Irvine, John Baptiste, 27, 28
Israel, 204, 208, 211

Jackson, Andrew, 5, 23, 34, 38, 47, 83
Jackson, Henry, 205
Jankus, Alfred P., 191, 192
Jaurett, Albert F., 102, 113
Jefferson, Thomas, 15, 16, 49, 50
John Birch Society, 215
Johnson, James Weldon, 99, 108, 109
Johnson, Lyndon, 202
Judicial system, Venezuelan, 53

Kamen-Kaye, Dorothy, 186
Kellogg, Frank B., 122
Kennan, George, 153
Kennedy, John F., 8, 214
Kennedy, Robert, 215
Kieffer, John, 155, 156
Kirkpatrick, Jeanne, 211
Kissinger, Henry, 199, 204, 206, 224
Knox, Philander, 114, 115, 124
Kornfeder, Joseph, 125

Labor, in Venezuela, 147, 173, 176, 177,
    179, 180; and labor law of 1928, 135
LaFeber, Walter, 63, 75
Lagunillas, 136, 141
Lander, Tomás, 48, 49
Larrazábal, Wolfgang, 164–66
Latin American Economic System, 219
Lavin, John, 190–92
League of Nations, 127, 137, 171
Lecuna, Vicente, 115, 126
Lehman, Herbert, 161
Leoni, Raúl, 173, 203, 217, 218
Leprosy, 83
Liberalism, 3, 4, 7, 11, 37, 40
Liberal party, 38, 48, 57, 95
Liberals, 38, 48–53, 56, 65, 66, 93, 94, 99,
    112
Libya, 211
Lieuwen, Edwin, 190
Linares Alcántara, Francisco, 115

Lindbergh, Charles, 124, 132
Llovera Páez, Luís Felipe, 149, 152
Long, Huey, 138, 192
Loomis, Francis B., 91, 95, 109, 133, 137;
  accused of corruption 106; career of,
  93–94; recalled as minister, 101; and
  Spanish-American War, 96, 97, 98
López Contreras, Eleazar, 146, 147, 151,
  171, 172, 191, 192
Lowry, Robert K., 19, 22
Lusinchi, Jaime, 211, 221

Macaulay, Alexander, 11, 22, 23
MacGregor, Gregor, 25, 26
Madero, Francisco I., 94, 110, 119
Madison, James, 14, 15, 18
Malloy, Neil M., 191, 192
Maracaibo sandbar, 72, 74, 135, 174
Márquez Bustillos, Victorino, 119
Marshall, George, 152
Martí, José, 110
Masonic lodges, 14
Materialism, 86, 112, 196, 197
Matos, Manuel Antonio, 100–102, 104,
  108, 111, 114, 115
Maza Zavala, Domingo Felipe, 194
McGoodwin, Preston, 119–21, 126, 132,
  137, 158
McKinley, William, 74, 94, 101
Medina Angarita, Isaías, 147, 148, 173
Mendoza, Eugenio, 137, 162, 165, 170, 171
Mexico, 57, 63, 133, 147. *See also* Díaz,
  Porfirio; Madero, Francisco I.
Miranda, Francisco, 14–17, 19, 21, 56, 183
Monagas, José Gregorio, 52
Monagas, José Tadeo, 38, 47, 49, 50, 52, 54,
  58
Monroe, James, 20, 28, 30, 31
Monroe Doctrine, 7–9, 31, 72, 87–89, 91, 96,
  100, 103–5, 114, 122; and Cipriano
  Castro, 100; under Kellogg, 122; and
  Nicaraguan intervention of 1909, 114;

Olney Corollary to, 8, 88, 89, 91;
  Roosevelt Corollary to, 8, 103, 104
Moreno, José Ignacio, 14
Múñoz Tébar, Jesús, 64, 84, 85

Nariño, Antonio, 23
National Association of Manufacturers,
  70, 183
National Pantheon, 67
National security, 2, 36
Neutrality legislation, U.S., 24, 26, 27, 28, 35
New Deal, 146, 151, 192
New National Ideal, 157, 193
Newspapers, 56, 97, 129
New York and Bermúdez Company, 73,
  100–102
Niagara Falls, 41
Nicaragua, 111, 118; filibustering in, 51, 56;
  and Sandinistas, 200, 217, 221, 222; and
  Somoza, 151, 154, 214; and Zelaya, 98,
  114
Nicholson, Meredith, 172
Nixon, Richard, 8, 165, 203, 204, 214
Non-Aligned Movement, 209
North American Association, 184, 185
North American Free Trade Agreement,
  219
Núñez, Enrique Bernardo, 196
Nweihed, Kaldone, 209

O'Beirne, James R., 63
O'Conner, Gerald, 185
Oil. *See* Petroleum
Olney, Richard, 8, 9, 88, 89, 93
Olney Corollary, 89, 91, 117
Onís, Luís de, 18, 29, 30
OPEC. *See* Organization of Petroleum
  Exporting Countries (OPEC)
Orchids, 70, 83
Orea, Telésforo de, 11, 18, 20, 21
Organization of American States (OAS), 9,
  200, 208, 213

Organization of Petroleum Exporting Countries (OPEC), 8, 10, 134, 199, 200, 202–8, 211, 224; founding of, 201, 202; and oil embargo of 1973, 204, 205

Orinoco River, 2, 42, 46, 48, 58, 70, 74, 80, 88, 139, 176

Páez, José Antonio, 46, 56, 66, 82; affection of, for the U.S., 55; and challenge to Bolívar, 33, 43; and dictatorship of 1861–63, 52, 55; leadership of, 46–53; sword of, given to John Pershing, 124; as symbol of Venezuela, 35, 38, 67; and U.S. support of, 47, 51

Páez, Ramón, 47, 84, 85

Paige, Leroy "Satchel," 189

Palestine, 211

Pampero Industries, 194, 198

Panama Canal, 2, 72, 91, 114–15, 140; and Chilean ambitions, 87; construction of, 69

Pan American Airways, 121, 132

Pan-Americanism, 9, 87, 90, 148, 213, 222, 224; and Bolívar, 31, 33, 67; and conference of 1889, 9, 68; and conference of 1954, 159; and Pan-American Union, 9, 128

Pan-American Society of the United States, 132

Parker, Frank, 103

Partido Liberal Nacionalista, 94

Partridge, Frank, 77, 78, 80

Patriotic Junta, 163–66

Pazos, Vicente, 25, 26

Pérez, Carlos Andrés, 204, 205, 213, 219, 221, 223; resignation of, 221

Pérez Alfonzo, Juan Pablo, 163, 201–2, 209; and founding of OPEC, 202

Pérez Guerrero, Manuel, 209, 211

Pérez Jiménez, Marcos, 8, 149, 152, 184, 191, 210; dictatorship of, 155–61, 163–64, 166; exile of, 197; extradition of, 215;

and Legion of Merit, 160; petroleum and economic policy of, 174–78, 194–95; as symbol of dictatorship, 166, 169

Pérez Soto, Vincencio, 136, 141

Perón, Juan, 149, 151, 157

Perry, Oliver H., 28–29, 48

Pershing, John, 124

Pétion, Alexandre, 32

Petkoff, Teodoro, 217

Petroleum: and Americanization of Venezuela, 178–84 passim; concessions, 92, 174; and economic growth and trade (1939–58), 168–77 passim; and Gómez policy, 133–39; legislation, 121–22, 134, 170, 173; nationalization of, 9, 204, 206, 172; and oil camps, 135, 139–42; and pollution, 136; and quotas, 174, 202; and security of oil fields, 125, 156, 158, 164, 178, 211; "sowing" of, 5, 172, 193–94, 196, 200, 207; and Venezuelan foreign policy, 8, 9, 200–207, 218–19

Phelps, William H., 130, 132, 183, 184

Pickering, Thomas, 16

Picón Salas, Mariano, 182, 183, 195, 199

Pile, William, 64–68, 72, 73, 80, 88, 185; as lobbyist for Guzmán Blanco, 77, 78

Plumacher, Eugene, 69, 71, 72, 87

Poinsett, Joel, 34, 43

Pollution, 136

Porter, Robert Ker, 43, 166

Positivism, 64, 109. *See also* Social Darwinism

Price, Henry M., 80, 81

Privateering, 23, 24, 27

Protocol of 1903, 102

Proudfit, Arthur, 159, 164

Public diplomacy, 204, 205

Puerto Rico, 30, 32, 114, 160, 189; independence for, proposed in UN, 211; and Spanish-American War, 97

Race, 4, 12; and African Americans, 99, 108, 109, 189; and social Darwinism, 83, 84; U.S. perceptions of, 1, 32, 33, 39, 45, 48, 50, 52, 53, 142, 189; Venezuelan perceptions of, 86, 107, 189, 212, 135, 155

Rangel, Domingo Alberto, 99, 171, 183; and Central American crisis, 223; and petroleum crisis of 1973–74, 206

Rayburn, Sam, 202

Reagan, Ronald, 200, 217, 221, 223

Red D Line, 71, 75

Reich, Otto, 211

Republican party, U.S., 91, 93, 94, 138, 184, 215

Reuters, 129

Reynolds, Thomas C., 81, 82, 185

Ritchie, Thomas, 16

Robertson, Ruth, 186

Rockefeller, Nelson, 175, 180, 182, 184, 185; as coordinator of inter-American affairs, 184

Rodó, José Enrique, 86, 111

Rodríguez, Simón, 14

Roosevelt, Eleanor, 161

Roosevelt, Franklin D., 8, 144, 146, 171, 180

Roosevelt, Theodore, 8, 91, 99, 101–4, 113, 169; and desire to remove Castro, 105

Root, Elihu, 99

Roscio, Juan Germán, 19

Royal Dutch–Shell, 133

Royall, Kenneth, 153

Rubottom, Roy, 161, 164, 166

Russell, Thomas, 64, 69, 78, 83

Santander, Francisco Paula de, 30–33

Schacht Aristeguieta, Efraín, 205

Scott, Alexander, 19

Scruggs, William, 64, 65, 67, 74, 75, 80, 93, 105; as lobbyist on British Guiana dispute, 88, 89; publications of, 89

Sears, Roebuck and Company, 175, 180, 187

Seguridad Nacional, 157, 160

Seijas, Rafael, 79

Seward, William, 37, 55, 57

Sherman, John, 16

Sherwell, William, 120–21, 128

Shields, Benjamin, 44–47, 49–51, 54, 56, 95

Shipping industry, 44, 69, 130, 175, 176

Shultz, George, 222, 223

Slavery, 32, 33, 40, 41

Smith, Moses, 16

Social Darwinism, 64, 65, 83, 107; in *Daily Journal*, 180

Socialist International, 162, 209, 217

Somosa Debayle, Anastasio, 222

Somoza, Anastasio, 8, 117, 154, 160, 166, 214

Soublette, Carlos, 48

Southern Methodist church, 82

Spain, 3, 42; and Hispanism, 96–97, 111–12, 195

Spanish-American War, 91, 92, 96–97

Stabler, Jordan H., 117, 122, 133, 134, 137

Standard Oil, 6, 94, 106, 133, 134, 138, 177, 178, 201, 205

Steele, Isaac, 46, 53, 54

Steel industry, 107, 157, 174, 176, 185, 218

Stilwell, Thomas, 65, 77

Táchira, 98, 99

Taft, William H., 105, 106

Talmage, David, 77

Tamanaco Hotel, 182, 196

Tamayo, Pío, 123

Tariki, Abdullah, 202

Territorial seas, 156, 210

Thacher, Solon O., 81

Third World, 199, 204, 210, 212, 213, 216–18, 224

Thornburg, Max, 173

Tío Conejo, 2, 7, 76, 79, 90, 108, 198, 213
Tío Tigre, 2, 76, 79, 108, 213
Toro, Fermín, 40–42
Toro Hardy, Alfredo, 223
Torres, Gumersindo, 134, 135
Torres, Manuel, 30
Tourism, 83, 182
Trade, binational: balance of, 70, 170; effect of banking and credit on, 131–32; and NAFTA, 220; in nineteenth century, 37, 43, 45, 69, 70; origins of, 11, 12, 13, 17, 18; and tariffs, 45, 74. *See also* Petroleum
Trade treaties, 74, 75, 131, 170; of Gran Colombia, 32, 43; of 1836, 44; of 1861, 74; of 1939, 76, 171, 177; of 1952, 176, 177, 218
Trescott, William E., 88
Trippe, Juan, 132
Trujillo, Rafael, 117, 152, 154, 214
Truman, Harry S, 154, 158
Turpin, Edward, 52

Unión Republicana Democrática, 154, 158, 159
United Nations, 9: Conference on Trade and Development (UNCTAD), 209; founding of, 148; "Group of 77" in, 209; and Law of the Sea, 209–10; Security Council, 211; and Venezuelan activism, 206; and Venezuelan domestic politics, 208
United Press, 118, 129
Urruela, Charles, 158, 186
Uslar Pietri, Arturo, 2, 76, 193
U.S. Steel, 174, 176, 185

Vade-Mecum, 81, 197
Vallenilla Lanz, Laureano, 112, 115, 127, 137
Vallenilla Lanz, Laureano, Jr., 163
Venezuelan American Chamber of Commerce (AmCham), 177–79, 181, 185

Venezuelan Basic Economy Corporation, 175, 184, 185
Versailles Peace Conference, 127
Vietnam War, 200
Villaba, Jóvito, 123, 158

Waldman, Jules, 179, 180
Walters, Vernon, 211
Warner and Quinlan, 100–101, 102
War of 1812, 21, 23, 24
Warren, Fletcher, 158–61, 181
Washington, George, 1, 4, 26, 68
Washington Post, 129
Waterton, Charles, 85
Welch, James, 138, 139, 215
Welles, Sumner, 121, 124, 173
West Indian Squadron, U.S., 49
Wiley, John C., 120
Williamson, John G. A., 38, 44, 46–49, 61; and negative views of Venezuelans, 39; and rivalry with Porter, 43
Wilson, Belford, 34
Wilson, Warden, 141
Wilson, Woodrow, 91, 92, 118–21, 131, 132; Mobile address of 1913 by, 119
Wolf, Franklin W., 144, 159

Xenophobia, 108

Yellow Liberals, 65, 93, 94, 99

Zamora, Ezequiel, 108, 109
Zea, Francisco Antonio, 28
Zelaya, José Santos, 92, 98, 114, 117
Zimbabwe, 212
Zumeta, César, 124, 127, 156, 168, 195, 199; career of, 110; and Castro, 110, 111; and Gómez, 112; and Hispanic culture, 110; positivism of, 112; and "Sick Continent," 111–12